# DEMANDING WORK

# DEMANDING WORK

## THE PARADOX OF JOB QUALITY IN THE AFFLUENT ECONOMY

*Francis Green*

PRINCETON UNIVERSITY PRESS  PRINCETON AND OXFORD

Copyright © 2006 by Princeton University Press

Published by Princeton University Press, 41 William Street, Princeton, New Jersey 08540

In the United Kingdom: Princeton University Press, 3 Market Place, Woodstock, Oxfordshire OX20 1SY

All Rights Reserved

ISBN: 0-691-11712-8

Library of Congress Cataloging-in-Publication Data

Green, Francis.
   Demanding work: the paradox of job quality in the affluent economy / by Francis Green.
      p.   cm.
   Includes bibliographical references and index.
   ISBN 0-691-11712-8 (hardcover: alk. paper)
   1. Quality of work life.   2. Job satisfaction.   3. Work—Social aspects.   I. Title.
HD6955.G717 2006
331-25'6—dc22                                                                    2005006272

British Library Cataloging-in-Publication Data is available

This book has been composed in Sabon

Printed on acid-free paper. ∞

pup.princeton.edu

Printed in the United States of America

10  9  8  7  6  5  4  3  2  1

This book is dedicated to my mother, **Rosamund,** to my late father, **Keith,** and to **Alison, Daniel, Robert,** and **Toby**

# Contents _____

# List of Illustrations

**Figures**

## Tables

# *Preface*

## The Quest for "More and Better Jobs"

THE LAST QUARTER of the twentieth century saw the creation of nearly a hundred million jobs in the labor markets of the advanced industrialized world. This achievement, in which every economy shared, testifies to the apparently enduring power of capitalism to generate the prospect of paid work for the citizens of rich nations. Yet what has been happening to the quality of work life experienced by the people doing these abundant jobs? Has the affluent economy, with rising material living standards, yielded a better work life for most of us? If not, why not? This book aims to answer these questions, as far as is currently possible, using the tools of the economist and with considerable help from other social sciences. It shows that job quality has indeed risen in certain respects: the average job pays higher wages and uses more skills. However, in other respects the quality of work life has become worse: wages have become much more unequal, work effort has been intensified and, at least in Britain, employees are more likely to be overqualified for the kind of work they do, while their influence over their daily work tasks has been diminished.

Such findings ought to arouse some concern for policy makers in developed economies. For much of the past twenty years, the main objective has been to create jobs and reduce unemployment. Since the turn of the century, however, the quality of work life has crept into the policy agenda. The rhetoric of national governments and supranational organizations now favors improvements in job quality as well as in the numbers employed. The Council of the European Union, following its meeting at Lisbon in spring 2000, declared that, as part of its long-term aim of becoming the most advanced economy in the world by 2010, it needed to prioritize the "quality of work." It set its civil servants the task of defining indicators of quality that could become the targets of European-led policy-making in member countries.[1] It was felt that a fuller evaluation of employment policies should include whether the jobs generated are satisfying and have some promise of extension and betterment, rather than being of the "dead-end" variety. Similar themes have been taken up by the International Labour Office, which has developed a concept of "decent work," and by the Organization of Economic Cooperation and Development which in 2003 sponsored a conference of employment ministers with the theme of moving toward "more and better jobs." An important catalyst for the new interest in quality was the somewhat reduced unemployment levels to be found in the United States and some European countries. The logic is that, once sufficient jobs have been generated, the next task is to concentrate on improving the quality of those jobs. Interest may also have stemmed from the widespread publicity afforded to problems of workplace stress, job insecurity and, for substantial minorities, persistent low pay.

My own interest in arriving at an improved understanding of the quality of work life was aroused in the mid-1990s by a widespread public perception that conditions for the workers of advanced economies had been deteriorating. In the harsh new world of global competition, life at work seemed in the eyes of many to be getting worse. In Britain, where I live, work stress became the occupational health hazard of the last decade. There was widespread talk of "time-famine" and other metaphorical allusions to how the increased demands of work life spilled over to other parts of life, so dislodging the "work-life balance." In the United States, employees were said to be caught in a "time squeeze," and work was "becoming nasty, brutish, and long."[2] Yet the phenomenon was not confined to the liberal market economies: an intensification of work effort and its consequences were being bemoaned almost everywhere I looked across the industrialized world. Work intensification, moreover, has been only one item of complaint: other concerns have included rising wage inequality in the majority of countries, and perceptions of decline in the numbers of career jobs that offered security and promotion prospects, at least for those lucky enough to get on the inside track. A substantial minority of the new jobs being created had the worst of all worlds, offering low pay, no prospects, insecurity, and tedious, hard work—in short, drudgery. This picture fits well with the more pessimistic and critical ideologies about global capitalism in modern times. It seemed a fairly dismal scenario, then, which the official concern with "better jobs" was set to confront at the start of the new millennium.

Yet this picture of work degradation presents an extraordinary paradox, considering that this has been an era of affluence and continued economic growth. The time may come when environmental degradation will require an accommodation to declining living standards—let us hope a peaceful one—but looking back over the past quarter century we see only rising affluence, on average, in the already-rich world. If it is true that the quality of work life is in serious decline, while the economy as a whole—at least as measured by the conventional standards of welfare—is becoming even more affluent, we surely have some explaining to do. After all, for many people work is an important part of their life: why not devote part of that affluence to improving the quality of jobs, as well as to buy-ing better cars and washing machines?

One explanation might be that the popular portrayal of a deteriorat-ing workplace is simply false. Purveyors of the dismal-workplace sce-nario could be accused of suffering from a distorted memory of how un-pleasant work life used to be—forgetting how low were the wages, how short the holidays, and how unsafe the working conditions. Horrific ac-cidents at work are sometimes given proper publicity, but the tragedies of earlier industrial disasters are hidden in the mists of time. The numer-ous workers chained to assembly lines in earlier generations can hardly be said to have enjoyed fulfilling work lives. With the articulation of these opposing descriptions of reality, all too easily there follows next a pantomime of the ideologies. Optimistic and pessimistic declarations about whether work life is getting better or worse are counterposed with little or no evidence in support.

Addressing factual disputes about how the world of work is changing is one vital manner in which the labor-economist scholar should enter the stage. The first objective of this book, then, is to construct a reliable account of the extent to which different key facets of work life are changing. The concept of job quality, for this purpose, will be entirely worker-centered. Skills, effort, discretion, wages, and risk are the main focal points, as dictated both by theories of the sources of well-being at work and by available evidence. The indicators I shall use are primarily quantitative.

The second objective of the book is to seek understanding of the sources of change in job quality. I construct an account of how some as-pects of job quality have been changing in terms of wider socioeconomic movements. Making links between the world of work and the broader political economy is not uncommon practice in popular discourse. Here, by using formal methods, I am able to begin to assess more comprehen-sively the importance of technical and organizational changes and of politico-economic developments such as the decline of union power, and to evaluate the role of modern management practices.

The conclusions should be of interest to social analysts and policy makers, as well as to economists. There will be some among my disci-plinary colleagues who will feel that the changing quality of work life is an improper subject for investigation in a hard science, primarily be-cause a good deal of the empirical base is drawn from subjective reports of workers about their jobs. Such data, it will be alleged, are so full of biases and errors as to be worthless. To any such critics—if they are not my own imaginary "straw men"—I respond with two points. First, complete distrust of the individual is absurdly misplaced: what is needed is a measured and critical approach, which draws on the contributions of fellow social scientists in designing instruments of work measurement, who are equally aware of the pitfalls of invalid or unreliable instruments. Second, trying to understand the sources of well-being at work is exactly what labor economics should, ultimately, be about. Implicitly much of it already is, through its many analyses of wage determination. But pay is not all there is to jobs. There is a parallel here with recent debates about "happiness" in economic life. Proponents and practitioners of "happiness" studies also assert that they are doing precisely what economics should be concerned with: explaining what makes people better off, not just what makes them wealthier in material riches. I devote one chapter of this book specifically to the understanding of national trends in job satisfaction, which is sometimes quaintly referred to as "happiness at work." Elsewhere I am concerned with aspects of job quality which are central to theories that link the quality of work life to human needs.

A lot can now be said about these aspects of work life. Though the picture of change is a long way from being comprehensive across the industrialized world, scientific study of these aspects of work life has been made possible, if still in a somewhat halting fashion, by the arrival of the high-quality social survey. It is not too fanciful to liken the arrival of this new tool of enquiry to the invention of a scientific instrument or technique in any of the natural sciences. As is well known, new instruments can sometimes transform both its knowledge base and the way a science is carried out. The social survey is not quite at that stage because its application has, as yet, been too piecemeal. Nevertheless, as I hope to demonstrate, a lot can be learned from social surveys about the workplaces of the late twentieth century industrialized world with what we already have at our disposal. The social survey series is a qualified triumph of interdisciplinary social science, whose wider value is yet to be fully recognized. Unfortunately, too little of this material is multinational in scope.

There are some provisos. First, the information contained in social surveys about the quality of work life is in many cases quite constrained. This limitation has come about, I believe, because labor sociologists and economists have lacked influence (or the will to participate) in the design of nationally representative social surveys. Considering the importance of work in most people's lives, our high-quality surveys ask remarkably little about this domain. A second proviso is that the quality of the survey itself is of prime importance. Some readers may be surprised to see the virtues of the social survey paraded, knowing the large number of poorly conducted surveys that have grown up to serve particular interests of immediate local or commercial concerns. This, however, is where

the independent analyst contributes, by selecting only properly conducted surveys whose value should not be undermined by the purveyors
of cheap survey findings or those contaminated by self-interest.

Good-quality surveys, with support from administrative data, enable
us to settle many of the intriguing issues about job quality in the modern
era. As I shall show, we can be confident that there has been an increase
in the average skill level of jobs in recent decades, even though there remains a very substantial tranche of nonroutine, low-skilled jobs which in
some countries is rising in proportion to the totality of jobs. In most
countries wages have risen, giving workers a share of economic growth
(the United States is a major exception). The risk of accidents has been
diminishing. These developments appear to vindicate the optimistic perspective about work in modern advanced capitalism, and can be accounted for by the progress of technologies, by successful economic
growth, and by more enlightened interventions by governments.

Set against these pluses, however, the survey series confirm the intensification of work effort in many countries. The surveys support evidence,
moreover, of a robust association between effort change and technical
and organizational innovations at the workplace. In Britain, there has
also been a distinct trend toward reduced personal autonomy in the
workplace. It might seem easy to brush aside such a finding, but it is
likely that economists have underestimated the direct importance for
well-being of exercising personal influence at work. The deteriorations
in autonomy and the intensification of work lie behind an observed decline in the job satisfaction and affective well-being of British workers,
even while their wages have been rising. The job satisfaction of German
workers has also declined, and virtually nowhere is there a sign of workers gaining in satisfaction.

Survey data series are also of considerable use for elucidating our understanding of job insecurity in the modern age. Contrary to a good deal
of popular commentary, the surveys do not reveal a secular increase in
insecurity in the modern era. Rather, they confirm what one might
naively predict, that the public's perception of the security of their jobs
largely tracks the state of the aggregate labor market. When the aggregate unemployment rate is low, few people fear for their job. In the mid-
1990s, however, a somewhat disproportionate share of workers were
feeling insecure in both the United States and Britain—particularly many
middle-class, well-educated workers. This broadened perception of insecurity retreated as expected in the late 1990s with the booming economy.

The pessimistic aspects of the findings I am going to report make the
new official search for "better jobs" at once timely and, given the evolution of an increasingly competitive global economy, quite problematic.

Though an economist, I have drawn on the wisdom of other social sciences, especially from sociologists and psychologists who have been writing about the quality of work life for many decades. I shall contrast, but also interweave, some different perspectives on the quality of work life, and use them collectively to generate an interdisciplinary account of how and why various aspects of quality of work life have been changing in recent decades. If I am successful, my economist readers will perhaps be stimulated to think further about the processes of valuation and change in work life, and to join with all labor analysts to press for continual improvements in the available data. For my readers from other social sciences, especially in the field of labor sociology, this book offers some new answers to old questions, using the basic tools of economics applied to medium and large nationally representative data sets. In so doing, I hope the book will further the case for quantitative studies in the field of sociology, not as a substitute for high-standard qualitative investigations or ethnographic research of work processes, but as a complement to these differing methodologies. For policy makers intent on designing policies to influence the world of work, an accurate summary account of change should be indispensable.

No one book, with such a broad canvas, could do more than paint a general picture of the most important workplace changes and to link particular developments with the wider transformations of the international economy. My scope, however, has been especially constrained by the relative scarcity of material for its chosen method. As a result, a preponderance of the discussion in this book concerns Britain, which for many purposes has some of the richest survey-based data series for the study of work life. Elsewhere the book goes where the data are, to say what it can about work-life changes in modern industrialized economies. It is hoped to contribute not only by enhancing understanding of the last quarter century, but also by demonstrating the value of the method, and so stimulating wider and more regular support of high-quality, survey-based research on life at the workplace. If successful, accounts that attempt a similarly wide perspective on workplace change in the next two decades could both be more comprehensive and have a broader geographical scope. For the present, I have largely used whatever good-quality survey series I could find. Doubtless there are and will be more, which can only bode well for the future of research into the quality of work life.

# Acknowledgments

THOUGH I WROTE this book myself, many of its constituents have been a collective endeavor. Alan Felstead collaborated with me in developing both the 1997 and 2001 Skills Surveys and many subsequent analyses. Duncan Gallie shared equally in the design and management of the 2001 Skills Survey, much of which drew on his earlier experience designing the Employment in Britain survey of 1992 and the Social Change and Economic Life Initiative of 1986. David Ashton has also been an important co-researcher on skills and education around the world. I owe these three an enormous intellectual and practical debt. Others have taken great trouble to read and comment on various drafts, including Paul Auerbach, Alan Carruth, Peter Skott, and Yu Zhu and three anonymous referees. To all of these people I give my thanks. I have also benefited greatly from excellent research assistance provided by Nicholas Tsitsianis.

Surveys nowadays are usually made available for public use by researchers, at some decent interval after they have been collected. The processes of depositing and retrieving data are immeasurably more fluent, and my task that much easier, than it would have been even a decade ago. The contribution of the many anonymous data archivists in harnessing new technology to enable this transformation deserves recognition. Funding sources for all surveys used are noted in the Data Set Appendix. For some of the surveys I also owe more direct acknowledgments. For funding the 2001 Skills Survey, on which several of the British-based analyses are founded, thanks are due to the U.K. Department for Education and Skills. The U.K. Economic and Social Research Council is acknowledged and thanked for its funding of the 1997 Skills Survey as part of its "Learning Society" program of research and, with regard to the material used in chapter 8, its funding of the project "Understanding Trends in Job Satisfaction." The ESRC is also indirectly responsible for support given me through its Research Centre at Oxford and Warwick Universities "Skills, knowledge and Organisational Performance," whose director, Ken Mayhew, has been a recurring source of encouragement and a generator of independent ideas about Britain's work environment. The Leverhulme Trust awarded me a Personal Research Fellowship in 1999, and it was this that enabled me to carry out most of my initial analyses of the intensification of work effort in Britain. Both the Skills Surveys were carried out professionally under the direction of Jon Hales at the National Center for Social Research, and I am grateful to him and his colleagues for their always courteous and thoughtful approach to survey management. More grandly I also thank the countless workers across many nations who took time to respond to surveys—an apparently selfless activity whose tedium appears only to be mitigated occasionally by the pleasure of talking to others about one's work. Their personal reports are, collectively, the lenses through which we social scientists can better understand the evolution of modern work life.

# List of Abbreviations ——————————————————

| | |
|---|---|
| EPI | Effort Pressure Index |
| EU | European Union |
| GDP | Gross Domestic Product |
| HRM | Human Resource Management |
| ICT | Information and Communications Technology |
| ILO | International Labor Office |
| OECD | Organization for Economic Cooperation and Development |

*For abbreviations of data sets, see Data Set Appendix.*

# DEMANDING WORK

# One

## Assessing Job Quality in the Affluent Economy

### The Paradox of Job Quality at the Millennium

Work is no mere passing show for a contemplative community of social scientists. Almost everyone gets to do it. Work itself is a major and defining part of most people's lives. It takes up a large proportion of their time on this earth, and profoundly molds their life-experiences. Writers about work are also their own subjects.

In the affluent economies of the industrialized world, life at work in the early twenty-first century has evolved in a curious and intriguing way. Workers have, with significant exceptions, been taking home increasing wages, exercising more acute mental skills, enjoying safer and more pleasant conditions at work, and spending less time there. Yet they have also been working much more intensely, experiencing greater mental strain, sometimes to the point of exhaustion. In many cases, work has come under increased and unwelcome control from above, leaving individual employees with less influence over their daily work lives and a correspondingly less fulfilling experience than before. In these ways, work in the recent era has become more demanding. Meanwhile, significant minorities of workers continue to endure great uncertainty regarding the future security of their employment. Overall, employees are getting no more satisfaction from their time at work than they used to, even though the material wealth of nations has been increasing.

The tension in these observations, all of which are to be described precisely and supported with evidence in this book, lies in the contrast between the increasing wealth in national economies and the ambiguous changes occurring in the quality of jobs. One might, on the face of it, expect increasing affluence to be devoted to improving all the important parts of life. Take, for example, an earlier period, the so-called "golden age of capitalism" that prevailed after World War II until the early 1970s. The central socioeconomic principle, which sufficed to prevent the explosion of conflict in the ever-larger workplaces that had been envisaged by Marx and others, was an implicit social compact between employers and the majority of workers: consent at the workplace, including acceptance of managers' control of the organization of work, was traded for a share, through increased wages, in the rising affluence that twentieth-century technologies were permitting. Superimposed on this social compact were the political and economic principles of Keynesianism, which rescued capitalism, at least for a while, from degenerating into a fragile mass-unemployment system by showing governments how to mitigate cumulative collapses of aggregate demand. While the U.S. economy had emerged from World War II being far more productive than European and Japanese capitalisms, modestly rising wages and improving work conditions (such as reduced hours, longer holidays, and safer workplaces) became the expectation of workers in all countries partaking in advanced capitalism. America's workers were already basking in the "affluent society," and the intellectual issue for economics had become, according to J. K. Galbraith's famous study, how to understand the construction of consumer demand once absolute poverty and wants had been diminished.[1] In Britain, the workforce was gradually shifting into newer, "cleaner" industries and into nonmanual occupations. With rising wages and greater security, and with most sections able to resist encroachments of managerial control, the average quality of working life was improving in that first genuine affluent age in history.[2] Prime Minister Harold Macmillan was able to secure re-election in 1959 on a slogan which probably resonated as much with the electorate's working life as with its wider experience of life: "You've never had it so good."

True, sociologists were debating whether the growing affluence was genuinely diminishing the differences between the traditional middle-class and working-class work experiences, and whether the creeping growth of bureaucracies and large-scale technologies would increase alienation among workers (Goldthorpe, 1969; Blauner, 1964); and it was being maintained that the cost of male manufacturing workers' rising pay had been a sacrifice of autonomy and intrinsic work satisfactions (Goldthorpe et al., 1968). Psychologists were already investigating the microconditions of work that engendered greater or lesser levels of satisfaction and worker motivation (Herzberg et al., 1957). Economics had less to say about the quality of work life, having already drawn in more closely the boundaries of the discipline. A long-standing contribution was the proposition that higher wages had a theoretically ambiguous impact on the work that people chose to do. An increase in wages made it more costly for workers to stay away from work, and this might mean that some workers would put up with longer hours and poorer work conditions if it gave them substantially more resources to enjoy in their leisure time. On the other hand, higher wages meant that people were more affluent, which could lead them to choose more leisure time and better conditions. In practice, male workers who had been working long, burdensome hours were choosing to reduce their hours, as they had done (supported by trades unions and political pressure) since the early nineteenth century. Overall, with relatively few exceptions the prevailing view, often unstated, was that *if* the conditions for affluence could be maintained, the quality of working life could and would continue to be improved in parallel.[3]

The current era, since the end of the golden age of capitalism in the 1970s, has continued to be one of growing wealth in all the industrialized nations. But it is different from the 1950s and 1960s in two crucial respects, whose significance merit some preliminary elaboration in the ensuing sections. First, much more is known than in earlier eras about what has been happening to the quality of work life, through the arrival in the investigators' toolkit of a powerful instrument, namely the consistent social survey series. Second, there have been enormous structural changes in the global economy, with ramifications reaching down to workplaces across whole nations; these transformations lie behind the many contradictory and ambiguous changes in the working lives of ordinary people to be investigated below.

## Revealing a History of the Present

The rise of the large-scale social survey, coupled with an expansion of official statistics capabilities throughout the industrialized world, has had major consequences for our understanding of life in the workplace. Simultaneously, the facility with which administrative and employment-based data can be gathered and processed has improved. Computers now enable complex databases to be analyzed with ease, and have transformed empirical research in the social sciences almost beyond recognition. Some of these social surveys reveal a great deal about trends in the quality of working life across the whole of a nation's workplaces.

This investigative method is largely unavailable to work historians of earlier periods. Of course, the social survey was not invented recently: it has a distinguished history going back at least as far as the 1880s when Charles Booth began publication of his *Life and Labour of the People in London* (Bulmer et al., 1991). What is new is that modern governments and other institutions have funded consistent series of high-quality social surveys, permitting the analysis of social change. It is fortunate that at least some of these series have included a focus on work. Just as the invention of a new measurement instrument normally transforms a field of science—in our times, think of genetic fingerprinting—so the embryonic development of representative social surveys is already advancing the understanding of social and economic change.[4]

The aim of this book is to use the instruments now available to develop a "history of the present." This phrase is intended to convey the intention to use the surveys to explain what has actually been happening in the present era, rather than to test the validity of higher-level theories. In spite of periodic disruptions, there are no nations which were industrialized thirty years ago that have not continued to grow. On average, the people of the OECD countries, the club of rich nations, had become by the time of the millennium nearly twice as rich as they had been in 1970. But what has been happening to the quality of working life in these years of affluence leading up to the third millennium? Are people using their first world affluence to buy themselves a more decent experience when they set out to earn their daily bread? If not, why not?

The informants of this history are, for the most part, the respondents to nationally representative surveys. For understanding the world of work, these informants are in an unrivaled position: they are the ones doing and experiencing the work, and for many aspects of work no other observers can generate more reliable information. Future historians of the current era will uncover many now-hidden documents, and will be able to reinterpret with hindsight the social, political, and economic forces impinging on work. But the social survey record is already in; it may be reinterpreted but cannot be expanded in retrospect.

The availability of consistent survey series, with workers' direct reports about their work, is especially felicitous, in view of widespread assertions that the quality of working life has changed fundamentally in the last decade or so. Claims, which vary in status from formal academic studies (e.g., Burchell et al., 1999; Cappelli et al., 1997) to popular social commentary (e.g., Toynbee, 2003), have often focused on the down side—a deteriorating work-life balance, increased workplace stress due to effort intensification, stagnant or declining wages for unskilled workers, rising insecurity. But counterbalancing claims of improvement are also celebrated, for example that many workers have become more "empowered," or that they are doing more skilled (and so more fulfilling) work (e.g., British Government, 1992). Taken together with rising wages, this mix of changes breaks any simple connection that one might have expected to find between rising affluence and improved quality of work life. Finding out whether these claims are supportable generalizations is one of the main contributions that social survey analyses can make: they lend an authoritative counterweight to the cult of the vignette, the nice or shocking story, which is too often the sole evidential method of popular or journalistic social science. Social surveys can also assist in tracing connections between the quality of work life and the major structural transformations of the global economy. They can yield an understanding of the proximate causes of changes in work-life quality, and by identifying the key factors can help to focus policy where it is most effective.

But survey analyses can only go so far. Though utilized here to construct a history of the present era, social surveys are not themselves good at uncovering deep processes of change—for this purpose surveys need to be used in a complementary way with ethnographic and case study methods. Nor do survey analyses displace the methods of the regular historian: they do not explain, for example, why or when computers were invented, why China entered the market for manufactured goods, or why Americans voted for President Ronald Reagan and his policies of minimum-wage reductions, and why Margaret Thatcher's policies of reducing union power triumphed in Britain. Such matters are the subject of a wider politico-economic canvass. Moreover, surveys that have relevant information about working lives are quite rare. Only a handful of suitable series of high-quality surveys exist. While low-quality surveys abound, typically purveyed by commercial concerns or interest groups, these often generate findings that are misleading because they are derived from unrepresentative samples; and they are rarely consistent over time. Still lacking are appropriate series of surveys in most developing or transitional countries—this is the prime reason for confining the analyses of this book to the advanced industrialized world (the "North").[5]

Analyses in these surveys mainly rely on subjective accounts by workers of their own lives. This source of information is not favored by some, but aversion is unwarranted. Data that have useful information and predictive value deserve, subject to ethical bounds, to be utilized in any science. Unbridled skepticism needs to be replaced by a systematic approach to careful validation and reliability-testing of data—the stuff of scholarly papers. Subjective reporting from individuals can reflect biases driven, for example, by respondents' unconscious need for social esteem or by poor recall of past events. Yet these biases and errors can be assessed, and a considered weight given to each set of findings. Set off against the biases are the circumstances that make for minimal measurement errors: individuals know a great deal about what happens in their own jobs—much more than is revealed, for example, in bureaucratic records.[6] The countless people who were selected by chance to be in these surveys became the collective representatives of working people in their national populations; they will be telling their own story in this book. Whose story is more accurate than theirs?

## The Changing World and the Everyday Workplace

If the experience of work is changing, it is not hard in broad terms to see why. The world economy has changed in several profound ways since the golden age of capitalism ran out of steam in the early 1970s. Though the end of this era was signaled finally by the collapse in 1973 of the postwar international monetary system, the roots of crisis lay deep in the contradictions of American military and economic hegemony, technological slowdown, tight labor markets, and growing shortages of raw materials (especially oil). High on the list of major transformations of modern economies since the 1970s are: the growth of service industries, and the corresponding rise of service occupations at all levels—from sales assistants to lawyers; technological changes, led by the progressive growth of computer power and software, which pervade all industries; new or reformulated ideologies of management, which come in both hard and soft versions, both designed ultimately to raise worker productivity; the progressive withdrawal of governments from active participation as producers of goods or services; and, not least, the globalization of trade and production and consequent intensification of international competition, developments which both lie behind the new technologies and management ideologies and impinge directly on working lives.

Service industries have grown more rapidly than production goods industries in the affluent economy, largely because of consumer demand. Since many services have to be delivered as they are generated, the customer becomes a major proximate controller of work flows, and there are corresponding requirements for workers to attend to their tasks at flexible times. One cannot store up nursing services, for example, when patients need care. Services are also highly heterogeneous in their skill requirements and in the extent to which they can be automated. The routine services are those that have most easily been replaced by new information and communication technologies. But these technologies create jobs as well as destroy them. Highly skilled workers, in particular, have been in greater demand across the industrial spectrum. Generic skills involved in information processing, communication, problem-solving, and team-working activities have come to the fore. However, many unskilled activities are also emphasized in the advance of the service economy— especially those nonroutine activities that are hard to automate. The affluent economy sees a return of servant occupations, there to pack bags, clean floors, and secure property—a renaissance which mocks earlier expectations that the servant class had disappeared forever in the first part of the twentieth century.

Many changes in the modern workplace can be traced to the global expansion of trade and the internationalization of manufacturing facilities. Well known is the public display of firms closing down plants located in an advanced industrial economy and opening up in a low-wage economy. The main impact of such relocations and of direct trade with low-wage economies may be yet to come, but their significance hitherto has often been exaggerated. Most trade still takes place between the advanced industrialized countries. The significance of trade, for the work-places of the North, lies with its link to competition. Trade expansion is part of an increasing competitiveness of modern industry, which puts businesses and their managers under continual pressure to defend existing markets and find new ones through aggressive cost-minimization and innovative expansion policies.

Alongside these increased pressures, however, managers in many countries have been handed more power, with the declining strength of trade unions and the appearance of more business-friendly government; at the same time they have been presented with new ideologies of control. There is rarely a consensus as to how management should run their labor processes. Strange dichotomies have arisen: managers have to choose between "soft" and "hard" human resource management (HRM) policies. Soft HRM policies are designed to engender workers' commitment and innovative practices, but they raise labor costs and lessen managers' ability to reduce those costs without breaking the "psychological contract" with workers. Hard HRM policies, by contrast, go hand in hand with "lean and mean" systems, where no implicit promises are made to workers, and where competitive pressures to reduce costs lead to a continual re-examination of production methods, using management tools like "business process re-engineering" and involving occasional downsizing of establishment workforces. The soft/hard HRM dichotomy is parallel to the putative choice for managers between a "high road" and a "low road" to profitability. The former involves high wages, high skills, security, and commitment; the latter, low wages, no training, and frequent layoffs. Managers' choices vary along this spectrum, and there are no established wisdoms to determine which approach generates the best performance.[7]

Managers' decisions which affect the quality of work life are now taken, however, in the context of an expansion in the range of work scenarios that emerge with the diffusion of computer and telecommunications technologies. In some apocalyptic visions, the possibilities for replacement of labor have been deemed to be so large as to herald vast reductions in employment, even the "end of work" (Rifkin, 1995). In a more considered overview of the evidence, Castells (1996) disposes of this fantasy and redirects attention to the systematic "individualization of labor in the labor process" (265). In the "network society," one sees the reversal of the previous trend toward socialization of production (larger workplaces, collective representation, and so on). The new technologies facilitate the customization of products, the development of decentralized businesses, the subcontracting of business functions, and the introduction of new business practices to control quality and performance within core businesses. These business developments present consequent demands for workers to be prepared with relevant new skills and to be willing to accept new forms of work. Indeed, contemporary technologies often directly facilitate new working arrangements such as telecommuting, working while traveling, or shift-working.

Nevertheless, the consequences of modern technologies for the quality of work life in this modern affluent economy are hard to trace in detail, and adhere to no ironclad law. There are many possible ways in which technologies can be used. Best practices are imperfectly known, because they are likely to vary from culture to culture, and because technologies and attitudes are forever changing. There may be no single optimal way to use technology. Even if there is, diffusion of awareness of best practice could be permanently blocked or could indefinitely lag behind the forces that are changing the optimum.[8] The implications for workers can be ambiguous and contradictory. Moreover, though workers' lives are the objects of study, workers are also subjects, real players in the game of workplace conflict and consent. The power and the culture of managers, the institutions of the labor market that may or may not foster cooperation and diffusion of best practice, and the partisan support of governments yield an irreducible indeterminacy to the quality of working lives.[9] For these reasons, the connections between technologies and working lives are only imperfectly understood by scholars.

To begin to understand the links between these changes and the quality of the work lives being experienced in modern industrial economies, it is necessary first to examine the ingredients of a "good job." Unfortunately, this is not a straightforward matter, not least because there are considerable differences of emphasis between the social sciences in this respect. The rest of this chapter sets out the approach to be used in this book. It then takes a first look at how social survey findings have been able to contribute to an understanding of changes in job quality.

## What Makes a Good Job?

There is a school of thought which maintains that, if one wants to know what sort of jobs are being generated in modern industrialized economies, one need only look at their wages. Pay is said to be the single most important factor defining the quality of a job. Moreover, wages generally are positively correlated with other favorable working conditions. Therefore, it is held that a picture of wages over time would not be substantially different from any more detailed picture of overall job quality.

Yet, is pay the overriding factor in job quality? If pay is increasing, does this mean the job is improving even if other aspects of the job, such as the amount of effort required, are deteriorating? To consider these questions, and to evaluate the significance of the nonpay aspects of work, a conceptual framework is needed. Differences among writers on the quality of work life stem at least in part from their different views of how human activities are to be evaluated.

The "quality of work life" or "job quality" is constituted by the set of work features which foster the well-being of the worker. This definition is *worker-centered*: it refers to what is good for the worker, not what an employer or customer might want (though these can affect the worker's well-being directly or indirectly). This book will focus only on paid work and will assume that there is normally a separable domain of work that is important for a person's overall well-being but nevertheless only one part of it. Though "work" and "job" are not universal but historical categories, discussion of how the boundary between work and nonwork could be defined is omitted. Even with these limitations, the notion of job quality is neither simple nor uncontested. Different notions are rooted in the major philosophical systems that have ordered the social sciences for at least two hundred years. Broadly, there are two ways of thinking about well-being and, hence, the quality of work life: the subjective and objective approaches.

In the subjective tradition, with its origins in nineteenth-century utilitarianism, a person's well-being is constituted by the extent to which he or she is able to satisfy personal tastes or preferences. Among the major subjective approaches to well-being is neoclassical economics, the dominant paradigm which governs the way most economists think about normative issues. The neoclassical approach to job quality is found in the theory of compensating differentials, which originated with Adam Smith and the classical tradition. Economics teaches that a job is an exchange of certain approximately specified obligations (hours, effort, duties, and so on) for a package of wages and other benefits. Both the obligations and the benefits are multifaceted. Neoclassical economic theory is purposefully silent on the relative importance of different obligations and benefits for a worker's well-being. The quality of work life is constituted by the overall utility function, which depends entirely on a subjective evaluation of the set of work characteristics. The valuation comes from the individual, and is quantified through market exchange. On the assumption of competitive market conditions, different jobs are predicted to offer packages of obligations and benefits that equate overall utility across jobs for the marginal worker. If competition is restricted, some jobs could confer greater utility than others, but access to the better jobs will be barred for some workers. Leaving aside such restrictions, wage differences for equally productive workers are thus interpreted as "compensating" differentials. Higher pay acts as the incentive to attract workers to less favored jobs. However, people are heterogeneous in their preferences

for benefits and their distaste for work obligations, and firms are heterogeneous in their capacity to supply benefits or to reduce the burden or risk
of work obligations. A matching process occurs in a competitive market,
in which workers with the least aversion to poor working conditions
gravitate toward high-paying companies that would find it most costly
to avert such conditions. Thereby is constructed the "hedonic wage function" that predicts a correlation between wages and less favored work
characteristics, among workers with similar skill.[10]

To many economists, the chief attraction of this subjective approach is
that it avoids having to lay down in advance, or from above, what really
matters in a job. Wants and needs are indistinguishable in this paradigm.
Nevertheless, in the progressive development of economics' claim to scientific status, the subjectivist approach to well-being has led economics
down ever-narrower routes. Despite the individual-oriented basis of the
discipline, ironically there arose an understandable but awkward distrust
of the individual as a source of empirical evidence. Individual evidence
about preferences, it was held, could not be used to make interpersonal
judgments of well-being. This conclusion led eventually to a rejection of
classical utilitarianism at the center of economics. The main criterion
upon which judgments could be made became the Pareto principle, which
states that welfare gains can only be said to occur if one or more persons'
lot improves while nobody loses.[11]

The distrust of the individual as a source of evidence had another
consequence greatly relevant to the task at hand. It meant that direct
survey and other evidence of workers' preferences have rarely been collected by economists, and usually are ignored altogether. Underlying
this distrust is the problem that preferences lack a set metric—either a
quantitative scale or, even, any universal point of origin. It is recognized
that people's assessments of their own situation and preferences are affected by norms, which themselves are unobserved and determined by
societal and historical factors. In addition, survey respondents are subject to many well-known biases. For these reasons, the standard episte-
mological approach of neoclassical economics—which is rooted in the
empiricist tradition—has led it to favor drawing inferences only from the
observed behavior of individuals. It is not what people say, but what
they do, that counts.

This latter criterion provides one possible justification for economics
to treat wages as the premier indicator of quality. Even if, in surveys,
only a minority of workers say that pay is a very important aspect of
their jobs, the wage rate is typically the most significant item over which
they enter into negotiations, or about which they go on strike. This could
be said to reveal workers' evaluation of wages as the main item of work

reward in most cases. A second justification is that pay is the monetized part of the reward, which through the market valuation process represents the basket of goods and services the workers can consume without borrowing. And, third, this market valuation also reveals that for most workers pay is the largest share of the labor costs which employers incur. The other elements of a person's job play only a minor part, or none at all, in the consumption domain.

Notwithstanding these reasons for prioritizing wages, in recent decades the power of the empiricist urge began to undermine the economists' conventional wisdom that data on preferences carry no useful information. Several economists have maintained that happiness data, based on instruments designed and validated within the tradition of empirical psychology, have application and relevance to economic theory and policy (Frey and Stutzer, 2002a, 2002b). Preferences about work as yet play only a small part in this recent tradition. But interest in "job satisfaction" has simmered for three decades and persists. The chief defense of the use of indices of job satisfaction in economics is that they have been robustly shown to be predictors of economic behavior—in particular, job mobility. Workers who say that they are dissatisfied with their job are more likely to quit (Freeman, 1978; Clark et al., 1998). Nevertheless, it is doubtful whether the use of job satisfaction data commands widespread support among economists.

Even among economists who do use job satisfaction data in their research, there is no consensus on its interpretation. The data are regarded by some as constituting a measure of the utility received from work, which is taken to equal well-being from work (e.g., Clark and Oswald, 1996; Frey and Stutzer, 2002a). Others regard job satisfaction as a useful predictor of labor market behavior, but doubt whether it captures well-being (Hamermesh, 2001; Levy-Garboua and Montmarquette, 2004). The difference of views hangs on the character of the norm against which preference and welfare judgments are formed. In particular, job satisfaction is assessed by workers in part in relation to what they expect from the job. Workers might be conditioned to expect a lot or a little from different jobs. This fact has led the doubters to conclude that job satisfaction is not a measure of utility. Nevertheless, it can be maintained that medium-term trends in job satisfaction in a population can be an indication of trends in well-being: this conclusion depends on an assumption that the norms against which satisfaction is measured change only slowly or not at all.

In a more radical departure from orthodoxy, the equation of utility with well-being, and the resulting policy implications, have been robustly criticized by heterodox economists and others drawing on moral philosophy (Hausman and McPherson, 1996, Chap. 6). In contrast to the subjective individualism of neoclassical economics, other major social science traditions have evolved objective, and frequently explicit, approaches to the quality of work life. These approaches are related to their fundamental concepts of human need and valuation, which differ from that of *homo economicus* at the heart of neoclassical economics.

The sociological tradition stems in part from Marx, who held that the fundamental characteristic that distinguished humans from other animals was the conscious planning of their productive activities. Building on this foundation, the sociological tradition has privileged the concept of skill as central to the quality of work life (e.g., Wood, 1982). The Tayloristic philosophy of pursuing an extensive detailed division of labor was seen as constituting not only a de-skilling of labor, but also a dehumanization, or "degradation," of labor—its objectification, and its alienation. In sociology, skilled work is seen as involving both complex operations and "autonomy" for the worker. Post-Taylorist and post-Fordist work organizations are viewed positively in this light, insofar as they herald greater worker involvement in their production activities at various levels, including having more influence and discretion over daily work tasks. This perspective on what counts as quality in a job is also taken by non-Marxist sociological schools, which, though they tend to envisage more optimistic trends in job quality within capitalism, place similar emphases on initiative and influence, skill acquisition, and participation.

Complementing this sociological tradition of concern with autonomy and involvement, occupational psychology has developed since the 1950s an impressive body of empirical knowledge about the correlates of job satisfaction and other measures of affective well-being. Underlying this work have been implicit or explicit theories of human need. The characteristics of high-quality work settings are derived using Maslow's theory of needs or other similar frameworks. This empirical work repeatedly confirmed the high importance to workers of being allowed discretion and trust in their jobs. Notable contributions of evidence in Britain came from the Tavistock Institute of Human Relations. The psychological tradition also affirmed the importance of the workplace as a social arena, and hence the relevance to the quality of work life of having good social relations among workers. In recent decades, one of the objectives of (academic) research has been to refine and improve the design of quality of work life instruments for survey usage in selected settings.

Drawing on the earlier work, the 1960s and 1970s saw the beginnings of a Quality of Work Life movement as a driver of social policy. This movement was most advanced, and appeared to have most effect, in the Scandinavian countries (Gallie, 2003). Such programs involved the development of policies designed to improve a range of areas of work life, including health and safety; the humanization of work (including limiting the division of labor); the promotion of worker involvement in decision-making; and security.

These factors are also emphasized in most modern accounts of work quality outside economics.[12] Surprisingly, such accounts usually do not include wages, which is often the only factor on the economist's list. This omission could be a matter of semantics, where the phrase "job quality" is taken to refer to factors other than the wage. Nevertheless, the economist's near-exclusive emphasis on wages, and the sociologist's focus on factors other than wages, create a potential obstacle to the development of understanding about job quality. The economist stands accused of not dirtying hands with hard-to-measure subjective aspects of work, the sociologist of ignoring the vulgar reality of workers' material rewards.

## An Interdisciplinary Perspective on Job Quality

To counter this tendency, it is useful to observe that there is a broad convergence of the sociological position on work quality with an application of the ideas of Amartya Sen who, among prominent economists, has perhaps done most in recent years to question the scientific and moral case for utilitarianism and individualism in economics. Out of his analysis of the problems facing developing economies, Sen proposed that valuation of human experiences can be conceived in different ways, relevant to the purpose of valuation. Assessment of the achievement of personal well-being is one main method of valuation. Another is through the achievement of "agency goals," that is, the pursuit of goals that may extend beyond the advancement of personal well-being (Sen, 1987, 1993). And, for each of these means of valuation, it is possible also to delineate and evaluate a person's freedom to achieve the objects of valuation. To assess the quality of life, Sen argues that it is important to know a person's "capabilities," which signifies the ability to carry out a range of "functionings" (either doing something or being something) (Sen, 1993). Thus, the ability to perform a range of activities, even if only one activity is chosen, is itself valuable. And, "doing activity $x$" is seen as inferior to "choosing and doing activity $x$."

The notion of capability can be applied in the domain of work life.[13] An individual whose job involves choosing a set of tasks $\tau$ from a wider set $T$ can be taken to have a higher quality of work life than one whose job precisely prescribes that tasks $\tau$ will be performed. The latter has but one choice, whether or not to partake in the exchange: take the job (and do tasks $\tau$) or quit. This person's quality of work life is higher than that of slaves who must do tasks $\tau$ by virtue of their enslavement, having no choice to quit; but less than that of workers who, through participation in the conception as well as the execution of the work, elect to perform the tasks.

Using Sen's approach, the way to evaluate the quality of a job is through the capabilities that are afforded to workers in the job to achieve well-being and to achieve agency goals. The capability to achieve well-being can be thought of as depending on the set of wages and other reward conditions, including future prospects (pensions, security, and so on), and on the range of tasks to be chosen from and actually carried out in the job. The capability to achieve agency goals can be thought of as depending on the extent to which the job enables the individual to pursue personal goals. For example, jobs that permit the satisfaction of providing a service to others could be seen as high quality in this respect, on the assumption that most people do possess such a goal. Alternatively, jobs which afford the possibility of developing fulfilling relations with other people could be considered high quality on the assumption that participating in cooperative action is a valued functioning (at least for many workers, if not all).

The value of the job will depend both on the range of functionings and on the valuation attached to each functioning. For most jobs, the *range* of types of material rewards is not that large: it chiefly embraces wages, bonuses, any fringe benefits, pensions, and holiday privileges. Though an ability to choose between these types of rewards might be valued in itself, the chief element of job quality is normally the magnitude of the rewards, primarily the wages on offer. In contrast, the range of possible work activities is potentially high. Through the freedom to choose between such activities, sometimes in different ways from day to day, a higher quality of work life can be achieved. The complexity and uncertainty surrounding most modern work processes ensures that it is normally impossible to write very precise job descriptions. The valuation of the work activities is thus likely to be significantly affected both by what those activities are and by the extent of genuine remaining choices among activities within the job. With regard to both the work activities and the wages, the range of capabilities need not be constrained by what the job offers immediately: a high-quality job might be one which offers the prospect of acquiring skills to be promoted or to move to other jobs with more highly valued tasks and higher wages.

The quality of jobs is one of the elements that contributes to a person's quality of life. Having access to a job is a positive indicator of living standards. Conditional on having work, a high-quality job is one which affords the worker a certain capability—the ability and the flexibility to perform a range of tasks (including the necessary sense of personal control), to draw on the comradeship of others working in cooperation, to choose from and pursue a range of agency goals, and to command an income that delivers high capability for consumption. This conception of high-quality work, derived by a simple application of Sen's valuation framework, is similar to the emphasis traditionally given in sociological accounts of job quality, with their focus on autonomy, skill, and social relations, but it includes also the present and prospective material rewards of the job.

This valuation framework admittedly does not provide a decisive means of relative valuation of the different aspects of work quality. Sen rejects a universal law of market valuation and suggests that the choice of items that receive high valuation should be appropriate to circumstances. The choice will be different for poor countries, from what it is in the industrialized world. Relatively good wages might, for example, figure more strongly in what makes for a good job in Bangladesh than it does in the United States. But what makes for an appropriate valuation of the various ingredients of job quality remains undecided. The choice is related to "underlying concerns and values," and there is no escape from declaring one's choice. This incompleteness is of course unsettling for anyone in search of a universally applicable approach to work quality. Sen's defense is that his framework of capabilities and functionings fares in this respect no worse than other evaluation frameworks (Sen, 1993–32).

This book will focus on skill, effort, personal discretion, wages, and risk as key indicators of job quality. There are, of course, many other aspects of jobs, but here the choice of job-quality aspects to be examined is driven both by the interdisciplinary conceptual and theoretical approach just outlined and by the constraints of available representative survey evidence. An additional motivating factor is that each of these aspects of job quality has potential links with major institutional and politico-economic changes that have been features of the modern era, including ongoing economic growth of service industries at the expense of manufacturing, globalization, technological change, and the liberalization of markets.

This approach to job quality is based ultimately on need and not premised exclusively upon individualism or upon a market-driven valuation. To justify including a job characteristic among the ingredients of job quality, it is not necessary that a compensating wage differential should be paid for it. Considerable weight is given to features of jobs emphasized in the psychological and sociological literatures, in addition to those more traditionally analyzed in economics literatures. Individuals are, however, still an important and indispensable part of the analysis. Indeed, the socio-psychological literature draws on analyses of individuals in arriving at the conclusion that intrinsic job features are very important in the determination of work quality; and the evidence on compensating wage differentials contributes important information on job quality. Individuals are legitimate informants of value but not its sole arbiters.

The following summarizes the aspects of job quality to be examined:

**1.** The skill involved in a job is considered because the utilization of skill is an end in itself, with intrinsic value. Engagement in complex production processes, requiring both conception and execution of tasks in various measures, is the hallmark of distinctively human production activity, and is the means by which people have the potential for self-fulfilment. Changes in skill requirements figure prominently and widely in debates about work life. In recent years an optimistic perspective has emerged through claims about the emergence of a "knowledge economy" in modern industrial nations, in which better knowledge and information are said to have become the keys to competitive success. The belief exists that the new economy requires jobs to become higher skilled throughout the economy.

In chapter 2 the discussion asks whether the average skill levels needed in jobs have really risen as asserted in this "knowledge economy" paradigm. Though this proposition is empirically confirmed for a number of countries, a more mixed picture arises in answer to the question of how far-reaching is the spread of the knowledge economy. In some countries there is suggestive evidence of a skill polarization taking place. Though the highly skilled jobs are the ones that have increased the most, in these countries there is also a disproportionate growth of low-skilled jobs. Though the upskilling is plainly associated, to some degree, with technological advances of the modern era—principally the computerization of jobs, there remains a demand for relatively low skilled jobs where the work has not yet been automated. The probable reason is that this low-skilled work is nevertheless nonroutine and not easily programmed for replacement by a machine.

Another worrying trend unearthed by social survey analysis is the growing tendency for workers and their qualifications to be poorly matched to their jobs. The supplies of qualified workers have expanded everywhere; in Britain this expansion of supply has proceeded at a faster pace than the increased demand for qualified workers.

**2.** Work effort is considered a key element of job quality, because it is an argument in the standard economists' utility function originating in 1871 with Jevons's labor supply theory, because it is central to a major stream of modern economic theory (efficiency wages theory), because of widespread perceptions in popular discourse that effort is being intensified in the modern era, and because there is psychological evidence linking high work effort to stress, which is the major growing occupational health hazard in industrialized countries.

Chapters 3 and 4 explore evidence about the trends in work effort, both in Britain and in a number of other countries in Europe and elsewhere. The picture is one of fairly widespread, though not universal, effort intensification in the workplaces of the advanced industrialized nations. Here, too, the evidence is in line with much popular comment. It is not so clear exactly *why* people are working harder. There are multiple causes, including declining union power, increased competitive forces, and in some cases greater managerial pressures to raise productivity. However, the evidence also robustly supports the hypothesis that changing technology and work organization are strongly associated with effort intensification.

**3.** The personal discretion of workers over their job tasks, and forms of participation in workplace decisions, are covered in chapter 5, with emphasis on the former. These aspects are implied by the capabilities approach, which leads to an attribution of high value to the process of determining and choosing one's activities, as is confirmed by a considerable body of empirical psychology.

The social survey evidence here, confined to just two countries (Britain and Finland), confounds the hopes of management gurus like Tom Peters and Rosabeth Kanter, as well as a strand of discourse among management theorists. Rather than the proposed steady rise in job quality as newly "empowered" workers are allocated more responsibilities and more autonomy, in Britain the trend is unambiguously toward a reduction in the scope for workers' personal discretion over the tasks that they must perform. It is hypothesized that new technologies may be part of the reason for workers experiencing less discretion; but the evidence is sketchy, and it is equally likely that managers have considerable leeway to determine the way that jobs are designed, and hence that their strategic decisions are an independent factor determining the extent of personal discretion. In Finland, the evidence points largely toward stability, though with some increases in personal discretion being observed. Two lessons can be drawn from this. On the one hand, it should teach skepticism of speculations about workplace trends that are borne of writers' imaginations rather than proper evidence; while, on the other hand, it is a reminder that institutional and cultural factors can induce quite different trends in different countries.

**4.** Pay is, for most workers, the prime source of income, as well as a key aspect of job quality. Chapter 6 presents a cross-national analysis of how pay has changed over recent decades. As expected, in most countries workers have been able to share in the fruits of economic growth, receiving raises in their real average pay. But there are a few exceptions, of which the most significant is the United States. Though American workers received the highest wages during the 1970s, this was no longer true by the turn of the century; for decades, the average pay had stagnated. Job quality is also affected by the fairness of wages—it is inhibited by discrimination and by unjustified inequalities.

There are also big differences across nations in the extent to which pay has become more unequal in recent decades: inequality has increased more in the "liberal market" economies, such as Britain or the United States. The considerable increases in American pay inequality, coupled with the failure of average pay levels to keep pace with economic growth, has meant decreases in pay in the lower half of the pay distribution for Americans, while those further up the pay scales have had their job rewards improved a great deal. Though technology has frequently been the assigned prime cause of the rises in inequality, and sometimes increased international trade with poorer industrializing countries such as China has been blamed, much of the evidence points to the significance of institutional and political factors, in particular the decline in union power and the political decision to reduce the real value of minimum wages during the 1980s.

5. Low risks and security are also key aspects of job quality. This book identifies health and safety as the most important aspects of intrinsic security. In this respect, job quality has been improving unambiguously in most countries: the chances of having a serious or fatal accident at work have declined over recent decades. Partly due to the decline in the proportions of workers involved in heavy industry, the improvements also reflect collective learning and improved regulation of workplaces. By contrast, insecurity of the job itself has been claimed in a good deal of popular discourse to be a distinctive feature of modern workplaces, reflecting a supposedly increased pace of organizational and technical change. The evidence, however, does not support the view that there is some secular decline in job security. There have been no dramatic declines in the stability of jobs (as measured by average job tenure). Perceptions of the risk of job loss are found (in Britain, the United States, and Germany) for the most part to track the movements of the aggregate unemployment rate. An exception is the mid-1990s, when perceptions of insecurity in both Britain and the United States were somewhat on the high side, especially among the higher educated sections of the workforce.

6. Changes in job satisfaction and indicators of affective well-being at work are covered in chapter 8. Their inclusion might be justified as proxies for changing utility and hence well-being, within the neoclassical tradition. For those unwilling to accept that assumption, trends in affective well-being should nevertheless be regarded as a significant component of a wider concept of well-being, and demanding of an explanation. It will not now do to dismiss trends in subjective data as lacking informational content or as irretrievably biased. The social survey evidence presents a picture of declining job satisfaction in Germany and in Britain; in the United States there is a remarkable stability in job satisfaction over a long period. The decline in job satisfaction of workers in Britain is found to be associated with the increases in average workloads and with the decline in personal discretion over job tasks.

There could be a temptation to regard the last set of features, the subjective measures of well-being, as the outputs of work-based happiness, while the inputs are the wages, effort, and other job characteristics. One could then estimate the determinants of job satisfaction, analogously to estimating a production function. Thus, one might in this view, trusting in the individual data, deduce what matters in a job from the estimated coefficients. Using this method, Clark (1998) finds that the content of the job and having good social relationships at work are the most highly valued aspects of job quality. An alternative to a direct well-being measure is to use as a dependent variable individuals' own evaluations of their job relative to an average job. Jencks et al. (1988) regress individuals' job evaluations on job characteristics, and use the resultant coefficients to project an index of job desirability for all jobs. However, to use either of these methods one has to endorse fully the subjective conception of work quality. The valuations are likely to change and to vary across societies. A practical drawback is that surveys of nationally representative samples carrying both subjective job quality indicators and rich details on the characteristics of jobs are scarce. It is preferable, at least for now, to regard the trends in wages, effort, autonomy, security, and environmental health of jobs as evidence *in themselves* of changes in the quality of work life.

## From Quality of Work Life to "Quality in Work"?

Clear thinking about what factors constitute for a good job is a natural prerequisite for understanding the changes affecting many millions of working lives in the present day. From that understanding can come more enlightened policy-making and strategies for all governments and agents seeking to make a difference. There is increasing interest in improving job quality, so it is not surprising that some governments and supranational organizations have also stepped in with their explicit or implicit conceptions. It is useful to compare two official conceptions of job quality with each other and with the approach used in this book.

The International Labor Office (ILO), which attempts to influence work through the agreement of standards and basic rights for workers across the world, has its own laudable concept of "decent work":

> The goal of decent work is best expressed through the eyes of people. It is about your job and future prospects; about your working conditions; about balancing work and family life, putting your kids through school or getting them out of child labor. It is about gender equality, equal recognition, and enabling women to make choices and take control of their lives. It is about

personal abilities to compete in the marketplace, keep up with new technological skills and remain healthy. It is about developing your entrepreneurial
skills, about receiving a fair share of the wealth that you have helped to create
and not being discriminated against; it is about having a voice in your workplace and your community. . . . For everybody, decent work is about securing
human dignity." (ILO, 2001: 7–8)

These criteria of decent work overlap with those to be used in this book,
but are broader. Though some aspects would be hard to measure, at least
the overall concept is unambiguous because it is, as it should be, worker-
centered. The ILO's problems start not with its vision but with the difficulties of addressing the "decent work deficit" around the world (Bruton
and Fairris, 1999), especially in developing countries.

Another supranational organization, the European Union (EU), also
expresses the desire to influence job quality. It may have more power
than the ILO to put policies into effect, but this is within the EU's own
member countries, whose economies for the most part are very much
richer than many of the economies under the remit of the ILO. Unfortunately, the EU's conceptualization of job quality is clouded by being sub-
sumed under the objective of raising the competitiveness of the European
economy. This confusion limits the extent to which EU-driven policy initiatives will be implemented in member countries to improve the quality
of work life. Nevertheless the EU's explicit attention to job quality has
highlighted the need for improvement in several aspects that are in the
interests of both employers and workers, including skills and workplace
safety.

Improving job quality became an explicit objective of the European
Union at the Lisbon Summit of the European Commission in March
2000, and the agenda was developed further at subsequent European
Council meetings in Stockholm and Nice (European Commission, 2001a,
2001b, 2002). Concern with "quality" was said to be at the heart of the
European Social Model, and, while it had already driven the development of social policymaking, employment policies had hitherto largely
been shaped by the objective of reducing social exclusion, which largely
meant maximizing employment opportunities. After the Lisbon summit,
however, policy evaluation, at least at the European level, was to be driven
by the idea that what was needed was not only more jobs, but better
jobs. The question, however, was how to define "better jobs." The Commission has therefore developed its own concept of "quality in work,"
which can be contrasted with the approach in this book.

The Commission sees quality as "taking into account" objective characteristics of the job, subjective views of workers, worker characteristics,
and the match between the worker and the job. This approach naturally

**TABLE 1.1.**
Dimensions of "Quality in Work," according to the European Commission

*Characteristics of the Job*

| | |
|---|---|
| i. | Intrinsic job quality |
| ii. | Skills, lifelong learning, and career development |

*The Work and Wider Labor Market Context*

| | |
|---|---|
| iii. | Gender equality |
| iv. | Health and safety at work |
| v. | Flexibility and security |
| vi. | Inclusion and access to the labor market |
| vii. | Work organization and work/life balance |
| viii. | Social dialogue and worker involvement |
| ix. | Diversity and nondiscrimination |
| x. | Overall work performance |

required more focus. With no guidelines as to what could be an appropriate single index of work quality, the Commission drew up a list of job characteristics, classified according to whether they were intrinsic features of the job or features of the work environment. This classification, it is claimed, gave the list of proposed indicators a "coherent framework and approach." It is stressed also that the associated policy framework should form a coherent whole. Considerable emphasis is placed on the claim that policies to raise the quality of jobs are consistent with the aim of increasing the employability of workers. In addition, the chosen features are said to provide a coherent assessment of the progress toward policy conformity with the goals of the Lisbon summit (European Commission, 2001a: 4). "Quality in work" is set to be monitored regularly, and the results used as part of the evaluation of the development of employment policies in member countries and at the EU level. This objective placed a significant constraint on the choice of quality indicators, in that the measures have to be available for all member countries.

The general features to be monitored are listed in table 1.1. Many of the features in table 1.1 have an obvious place in social and employment policies. In fact, the list appears to be largely driven by pre-existing policy objectives of the European Commission, rather than any explicit reference to social or economic theories, and the drive for better jobs thus has the appearance of a repackaging exercise. Moreover, this official interpretation of the concept of job quality shows an ambiguity that is nicely captured in the phrase "quality in work" which appears to merge in one concept the interests of workers and their employers. The tension in the concept shows itself both in what is left out and in what is included.

Even though one of the sources of evidence on work intensification in European countries is the European Foundation for Living and Working Conditions (an EU research institution), indicators of work effort are not on the list. This exclusion cannot be because of a distaste for subjective measures, since job satisfaction is proposed as a key indicator of intrinsic job quality. One suspects that work effort is less easy to include because of the built-in ambiguity in the Commission's concept of "quality in work": effort is conflictual and contested, and indicators of effort could imply opposite values for employers and employees. Similarly, one wonders why average wages should be excluded from the list: the reason, again, may be the embarrassment surrounding whether high wages are to be applauded or deplored. Pay is only included indirectly as an aspect of gender equality and as contributing to an indicator on mobility (which is itself part of "intrinsic job quality").

So much for omissions. The list also includes measures that are business oriented, and not directly part of the quality of workers' lives. As is typical among official analyses the world over, potential conflicts of interest between workers and employers are underplayed. Thus, it is asserted that "quality can, and must, go hand in hand with improving efficiency, especially as far as public finances and labour market incentives are concerned" (European Commission, 2001a: 5). De-emphasizing the underlying potential for conflict may be essential, if "quality in work" objectives are to be made compatible with the objective of raising competitiveness in the "knowledge economy." In the Commission's analysis, high quality in work is indicated by good performance, for example through productivity indicators (see item (x) in table 1.1). However, this hardly rings true for the worker who is stressed and exhausted as a result of performing so well; and the flexible labor market that is deemed profitable for employers may not be conducive to security and peace of mind on the part of employees obliged to take temporary and otherwise insecure employment.[14] Such tensions are apt to test the neutrality of many analyses by national or supranational governments.

## How to Measure a Good Job: Surveys of the Quality of Work Life

What are the opportunities and constraints of a survey-based approach to work quality measurement? The quality of work life is not easily measured. The concept is complex and lacks an obvious unitary index. Essential components of work quality are in practice measurable primarily through the reports of workers. Any comprehensive measure is thus affected by the potential limitations (e.g., social esteem bias), as well as the advantages (e.g., first-hand knowledge) of subjective data. Nevertheless, the raison d'être for this book is that acceptable quantitative measures are now available in a number of countries. In the last thirty years, surveys have evolved into a widely used instrument of social enquiry. Hitherto, representative large-scale survey methods have been used less frequently for quality of work life issues than for other areas of social life. Survey methods can be inferior to, say, ethnographic methods, for the purpose of uncovering processes, ideologies, and conflicts at the workplace. But, for their generalizability to large populations of interest, their ability to uncover structural changes, and their transparency, survey methods are indispensable.[15]

The quality of the survey, however, is crucial. Many are compromised by poor design, insufficient finance, undue selectivity in their choice of sample population, or overdependence on survey sponsors' nonresearch objectives. Unfortunately, surveys of work issues are no exception, perhaps because interests are especially prone to intrude in this most delicate and central of areas. Also common is the loose use of statistics on work in popular discourse. The general principles that drive the choice of surveys of work used in this book are:

- Sampling methods need to be of sufficiently high quality. This criterion normally entails the use of some form of random sampling procedure.
- The achieved sample should be representative of a nation's workforce, or at least a subgroup forming the large majority.
- There needs to be a good response rate—if possible, explicitly reported.
- The questionnaire needs to contain well-designed instruments for measuring aspects of work quality.
- The surveys need to be able to address the issue of change, preferably through comparison within a series of surveys, or if not, through valid change questions within a single cross-section.

The surveys drawn upon directly in this book are described in the Data Set Appendix. Inevitably, their scope is selective, in terms of both geography and subject matter. This is not a comprehensive account of all aspects of work life across the industrialized world, and does not touch on work life in poor countries. Perhaps such a picture could be drawn up in the future, if the means and methods of social and economic analysis improve as much in the next thirty years as they have in the past. The more modest aim here is to arrive at a picture and an understanding of changes in work life from the workers' perspective, across a reasonable range of countries where the data allow.

# *Two*

## The Quality of Work Life in the "Knowledge Economy"

### An Optimistic Outlook

Among all forms of recent social and economic change, the development of the "knowledge economy" is the transformation which has, apparently, the rosiest implications for the quality of work life in the modern era. According to this model of the modern industrialized world, knowledge and information have become the main drivers of competitive advantage and the route to securing high economic growth. Underlying the shift from a resource-based to a knowledge-based economy has been the revolution in information and communication technologies, which has facilitated enormous changes in the way companies relate to their markets, and how they communicate among themselves and organize themselves internally. Furthermore, rapid scientific progress, accelerated learning, and diffusion across national boundaries of best practices, as well as increasing demand for knowledge-based services that come with rising incomes, have contributed to the preeminence of knowledge-based sectors. Industries such as pharmaceuticals, financial and professional services, or the communications industries, have grown in proportion to the economy. These, however, are just the leading sectors. The knowledge economy is said to embrace all areas, and the tale of its emergence is now ubiquitous in policy discourse across the industrialized world. Together with a wider rhetoric about the modern function of skill in raising productivity, the knowledge economy paradigm has underpinned expansive education policies, transforming them into branches of economic policy. Simultaneously, an important aspect of conventional economic growth theory has come to be centered on the role of human capital in delivering increasing returns and cumulatively higher growth rates.

An optimistic outlook for job quality emerges because, in this perspective, the new jobs ushered in with the knowledge economy entail a more satisfying exercise of human skills and abilities. According to the British government, for example, "The emerging economy puts a premium on skills and knowledge at all levels but particularly on creativity and the ability to innovate, information and communication technologies (ICT) skills, other technical skills as well as the basic ability to read and write."[1] It follows that workers should be less alienated from their work because they are more often engaged in complex production processes that require thinking and planning activities—that is, they are involved more in the process of conception of work, and not just in its execution. Even those workers at the bottom of the occupational hierarchy can benefit from the drive to develop basic skills of literacy and numeracy which are now needed in almost all jobs. The knowledge economy also carries with it a dynamic imperative to engage in lifelong learning. Superior knowledge of production processes cannot be maintained in a competitive economy without continual renewal and development. Thus, many jobs require workers to engage periodically in training. Workers in these jobs therefore may enjoy the additional satisfaction of learning new skills. Apart from any impact that the utilization of more skills might have on wages, therefore, the knowledge economy is directly beneficial for the quality of work life.

The rhetoric associated with the rise of the knowledge economy concerns educational policy makers and employers, as well as individuals. For policymakers, improving workforce skill has become the rhetorical key to making nations or regions the locations for high-quality work. The U.S. economy in the 1980s, it was said, was at risk from a skills crisis, which it needed to resolve by improving its education system. For employers, deploring the deficiency of their employees' skills became a widespread indulgence across continents. For individuals, the imperative to get educated in order to get on is reflected in a substantial private return to education participation that exceeds the return to other forms of investment, as well as in widespread government exhortation. In many countries, educational achievement has become the route to social advancement, and for many at the top of society, the way to preserve their advantage is through privileged (because expensive) access to excellent educational opportunity.[2] Across the industrialized world there is a transformation in the lives of teenagers, as they become subject to the increasing pressures of exams.

Yet, is the scenario of the knowledge economy accurate and does it genuinely reflect these vaunted positive implications for work and for education policies? As Keep and Mayhew (1999) have pointed out, the knowledge economy could be generating a market for a range of types of skills at different levels throughout the economy, some of which do not necessarily require greater formal education. Moreover, whether the potentially positive implications of the knowledge economy extend to lower as well as upper levels of society is open to question, although it is easy to see how there could develop a polarization of the labor force between high-skill and low-skill jobs. To address these issues, this chapter will briefly delineate the hypotheses about skill demands contained within the idea of the knowledge economy. After reviewing how skills can be measured, the survey evidence on changing skill utilization is then scrutinized.

A further concern is that the technologies generating a demand for new skills in the knowledge economy may also be having less felicitous consequences for work itself. This question will be addressed in the subsequent two chapters, but at this point it will be necessary to review evidence about the links between new technologies and the demand for skills.

A final issue to be examined with survey evidence concerns whether there is a mismatch between the output of expanding skill-formation systems and the changing skill demands that are envisaged in the knowledge economy. Skill formation systems are slow to adjust, and because education and training are long-term investments it is common for individuals to find themselves in jobs in which their qualifications are not being fully utilized or, conversely, are insufficient for modern requirements. The rhetoric of the knowledge economy has supported the expansion of education in many countries, but has the economy delivered the jobs to match the increased numbers of qualified workers?

## Theories of the Changing Demand for Skill

The thesis and the rhetoric of the knowledge economy run counter to a major historical stream of writing within sociology, which argued that within capitalist production processes there was an inherent imperative to extend the division of labor, and with it managerial control over production. That proposition was expressed most clearly in the work of Harry Braverman (1974), but the idea's origin lies first in Adam Smith's *Wealth of Nations*, which described the division of labor as simultaneously the motor of economic growth and the source of a boring work life, and then later with the radical critique of capitalism by Karl Marx. The idea later found ironic expression in the work of Frederick Winslow Taylor, who originated "scientific management," which turned the human-centered writings of Marx on their head by advocating a systematic extension of the division of labor and unlimited control by managers of the labor process, as the chief means of achieving greater productivity. According to Braverman, twentieth-century managers were steadily taking control of the production process out of the hands of craft workers, who then become progressively under-skilled. The work itself becomes ever more repetitive and alienating. These theses influenced a substantial body of detailed empirical and subsequent theoretical work in the last thirty years. However, despite their influence, Braverman's ideas have been widely debated and criticized, not least for ignoring workers' resistance, for taking the United States to be the only capitalist model, for its unjustified emphasis on control (rather than profit) as the prime capitalist objective, and for undue generalizing from the experiences of craft workers to all other occupations (Wood, 1982, 1989).

Other schools of sociology have taken a more sanguine view, namely that technological progress in an increasingly industrialized economy brings with it a steadily increasing demand for skill. Theorists in the 1950s and 1960s were already predicting that automation would progressively limit the demand for low-level and routine jobs, in the process blurring the distinction between low-level nonmanual and manual work (Blauner, 1964). The development of automation did not take off, however, until the 1980s, by which time it was being underpinned by the new micro-electronic technologies (Gallie et al., 1998). Parallel to this stream of thought, economists in the 1980s and 1990s, beginning to address the astounding increases in wage inequality that first occurred from around the late 1970s in the United States and elsewhere, argued that a burst of technological change could have been the reason for the rising inequality. It was supposed that technological change was "skill-biased"—that is, leading to decreases in the relative demand for low-skilled labor compared with the demand for high-skilled labor. The proposition was that an acceleration of the demand for skilled labor, brought on by the spurt of technological progress, had led to long periods of demand exceeding the supply of skilled labor, which was expanding at a more modest and steady rate.[3]

The knowledge economy paradigm has become the embodiment of this same thesis for the present day. With it comes as well the focus on new management skills needed to coordinate the process of seeking competitive advantage through knowledge management. These management skills are said to develop alongside teamwork skills, and it is argued to be a requirement that greater proportions of the workforce are empowered to become managers of their own work schedules, that traditional hierarchies are being and should be "de-layered," and that there is and should be a greater reliance on trust in the workplace. Here is one place where the more abstruse outpourings of theorists ride on the same tracks as a significant strand of the popular management literature to be found in airport lounges.

Just as the direction of change of skill remained a subject of sharp controversy among sociologists for many years, there is as yet no consensus of opinion among economists as to whether skill-biased technological change is the best explanation for increasing wage inequality. Nor is there any explicit evidence that there was an *acceleration* of the demand for skills in recent decades. Nevertheless, it is widely held among economists that the direction of skill change is upward, and that this process is linked in part to technical and organizational changes. If skill is an indicator of quality, one might take this as evidence that capitalism is delivering an increasing quality of work life in the modern era. But before concluding positively, three matters must be properly investigated: first, that skills demands are indeed increasing overall and for a broad cross-section of jobs; second, that the skills demands are being matched by rising skill supplies; third, that more skilled jobs are, as expected, delivering better-quality work.

None of these conditions deserve automatic acceptance. Not least, there is no necessity for skill change to be upward. The de-skilling school among sociologists can point to periods of history, like the onset of scientific management, showing very many instances of destruction of craft-level skills in manual and nonmanual jobs, and replacement of skilled with less-skilled jobs. Despite rising education levels in all industrialized countries in recent years, it is by no means obvious that skill levels at work *must* have been rising. Employers may have been increasingly driven to take on employees with qualifications which are not related in level or type to the simple nature of the tasks that the work involves. There needs to be some more convincing evidence about the jobs themselves.

## The Concept and Measurement of Skill

To set the stage, consider first how different disciplines have evolved contrasting, if overlapping, conceptions of what "skill" means. In psychology, a skill is the competence to perform specified tasks, and is distinguished from "ability," which is the general capability that an individual possesses when first beginning to perform tasks, and also from "knowledge," which is the body of information necessary for competent performance. In sociology, the primary indication of skill is the degree of complexity of work, but skill is also intimately related to the autonomy of the worker. Sociologists distinguish between job skill, which resides in the job specification, and person skill. They also point out that the designation of jobs as "skilled" or otherwise is contestable and often "socially constructed"—that is, determined in part by the configuration of power relations at the workplace. The label "skilled," it is held, contributes to the valuation of jobs in the labor market. The social and economic relations in the environment in which skills are deployed are considered highly important.

For economists, skill is a more general concept—namely, a characteristic of individuals that can be acquired and that enables them to produce valued services at work. It is a component of human capital. As such, skill is conceptually the same as, for example, health, since both good health and skill can be invested in, enabling a stream of revenues to be earned. Skills are also conceptually equivalent to such behavioral traits, as being honest, reliable, or well-motivated, because these too are productive of market values and are acquirable. These overlapping but different conceptions of skill can easily interact with the term in everyday usage to engender confusion in social discourse.

Explicit discussion of the measurement of skill can help to avoid misunderstanding. Table 2.1 shows six different ways in which skills have been measured in empirical work in recent decades. Each has advantages and disadvantages. Most relevant to the knowledge economy paradigm is the measurement of job skill. While length of education or qualifications achieved by the workforce are relatively easy indicators to collect and can sometimes be made internationally comparable, both have a loose connection to skills actually used in jobs. Occupational classification has a better link with job skill, but even so the hierarchies of skills among occupations are contestable, uncertain, and changing. Direct literacy and numeracy test scores also exist to measure person skills, but such tests cover only a limited range of skills and are rare because they are expensive to administer. Self-assessment of person skill is also possible, but has been used even more rarely. The most satisfactory approach to gauging job skills and how they have changed is through indicators of job requirements (see row 6 of table 2.1). Job skill requirements can be obtained as secondary data from the commercial practice of job analysis, using the few proprietary databases that have been made available to researchers, from expert assessments of occupations, or, alternatively, from specially designed social surveys.[4]

### The Rising Level of Skill

The evidence regarding job requirements shows that, taken on the whole, the level of job skills has indeed been rising in the industrialized countries. There are many studies, worldwide, documenting modest trends toward greater proportions of higher-skilled occupations in industrialized economies. Examples for Canada and for Britain are given, respectively, in Lavoie et al. (2003) and DfEE (2000). In the United States, researchers have also turned to the *Dictionary of Occupational Titles,* and used assessments of a range of skills attributed to each title by experts. The skills can be combined into three indices measuring "substantive complexity," "interactive skills," and "motor skills." Across the whole economy, substantive complexity and interactive skills increased steadily from 1950 to

**TABLE 2.1.**
Ways of Measuring Workplace Skills

| Method(s) | Example(s) | Advantage(s) | Disadvantage(s) |
|---|---|---|---|
| *Qualifications* | | | |
| The proportions at each level (often limited to college or noncollege) | Giret and Masjuan (1999) Steedman and Murray (2001) | Objective; long-term trends available | Loose connection of academic qualifications with job skills |
| *Education Length* | | | |
| Average years of schooling, or proportions with many years | Barro and Lee (2001) | Objective; long-term trends available; internationally comparable | Variable quality of education, and loose link with job skills |
| *Occupation* | | | |
| The proportions in higher-skilled occupations | Machin and Van Reenen (1998) Gregory et al. (2001) | Easily available from labor force surveys or censuses; sometimes internationally comparable | Skills change within occupations; the hierarchy of skill among occupations is contestable and changing |
| *Tests* | | | |
| Scores from literacy and numeracy tests | OECD et al. (1997) Freeman and Schettkatt (2001) | Objective; international comparisons possible | Narrow range of skills; expensive to administer; trend data rare |
| *Self-Assessment* | | | |
| Survey-based individual reports about themselves | Bynner (1994) | Wide range of skills | Subjective, and skill assessment associated with self-esteem |
| *Job Requirements* | | | |
| Sourced from commercial job analyses, expert assessments of occupations, or surveys of individuals or employers | Cappelli (1993) Holzer (1998) Howell and Wolff (1991) Ashton et al. (1999a) Felstead et al. (2002) Autor et al. (2003a) Handel (2000) | Wide range of skills; intimately connected to jobs | Job skill requirement could differ from person skill; subjective; only measures skills of those employed |

1990, while motor skills began to decline after 1970 (Wolff, 2003). The pace of the growth of skills appears to have slowed in the 1980s (Howell and Wolff, 1991). However, their method does not capture changing skill requirements within detailed occupations. If within-occupation changes were upward, the rise in skills will have been greater. Evidence from detailed job analyses carried out over time by private consultants Hay Associates suggests that, within the large number of jobs covered by their company, skill requirements had indeed been increasing in a range of clerical and production jobs from 1978 to 1986 (Cappelli, 1993).

The story of rising skill is confirmed by individual-level evidence on job requirements for a similar period in the United States. The proportion of jobs requiring a college degree rose from 10 percent in 1969 to 23 percent in 1985. The changed requirements also reached the lower end of the labor market as, over the same period, the proportion of jobs for which less than a high school education would suffice fell from 36 percent to 13 percent (Handel, 2000). Between 1977 and 1985 there was also a decline, from 29 percent to 22 percent, in the proportion of jobs for which less than a month would be required to "learn to do the job reasonably well."

In Germany also there has been a steady rise in the qualification requirements of jobs. Table 2.2, taken from the German Socioeconomic Panel, shows this trend. To maintain a consistent picture on either side of re-unification, the table excludes jobs located in East Germany. It shows that, between 1985 and 1997, the proportion of jobs with high education or training qualification requirements rose by nearly 5 percentage points to 16 percent, while the proportion with little or no qualification requirements fell from 32 percent to 27 percent.[5]

In Britain, even more recent evidence derived from job requirements data also confirms that work is, on average, increasingly requiring higher levels of skill (Ashton et al., 1999a; Gallie, 1996; Gallie et al., 1998; Felstead et al., 2002). Some of the most up-to-date evidence is shown in table 2.3, panel (a). For example, jobs for which no qualifications would be required to obtain them amounted to 38 percent of all jobs in 1986, but only 26 percent of jobs in 2001. At the other end of the scale, the proportion of jobs requiring professional or degree qualifications rose from 20 percent to 29 percent over the same interval. It might be argued that this could be simply reflecting a creeping credentialism, whereby employers are obliged to keep raising their requirements in order to recruit employees of constant ability, simply because of the rising tide of qualifications emerging from schools over the period. To consider this, questions were designed to elicit job-holders' judgments about whether the qualifications required from recruits were also necessary to do the job competently. The responses to these questions reveal *some* evidence

**TABLE 2.2.**
Trends in Qualification Requirements, Germany, 1985–1997

| | Qualification Requirement | | |
| --- | --- | --- | --- |
| | Low (%) | Medium (%) | High (%) |
| 1985 | 32.2 | 56.3 | 11.5 |
| 1986 | 32.2 | 56.1 | 11.8 |
| 1987 | 33.6 | 54.8 | 11.6 |
| 1988 | 33.1 | 55.0 | 11.9 |
| 1989 | 31.7 | 56.0 | 12.3 |
| 1990 | 33.2 | 55.0 | 11.9 |
| 1991 | 33.2 | 55.0 | 11.9 |
| 1992 | 30.5 | 56.8 | 12.7 |
| 1993 | 30.7 | 55.8 | 13.5 |
| 1994 | 29.1 | 56.1 | 14.8 |
| 1995 | 26.5 | 57.3 | 16.2 |
| 1996 | 28.3 | 55.1 | 16.7 |
| 1997 | 27.2 | 56.8 | 16.1 |

*Source*: GSOEP

*Note*: Respondents were asked about the education and training requirements of their job at the point of job entry. "Low" training means either: no education/training requirements, or only an introduction to job or on-the-job training. "Medium" training means completed vocational training or formal courses of post-compulsory education. "High" training means college education or equivalent.

of increasing credentialism over this period, especially with respect to middle- and low-level qualifications (Felstead et al., 2002: 49–50). For example, where a level 3 qualification (A-level, or the equivalent of high school diploma) was required by an employer, some 77 percent of employees in 1986 reported this was fairly necessary or essential to do the job competently; this same proportion had fallen to 70 percent by 2001. Notwithstanding this evidence, employers' requirements for qualifications that are also necessary to do the job have been rising. Panel (b) gives an example: the demand for graduate-level qualifications to get and do jobs rose from 7 percent to 13 percent over the 1986–2001 period.

Figure 2.1 highlights the similarity in the upskilling story emerging from skill requirements data in the United States, Germany, and Britain. The figure also shows the differences in the timing and extent of employers' use of highly educated labor: in the United States, utilization of college-educated labor was already relatively high by the mid-1980s.

Required qualifications are only one indicator of the ability needed to do complex jobs. Another element is the cumulative amount of time spent training for the type of work now being done. This indicator also

**TABLE 2.3.**
Trends in Broad Skills, Britain, 1986–2001

|                            | 1986   | 1992   | 1997   | 2001   |
|----------------------------|--------|--------|--------|--------|
| *(a) Highest Qualification Required(%)* [1] |        |        |        |        |
| Degree or                  |        |        |        |        |
| Professional               | 20.2   | 25.5   | 24.3   | 29.2   |
| Level 3                    | 15.2   | 16.6   | 13.8   | 16.3   |
| Level 2                    | 18.5   | 19.0   | 21.2   | 15.9   |
| Level 1                    | 7.7    | 5.0    | 9.2    | 12.1   |
| No qualifications          | 38.4   | 34.0   | 31.5   | 26.5   |
| *(b) Jobs Requiring Graduate Skills to Do Them(%)* [2] |        |        |        |        |
|                            | 7.5    | n.a.   | 10.6   | 13.4   |
| *(c) Training Time(%)* [3] |        |        |        |        |
| >2 years                   | 22.4   | 21.9   | 28.9   | 23.6   |
| <3 months                  | 66.0   | 62.6   | 57.0   | 61.1   |
| *(d) Learning Time (Employees only)(%)* [4] |        |        |        |        |
| >6 months                  | 43.7   | 45.0   | 49.2   | 50.9   |
| <1 month                   | 27.1   | 22.3   | 21.4   | 20.2   |
| *(e) Composite Skill Index (Average Score)* [5] |        |        |        |        |
|                            | −0.183 | −0.010 | 0.085  | 0.123  |

*Source*: SCELI, EIB, 1997 and 2001 Skills Surveys.
*Notes*:

[1] Respondents were asked: "If they were applying today, what qualifications, if any, would someone need to *get* the type of job you have now?" A range of options was given. From this the highest qualification level was derived. Level 3 is equivalent to A-level, the qualification normally taken by 18-year-old school leavers. Level 2 is equivalent to the higher range of achievement at O-Level or General Certificate of Secondary Education, the qualification normally taken at age 16. The lower range of achievement at this age, or other low qualification, is termed Level 1. Levels correspond to the U.K. system of National Vocational Qualifications.

[2] Graduate skills are deemed to be required to do jobs if they are required to get jobs *and* are reported to be "essential" or "fairly necessary" to carry out the job competently.

[3] Respondents were asked: "Since completing full-time education, have you ever had, or are you currently undertaking, training for the type of work that you currently do? Respondents answering "yes" were then asked: "How long, in total, did (or will) that training last?" A range of options was given.

[4] Respondents were asked: "How long did it take for you after you first started doing this type of job to learn to do it well?"

[5] The Composite Skill Index is the first principal component derived from cardinal indices of the three measures: highest qualification required, required training time, and required learning time. This measure is the best available single index of the broad level of job skills actually used in jobs in Britain. It has mean zero over the pooled sample of all years, and applies to employees only.

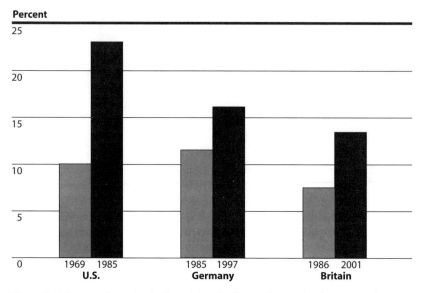

Figure 2.1. Proportion of Jobs Requiring College-Educated Labor: United States, 1969 and 1985; Germany, 1985 and 1997; Britain, 1986 and 2001
  *Source*: Tables 2.2 and 2.3 and Handel (2000).

shows an increase over the 1986–2001 period, though with a drop in the late 1990s. Thus, the proportion of workers in Britain whose work had required no or fewer than three months' training fell from 66 percent to 61 percent. Yet another source of broad skill acquisition is through learning while doing the job. Respondents were asked how long it took them to learn to do a job well. The presumption was that jobs that could be done well only after a substantive learning period were, on the whole, more complex than jobs that could be picked up very quickly.[6] This indicator also tells a similar story of increasing skill. In 1986, 44 percent of jobs had taken at least six months to learn. By 2001, this proportion had risen to 51 percent.

Educational qualifications, training time, and learning time each capture, if imperfectly, alternative inputs generating the ability to perform complex work tasks. While they tell broadly consistent stories, it is convenient for subsequent analysis to construct a single index from these three. The Composite Skill Index is a weighted average of the indices measuring qualification requirement, training requirement, and learning requirement.[7] As can be seen in panel (e) of table 2.3, the average value of this index rises over each subperiod throughout 1986 to 2001. Taken together, the trend in these three indicators and in the Composite Skill

Index add up to a fairly robust story of upskilling in the British workforce, even if the changes over fifteen years remain relatively modest. The story is consistent with other analyses that have shown increasing proportions among those employed in higher-level, nonmanual jobs,[8] and with occasional subjective reports of employers and employees that skill levels are rising. It is also consistent with findings from Britain and elsewhere that returns to educational achievements have been maintained, or even increased, despite considerable increases in the number of people with high educational achievements available in the workforce. A simple supply-and-demand framework can be invoked to draw the inference that the demand for people with higher achievements therefore must have increased as well.

Supplementing the evidence on broad job skills, case studies and employers' reports also point to increasing demand for certain generic skills, including problem-solving, communication, and IT skills, as well as the basic skills of literacy and numeracy. The job analysis method used in the 1997 and 2001 Skills Surveys also now furnishes formal evidence in support. This method makes it possible to compute indices of the usage and importance of several generic activities within jobs. The skills measured include literacy, physical skills, numeracy, technical know-how, high-level communication, planning, client communication, horizontal communication, problem-solving, checking skills, and computing skills. With the exception of physical skills, all others showed an increase between 1997 and 2001 (Felstead et al., 2002). This is too short a period to establish a long-term trend, even if the story is consistent with that obtained from other indicators and other sources. For most generic skills, the rise was modest, though statistically significant. Computing skills, however, were in rapidly increasing demand at this time.

## Skills Polarization?

A potential issue for the quality of work life in an upskilling economy could be that only some jobs are changing while others are left behind or de-skilled as managers seek to gain tighter control over labor processes. Many such transformations are indeed found: Lloyd (1997), for example, has found de-skilling in the clothing industry, Hjalager (1999) in restaurants. Moreover, not only the very high wage jobs have been growing in recent decades; also among the fastest-growing jobs in Britain are low-paying jobs such as security and protective service workers in the business services industries; window dressers, floral arrangers, and telephone sales persons in the hotel and catering industry; the matrons, house parents, welfare, community, and youth workers in the public administration and sanitation industries (Goos and Manning, 2003). Such jobs are not those that spring to mind with the vision of the knowledge economy.

These examples suggest not only that there are exceptions to the average upskilling trend, but that there may also be a polarization of skill taking place. Supporting that idea is the general finding in many countries that access to training is far greater for better educated workers. Most low-educated workers do not receive substantial amounts of training. Yet the evidence on skill polarization is mixed. In Britain, a key difference between 2001 and 1986 is the falling proportion of jobs requiring very low skill requirements. It is not only the very high skilled jobs that have been getting more populous: rather there is a general upward shift in skill distribution overall. A similar finding for the earlier period in the United States is reported by Handel (2000): the distribution of job skill requirements became less unequal between 1969 and 1985.

Both these pieces of evidence, however, rely on medium-sized survey samples that do not permit disaggregation to a detailed occupational classification. An alternative way to look for polarization is to rank jobs by their wage rate and to investigate whether middle-ranking jobs are experiencing lower growth in employment than either higher or lower wage groups. Over the relatively short period from 1993 to 1999, employment growth was greatest in the highest paid sectors of the labor market in the United States, Germany, Italy, Switzerland, France, Denmark, Greece, Belgium, the United Kingdom, the Netherlands, and Spain: the only exception among those analyzed was Ireland (OECD, 2001). This finding is fully consistent with the picture of the knowledge economy. Elements of polarization, where the next highest growth rate was to be found in the low-paid sector, were, however, also found in Belgium, the Netherlands, and the United Kingdom. For the United Kingdom, Goos and Manning (2003), using information on initial median wages and demand growth over 1979 to 1999 for three-digit occupations in Britain, report a similar picture. They find that, just as in the knowledge economy paradigm, it was largely the high-wage jobs that grew the most over the two decades. Yet the lowest-wage jobs also were growing faster than the middle-ranking jobs. Unless, for some reason, the middle ranking jobs were experiencing a high level of within-occupation upskilling (and there is no reason to expect this), Goos's and Manning's finding suggests that there may have been a process of polarization in the quality of jobs. Such a process is not consistent with the assumption that technological change is universally skill-biased.[9]

## Skill, Technology, and Work Organization

Whether the increasing skill level of jobs improves the quality of work life may depend on the reasons jobs are being upskilled. One possible reason might be that workers in the industrialized world are becoming better educated and more skilled. This could lead employers to substitute skilled for unskilled labor as the skilled labor becomes less scarce and available at lower wages. There is, however, no evidence that the relative wages of skilled labor are generally declining—if anything the reverse is true. Rather, jobs in the industrialized world are becoming more skilled primarily because of changes on the demand side. Two schools of thought vie for support in explaining the switch in demand in favor of more skilled labor. One sees the entry of third world countries into the global market for manufactured goods from the 1970s onward as the trigger for the establishment of a new comparative advantage in the industrialized world for goods and services that are intensive in the use of skilled labor. The other sees exogenous technological change arising in the industrialized world as the prime source. The resolution of that debate has implications for explanations of the increase in wage inequality: the key issue is which new sources of increased demand for skill were sufficient to generate a large enough acceleration of the demand for skills and thereby raise the price of skill. But, however that issue is empirically resolved, the relevant question for understanding the direct implications of skill change for the quality of work life is: what are the proximate sources of the rising demand for skill? The significance of technological change in practice is especially pertinent, because technological changes also have other consequences for job quality, to be considered in subsequent chapters.

The formal statistical evidence for a positive relationship between technical and organizational change and increasing skills comes from multiple sources, and many countries. Here are some examples of each type of evidence:

- There is a correlation across countries in the specific industries that are increasing workforce skills the most (Machin and van Reenen, 1998). Technical change can account for this international similarity, since many technologies are likely to be specific to particular industries, but available for adoption anywhere.
- Skill increases are associated with expenditures in firms and industries on research and development (Hollanders and ter Weel, 2002).
- Skills are associated with investment in and use of computers, the paradigm of new technology in the modern era (Haskel and Heden, 1999; Green et al., 2003b; Krueger, 1993).

- Technical and organizational changes experienced in establishments are correlated, and both are associated with rising skill requirements (Greenan, 2003; Caroli and Van Reenen, 2001; Bresnahan et al., 2002; Gera et al., 2001).
- New forms of flexible production processes, and modern management policies like quality improvement circles and other employee involvement practices, are associated with increasing skill requirements (Gale et al., 2002; Green et al., 2001; Appelbaum et al., 2000).

The relationship between computerization of the workplace and the demand for skills is both robust and substantial. The strength of the relationship is illustrated by the analysis shown in table 2.4, which extends a similar one reported in Green et al. (2003b).

The rise in the Composite Skill Index can be decomposed, using a standard technique originally suggested by Oaxaca (1973), into two parts, one the result of the spread of "advanced technology" (computerized or automated equipment), the other a residual comprising all other sources of change. In every year, the association between the "advanced technology" variable and skill use is positive and high. The decomposition shows that most of the rise over each subperiod between 1986 and 2001 can be accounted for by the rise in the proportion of jobs involving advanced technology (table 2.4). In a parallel analysis of

TABLE 2.4.
Computers and the Rise in Skill Demand, Britain, 1986–2001

|  | 1986–1992 (%) | 1992–2001 (%) | 1986–2001 (%) |
| --- | --- | --- | --- |
| Proportion of rise in skill accounted for by rise in usage of computers or automated equipment:[1] |  |  |  |
| Composite Skill Index[2] | 91.1 | 102.1 | 99.6 |
| Graduate skills[3] |  |  | 87.8 |

*Source*: SCELI, EIB, 2001 Skills Survey.
*Notes*:

[1] The proportions are estimated from a regression of the Composite Skill Index on a dummy variable representing usage of computers or automated equipment in each year, and calculated using Oaxaca's standard decomposition; in the case of graduate skill, the estimate is obtained from a linear probability model of the probability that a job requires graduate skill; an alternative estimate can be obtained from a probit model, but with a similar finding.

[2] See table 2.3, note 5.

[3] See table 2.3, note 2.

the whole 1986–2001 period, the increase in the demand for graduate skills can also be accounted for largely by the increase in computer usage. One can also tell this story the other way round. If, hypothetically, there had been no increase in the proportion of jobs using computers or automated equipment, the change in the demand for skills would have been very much smaller, and statistically not different from zero. This analysis demonstrates that new computerized and automated technologies, whatever their ultimate origin and whatever other complementary changes in techniques and in work organization were associated with them, were the main source of changes in skill demand in Britain.

Large though it is, the impact of modern automated technologies on skills needs to be differentiated. Computers are good at replacing functions that can be explicitly codified and hence programmed (Levy and Murnane, 2004). They extend the progressive and traditional effect of capital investment in replacing and superseding human effort into the sphere of many routine, nonmanual activities. Autor et al. (2003a) find that the industries that involved intensive use of routine manual and cognitive tasks were those that invested first and most extensively in computerization, displacing many jobs in the process. However, computers are not so good at replacing non-routine activities—such as problem-solving, interpersonal communication, or activities that require hand-eye coordination. Many nonroutine activities remain relatively low-paid, and if the demand for them has continued to rise while their productivity is not touched by the computer revolution, this can account for the findings of job polarization referred to above.

Autor and colleagues also find an increased intensity of jobs using nonroutine cognitive skills, which are likely to be complementary with automated technologies in their effects on productivity. Despite instances of de-skilling referred to above, other case studies support the formal statistical evidence. For example, it has been found that the introduction of new technologies is accompanied by a need for more diagnostic and problem-solving skills, for communication and other interpersonal skills, for more technical know-how, and for mathematical skills (Autor et al., 2003b; Bartel et al., 2003; Ballantine and Ferguson, 2003). Higher product specifications associated with more automated production have also been linked to greater demand for skill (Mason et al., 1994).

The nature of the association between computer technology and skill has probably changed over recent decades. While mainframe computerization had been responsible for the automation of very many routine nonmanual tasks from as early as the 1960s, the most significant aspect of the new computer technologies of the 1980s and 1990s is that personal computer networks enabled companies to devise innovative ways of working and of relating to customers, thereby transforming both work organization and the skills required of workers (Bresnahan, 1999). In short, upskilling was the consequence of complementary changes in both the technologies and forms of work organization.

## The Skills Balance

So far the skills as revealed by job requirements have been treated as direct indicators in themselves of the quality of work life. Yet a job of a certain skill does not translate automatically into a certain quality of work life. The job-holder's skill may not match that required by the job. On the one hand, concern is frequently expressed that workers' skills are less than those required. In the United States, the expressed fear in the late 1980s was that the education system was failing to produce enough skilled workers to meet expected demand. In Germany, more recently, the poor performance of teenagers in the Programme for International Student Assessment (PISA) tests of core skills opened a public debate on the adequacy of the German schooling system. In Britain, the perception that there was a skills deficit, which was manifest in extensive skills shortages whenever the economy began to grow faster than normal, drove the Labor government in the late 1990s to set up a "National Skills Task Force."

On the other hand, fears are also expressed, more commonly by academic writers and others independent of the educational policy-making network, of a growing risk of "over-education," whereby workers take jobs that require lower qualifications than the ones they possess, and displace or "bump down" workers with lower qualifications into jobs that require no qualifications at all. Though qualification is not the same as skill, over-education is already a nontrivial issue in a number of countries (Borghans and de Grip, 2000). In Britain in 1986, approximately 30 percent of workers were over-educated for their jobs' qualification requirements; also, about one in five workers tend to be "under-educated," meaning that anyone now applying for the same job would require a higher qualification than the job-holder possesses.

Though this indicates a high proportion of mismatched workers, similar estimates are found in other countries (Handel, 2000; Green et al., 2002). Indeed, employees' qualifications have always been quite loosely matched with job requirements. The issue, however, is that the proportion over-educated has been creeping upward: in Britain it had increased to 37 percent in 2001 (see figure 2.2). This rise is primarily associated with an increase in the extent to which higher levels of academic (rather than voca-

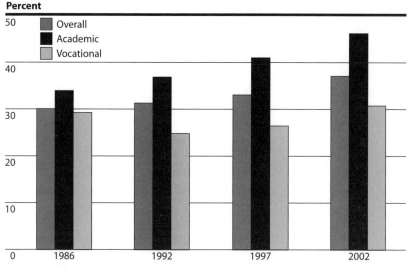

Figure 2.2. Over-Qualification in Britain, 1986–2001
Source: SCELI, EIB, 1997 and 2001 Skills Surveys.
Note: Proportion of workers holding qualifications above those required for current recruitment to job.

tional) qualifications are being achieved compared with what employers are asking for. Reflecting this individual experience of over-education, an aggregate qualifications imbalance developed during the 1990s: many more low-level qualifications were being supplied in the workforce, but the growth of jobs demanding low-level qualifications was much less. By 2001, there was an excess supply of around 4.4 million low-qualified workers. At the same time, the number of jobs requiring no qualifications outnumbered workers holding no qualifications at all by some 3.6 million. Meanwhile, although demand and supply for higher-level qualifications remained in rough balance through the 1990s (Felstead et al., 2002: 45–46),[10] in the current decade employers are seeking additional signs of character and commitment in order to select recruits (Brown and Hesketh, 2004).

If individuals possess too few skills to carry out their jobs, the quality of that experience is diminished, something that is typically experienced as work strain (Warr, 1987). If workers are unable to utilize their achieved qualifications, this also lowers the quality of their experience, entailing a loss of wages (Hartog, 2000). The problem appears to be becoming more serious in Britain. How far this matters for the job satisfaction of workers is examined in chapter 8.

### Conclusion: A Mixed Verdict

The concept of the knowledge economy, as a descriptor of twenty-first-century industrialized economies, may be a flawed one, in that it captures only imperfectly the quantitative and qualitative range of knowledge and skills required at work. Yet its optimistic implications for the quality of work life nonetheless appear to be valid from one perspective: in general, workers are now doing somewhat more complex jobs than they used to. The broad skills indicators each capture in some way the complexity of the tasks involved at work. In general, more complex sets of tasks require more learning, more training, and better educated recruits; they entail the exercise of a wider and deeper set of generic skills. Yet against this upbeat verdict there are some significant counterbalancing features.

First, the various measures of skill do not explicitly capture the autonomy of workers, also an intrinsic aspect of high quality work. Skill and autonomy are likely to be closely related, but it does not follow that changes in the complexity of work processes are mirrored by similar changes in autonomy. Compared with the measures of skill described and utilized in this chapter, representative indicators of the different facets of autonomy are more rare. As will be seen in chapter 5, the verdict from the formal evidence is not always in tune with the rhetoric of the knowledge economy; it is more pessimistic about trends in the quality of work life in Britain.

A second caveat is the potential for polarization of jobs within a knowledge economy, with growing proportions of hard-to-automate yet low-skilled service jobs, as well as of high-skilled jobs. Skills polarization is a more significant phenomenon in some countries than others. With generally expanding education systems, the polarization of skill demands also makes it more likely that imbalances in skills supply and demand will occur. Either inadequate personal skills or under-utilized skills can be a problem for anyone's quality of work life. The demand/supply balance is not readily measurable, except with regard to one skills measure, the required qualification level. In the case of Britain, the demand for qualified workers in the low to middle end of the spectrum did not expand fast enough since the mid-1980s to match the extra supplies of qualified workers.

The most remarkable aspect of the body of evidence on the reasons for changing skills demands is the overriding role of technical and organizational changes at work. Whether the origins of these technological changes lie in global economic transformation, in the changing balance of power between capital and labor, or in the autonomous progress of knowledge, the proximate association of computerization and of new forms of work organization with higher skill levels seems beyond dispute. Nevertheless, there are some types of task that computerization has not been able to touch—primarily jobs requiring nonroutine tasks—and there is still a growing demand for many of these.

No verdict on the overall quality of work life can be approached without also looking at other implications for employees of these technological changes. Of these other implications, perhaps the most striking are the increasing demands and pressures that jobs in the "knowledge economy" are placing upon workers, which are to be examined in the next chapter.

# Three

## Late Twentieth-Century Trends in Work Effort

### Working Hours, Work Effort, and the Quality of Work Life

In the last two decades, despite improved living standards, commentators in industrialized countries have increasingly noted and deplored a sense of increasing work pressure. While the exact nature of this increasing work pressure appears to vary from one account to another, the issue is frequently linked to ill health, either metaphorically or literally (as an "epidemic of stress"). A culture of long hours at work came to be dubbed the new "British disease," elevating the problem to a status usually accorded to only the most treasured of scapegoats.[1] Long hours for men, in particular, came to be seen as a constraint on the transformation of the household division of labor, held out as part of the feminist project.[2] Meanwhile commentators in the United States lamented the epidemic of "hurry sickness," a virus engineered in California that causes people to fear that "time is running out and it's driving us crazy."[3] For Gallie et al. (1998), the issue is more one of hard work and tension in the workplace, tight deadlines, and increased task flexibility. In their study of changes in the quality of work life in Britain up until 1992, they found a pervasive experience of rising work pressure, which went hand in hand with perceived increases in skill requirements. Similarly, in France, deteriorating workplace health has been attributed to rising pressures on the pace of work (Cartron and Gollac, 2002). For those with a campaigning perspective, increasing work pressure embraces both harder work and longer and more unsociable hours, and is deemed to be self-evidently associated with increasing job insecurity and health risks.[4]

Expressed concern is epitomized in the growth of the "stress" industry, that army of occupational psychologists whose job it is to find ways of relieving the adverse effects of overwork on mental and physical health. Workplace stress emerged as a political and social issue primarily in the 1990s. With headlines such as "Work can damage your health"[5] and reports of "stress at work rising sharply,"[6] the ballooning media coverage appeared to have discovered a new and growing problem.[7] Yet stress is only the extreme manifestation of increased pressures at work.[8] Experiences of less extreme pressures may also be undesirable. Economics assumes that this is so. In the neoclassical model of labor supply, it may be conceded that up to a point workers may prefer more effort to less, even for the same wage. However, employers will always ask employees to work beyond that point because both gain from doing so. From then on, increasing effort is assumed to reduce the worker's utility, and each extra unit of effort brings successively larger reductions in utility— this is the so-called "law of increasing marginal disutility of effort." In equilibrium the marginal disutility of effort is equated to the marginal utility of the wages earned. Remarkably, more than a century since Stanley Jevons first proposed this now-standard model, evidence on the disutility of effort remains largely only indirect, being implicit in estimates of labor supply elasticities. Little information exists about how much welfare and the quality of work life are affected by increases in work effort. What is available is a certain amount of psychological evidence about the impact of work overload on well-being (e.g., Warr, 1987; Van den Berg and Schalk, 1997; Johnson et al., 1998).

Despite popular commentary, the cited evidence to support the general proposition that late twentieth-century industrialized capitalism was an era of increasing work pressure has been rather limited. When considered just in terms of average work hours, in most countries people work on average far *less* than they did in the immediate postwar decades, when the working year already had been reduced by about one-third from what had been normal toward the end of the nineteenth century (Madison, 1982). The continued reductions work hours in the late twentieth century enabled working men and women to have more free time, more sleep, more holidays, and more time to attend to family responsibilities (Robinson, 1991). In recent decades work hours have continued to decline in many industrialized nations. Average annual work hours have fallen since the early 1980s in Belgium, Finland, France, Germany, Ireland, Italy, the Republic of Korea, Japan, and Norway (see table 3.1). Meanwhile, in another group of countries annual hours changed relatively little since 1983: these include Greece, Sweden, the United Kingdom, the United States, Canada, and Australia. In no industrialized nation has there been a dramatic rise in average working hours. All that could be said is that, during the 1980s and 1990s, in some countries average hours did not continue their long-term historic fall.[9] In Britain, the average weekly hours of work had fallen for three successive decades up to the 1980s, but remained relatively steady at around 37 hours during the 1980s and 1990s. Even so, since the late 1990s a new reduction set in, with average weekly hours falling to 35.7 by early 2003.[10] These statistics fail to bear out the feeling that work pressure is mounting.

This disjuncture between widespread perceptions and the most obvious nationally representative statistic warrants investigation: either perceptions of increasing pressures of work on life are based on a popular

TABLE 3.1.
Average Annual Hours Actually Worked per Employed Person

|                | 1979  | 1983  | 1990  | 2003  |
|----------------|-------|-------|-------|-------|
| Australia      | 1,904 | 1,853 | 1,866 | 1,814 |
| Belgium        | —     | 1,696 | 1,690 | 1,542 |
| Canada         | 1,785 | 1,735 | 1,788 | 1,718 |
| Finland        | —     | 1,809 | 1,763 | 1,669 |
| France         | 1,764 | 1,672 | 1,618 | 1,453 |
| West Germany   | 1,758 | 1,692 | 1,566 | 1,429 |
| Greece         | —     | 1,990 | 1,919 | 1,938 |
| Ireland        | —     | 1,902 | 1,911 | 1,613 |
| Italy          | 1,697 | 1,674 | 1,655 | 1,591 |
| Japan          | 2,126 | 2,095 | 2,031 | 1,801 |
| Korea          | —     | 2,734 | 2,514 | 2,390 |
| Norway         | 1,514 | 1,485 | 1,432 | 1,337 |
| Sweden         | 1,530 | 1,532 | 1,561 | 1,564 |
| United Kingdom | 1,815 | 1,713 | 1,767 | 1,673 |
| United States  | 1,833 | 1,819 | 1,829 | 1,792 |

Source: OECD (2004).

Note: The data show comparisons of trends, but are unsuitable for precisely comparing hours in a given year, because of differences in sources.

illusion, or the perceptions relate to something other than the average of work hours. The former is hardly plausible. The perception is not an invention of commentators in search of a story. It can be seen in formal surveys of individuals: for example, in successive time use surveys the proportion of Americans reporting that they "always feel rushed" rose from 24 percent in 1965 to 38 percent in 1992 (Clarkberg, 1999).

The public sense of increasing work pressure in many countries reflects two different aspects of change in the modern workplace. First, part of the expressed concern comes from pressures on the time balance between work and nonwork (the so-called "work-life balance"), which are reflected in statistics about the households' (not the individuals') average working time.[11] The flip side of the rise of the workless household (Gregg et al., 1999) is the growing proportion of households where all adults are working. Although each employed person is working, on average, no longer than before, the total hours per working household can be increasing. And so it is. For example, in Britain the mean hours worked in two adult working households rose from fifty-four to sixty hours per week between 1981 and 1998 (Green, 2001). In the United States, the mean number of weekly hours married couples worked rose from 53 to 63 hours between 1970 and 1998, mainly because more such couples became dual-earner households (Jacobs and Gerson, 2001).[12] Experience of conflict between work time and other activities is most acute among working people with children (OECD, 2004: 45). Across OECD countries, the proportion of two-adult families working more than a total of 60 weekly hours rose from 35 percent in 1985 to 47 percent in 2002. Taking a household perspective, it is not surprising that greater total household working hours are associated with a heightened sense of time pressure.[13] As might be expected, there has followed an increased demand for employers to provide flexible employment practices to suit people's private lives, sometimes driven by policy initiatives (Hasluck et al., 2000; OECD, 2004: 50).

In addition to the rise in household hours for those in multiple-worker households, for all workers a second source of growing pressure may have been increases in effort intensity while at work. Changes in effort intensity, however, are not so easily captured by a simple metric, and hence the thesis of rising intensity is less easy to establish. The main question for this chapter, therefore, is: what statistical support is there for the proposition that work intensification has been taking place in industrialized countries? Given that the process is found to be both widespread and significant, explanations are called for, but these are postponed till chapter 4.

### The Concept and Measurement of Work Effort

"Work effort" is an ambiguous term, so before proceeding to examine trends it is essential to clarify both its meaning and the methods through which it may be measured. First, one can distinguish the time spent at work from "work effort" or synonymously "work intensity," meaning the intensity of labor effort during that time at work.[14]

Since work effort is sometimes conflated with the related concept of "performance," or with "efficiency," or even "skill," it is also useful to make their relationships and conceptual differences explicit, as follows. "Performance" is constituted by the extent to which an individual performs contractual tasks (and is synonymous with the individual's "productivity"). An individual's performance is raised both by greater skill and by increased work intensity. There is scope for a trade-off between these two substitutes. One thinks of the person who wins a game with "effortless superiority," or of the opposite extreme epitomized in the tortoise's fabled victory over the hare. Stress specialists, in invoking the mantra "work smart not hard," appear to favor a slightly less relaxed hare.[15]

An individual's performance is "efficient" if it could *not* be improved without raising either skill or work intensity or both. By the same token, performance is inefficient if it *could* be raised without working harder or using greater skill—for example, through a different ordering of work tasks. However, a rise in performance that is brought about by increasing work intensity does not in itself signify an increase in efficiency; rather, it is simply a matter of raising an input to increase the output.[16] Misunderstanding of this fundamental, if simple, point is the source of one of the most frequent generic mistakes in economic commentary, whereby productivity gains are erroneously taken to *be* efficiency gains. Extending the analysis beyond the individual, each worker's performance is then related to the organization's output, but this relationship is mediated by the organization's efficiency. Thus, the organization is inefficient if its output could be increased without an increase in any of its workers' performances.

This simple framework allows one to encompass a number of managerial and organizational developments in recent years. For example, multi-skilling may be a process of raising skill levels as well as a process of work intensification (the latter because, for example, it reduces idle work time while waiting for other skilled workers to mend broken-down machines). Just In Time or Total Quality Management methods, frequently hailed as progenitors of large increases in an organization's efficiency, operate also by stepping up work intensity and hence individual performance. Teamworking, one of the most widespread management innovations of the last decade, can be seen as having multiple effects, insofar as it putatively generates new skills, induces employees to work harder, and also engenders greater organizational efficiency. The multiplicity of effects underlies the critique of such innovations (e.g., Taplin, 1995): the extent to which either greater skill, or removal of inefficiency, or work intensification are the sources of greater productivity is contested.

Despite its centrality in the determination of work quality, work intensity is not one of the social indicators that the European Union is now collecting in its synthesis of work quality indicators (see chapter 1). This may be partly because it is reluctant to take on board an indicator whose effects on employees' welfare and on employers' interests run in opposite directions. But it may also be because of an understandable hesitation in the face of the problem of measurement. Conceptually, work effort is the rate of physical and/or mental input to work tasks during the working day. But what are the units of work effort? They depend on the specific tasks, but measuring even physical effort (separately from outcomes) cannot be done except in restricted circumstances; mental effort is that much harder. In part, effort is inversely linked to the "porosity" of the working day, meaning those gaps between tasks during which the body or mind rests. Yet a gradation of effort is also exercised during task performance, which is hard to measure except in very confined circumstances. The problem of measurement of effort can be resolved, however, by calibration against a social norm, which can be assumed to impinge on people's perceptions of their own effort. In nonexperimental settings, when judgments about effort are made by case study researchers or by survey respondents, these are always judgments of effort relative to some norm. As long as those reporting on effort have a (within bounds) consistent perception of the effort norm, their reports may be regarded as valid effort data for purposes of analysis. The condition of consistency is achieved if it is assumed that, over time, effort norms change relatively little or not at all. Then, changes in self-reported measures of effort are cleansed of the "fixed effect," that is, the influence of the effort norm on reported effort levels.

The chief advantage of self-report is that the workers themselves are likely to be best informed.[17] Nevertheless, the potential for biased reporting on contested features like work effort is clear. A few checks on the reliability of self-reported effort have been made in experimental settings.[18] Subjective measures of effort correlated well with laboratory-based measures of physical and mental effort, though the scope for tests of the association with mental effort was very limited. Further evaluation of self-reported effort change data primarily involves checks on its content validity. One can ask: do the measures of work effort and effort change relate to other variables in expected ways? Reliability checks also need to be made by drawing where possible on multiple sources.

Existing studies have identified effort changes through organizational or sectoral case studies, through quantifiable proxies (such as the industrial injury rate, or indicators of the removal of restrictive practices), or through subjective survey responses. Often the latter method relies on respondents' recall of work effort in previous years and judgments about whether work effort has risen or fallen.[19] A preferable approach is to compare responses at different times to identical questions on effort levels, since this method avoids relying on respondents' accurate recall of previous work situations, and is not biased by any life-cycle changes within a cohort.

To sum up, while the definition and measurement of work hours are normally unproblematic, work intensity needs careful attention to allow conceptual distinction from organizational efficiency, individual performance, and skill. Although direct measures of the level of effort are impossible in most practical circumstances, measures of relative effort and, by extension, effort change, are by contrast quite feasible.

### Work Intensification in Britain

It happens that Britain is the country where the survey evidence makes it easiest to build a picture of changes in work effort in recent decades. But even here, the story does not begin until the 1980s. Unlike long-term trends in working hours, there is no appealing way of gauging trends in work intensity before that time.[20] The only outcome proxy variable with a sufficient run of data concerns industrial injuries. The fatality rate in manufacturing industry fell progressively from 1960 through 1980, before rising in the first half of the 1980s (Nichols, 1997). While this series is taken as evidence of labor intensification in the 1980s, Nichols himself has drawn attention to the limitations of this approach (Nichols, 1991) and he does not take the pre-1980 fall as evidence of falling work intensity. Industrial injuries and fatalities are probably too loosely linked to work intensity.

The picture of changes in work effort becomes clearer in subsequent decades as the quality of the data improves.

### The 1980s

The issue of the extent of labor intensification has been especially important in the evaluation and characterization of productivity changes in the Thatcher period (Nolan, 1989; Guest, 1990; Edwards and Whitson, 1991). Certain studies indicate that indeed work effort did rise. Thus, Elger (1990) characterized the 1980s as a period of work intensification in manufacturing on the basis of a review of case studies and flexibility deals. Tomaney (1990) arrives at a similar conclusion, maintaining that the main emphasis of moves toward a more flexible workplace in the United Kingdom was to "raise the rate of capital utilisation through a reintegration of work tasks." Through a selective review of sectoral and case studies, he suggests that the intensification of effort is the main route to increased productivity, rather than increased skill. Nichols (1991) infers a rise in work effort in the early 1980s from the combination of high productivity growth and very low investment in the manufacturing industry. These conclusions are consistent with the findings of Batstone and Gourlay (1986) who, using the subjective recall method, find increases in effort between 1979 and 1984 reported by shop stewards in a range of manufacturing plants.

And yet, selective reporting of firms or sectors could be giving a biased picture, in that cases with no work intensification might remain unpublished. Where workers' lives are unchanged or get better, it tends not to make for such good copy. Representative survey-based methods are

**TABLE 3.2.**
Effort Change, 1981–1986

| Change over previous five years | Work Speed (%) | Required Effort (%) |
|---|---|---|
| Increase | 38.0 | 55.9 |
| Little or no change | 54.3 | 36.1 |
| Decrease | 7.7 | 8.1 |

*Source*: SCELI.

less prone to this bias. The Social Change and Economic Life Initiative (SCELI) is an independent data source with respect to the work intensification debate for the early 1980s. Respondents were asked to consider the job they had held five years previously (if they had had one), and to say whether there had been a "significant increase," a "significant decrease," or "little or no change" between then and their current job with regard to, among other things: "how fast you work" and "the effort you have to put into your job." Their responses are given in table 3.2. The evidence is unequivocal: on both counts, a substantial number of workers experienced an intensification of their labor.[21] Unsurprisingly, the two variables are highly correlated (the Spearman rank correlation coefficient is 0.44).

The story for the latter half of the 1980s is picked up in part by a question asked in the 1990 Workplace Industrial Relations Survey (WIRS90).[22] As part of this survey of over two thousand establishments with at least twenty-five workers, representatives of manual and nonmanual workers were each interviewed on a range of industrial relations issues. Unfortunately, not all establishments had worker representatives who were interviewed. Most establishments that did recognized trade unions. On the issue of changing work effort, respondents were each asked how "the intensity or the pace of work for most manual (nonmanual) workers" compared with "three years ago."

The responses summarized in table 3.3 are again unequivocal: they show a strong balance of establishments where labor intensification took place during this period.

These findings are consistent with those of Edwards and Whitston (1991) for approximately the same period: they report increased effort levels between 1987 and 1989 among respondents in four organizations. Further confirmation of labor intensification in the late 1980s derives from Employment in Britain, a representative individual-based survey conducted in 1992. Respondents were asked to report their experience of change in effort. Table 3.4 shows findings in relation to that variable alone alongside the findings of Gallie et al. (1998) regarding changing

**TABLE 3.3.**
Effort Change, 1987–1990

| Workers' effort compared with three years previously | Manual Workers[†] (% of establishments) | Nonmanual Workers[‡] (% of establishments) |
|---|---|---|
| "A lot higher" | 30 | 46 |
| "A little higher" | 26 | 22 |
| "About the same" | 36 | 27 |
| "A little lower" | 6 | 4 |
| "A lot lower" | 1 | 1 |

Source: WIRS90.

Notes: Percentages are weighted to take account of oversampling of smaller establishments; respondents were the respective representatives of manual and nonmanual workers in the plants.

[†] base = 715 establishments; [‡] base = 675 establishments.

workplace stress, as derived from the same data. Respondents were asked, as in the SCELI survey in 1986, to compare their current situation with their job five years previously. Respondents were asked about "the effort you have to put into your job" and about "the stress involved in the job." The responses are consistent with the evidence from WIRS90 (that covers an overlapping period), with three out of five reporting increased work effort and more than half registering increased stress.

A telling feature of the findings from tables 3.1, 3.2, and 3.3 is evidence that the increase in work effort was found across the whole economy, though a disadvantage is that they are all based on backward-looking survey questions, which is not ideal. Taken together with the other case study and sectoral evidence, however, they present a consistent view that a substantial degree of work intensification took place through the 1980s and into the early 1990s. While no one piece of evidence is convincing on its own, the consistency of findings using different methods is impressive.

### The 1990s

A possible scenario is that the 1980s could have approached saturation in work effort levels, so that the intensification of labor would slow down or cease during the 1990s. Yet the picture for most of the 1990s is one of continued work intensification.

As part of an investigation of Total Quality Management (TQM), Edwards et al. (1998) found evidence of substantial increases in effort in the 1990s. Of their sample of workers in six large organizations in 1995, three out of four employees reported working "a lot harder" or "a little

**TABLE 3.4.**
Effort Change, 1987–1992

| Change over previous five years* | Required Effort (%) | Stress (%) |
|---|---|---|
| Increased | 61.5 | 53.4 |
| Little or no change | 31.1 | 34.2 |
| Decreased | 7.5 | 12.1 |

Source: EIB.

* If not in a job five years ago, since job nearest to that time.

harder" than three years earlier. Knights and McCabe (1998), in their detailed study of organizational innovations in the financial services industry, which had undergone a period of substantial restructuring, also found evidence of significant work intensification. In a similar vein, Burchell et al. (1999) report that among twenty organizations investigated in 1997–1998, more than three out of five employees reported increased effort and increased speed of work over the previous five years, with only one in twenty registering decreases. A survey by the Institute of Management reported that as many as four out of five managers said their workloads had greatly increased.[23] Yet, these studies and surveys are restricted in scope, and could be giving a selective picture.

Table 3.5 uses the best available method—the comparison over time of consistent representative surveys—to examine effort change between 1992 and 2001. Four common questions capturing subjective estimates of work effort were asked in the surveys Employment in Britain, the 1997 and 2001 Skills Surveys, and in Working in Britain, though only one of these was asked in all the surveys. Respondents were asked how much they agreed or disagreed with the statement "I work under a great deal of tension." Later in the interview they were asked: "How often does your work involve working at very high speed?" The other two questions were: " 'My job requires that I work very hard.' Do you strongly agree, agree, disagree, or strongly disagree with this statement?" and "How much effort do you put into your job *beyond* what is required?"[24] The first of these attempts to pick up the extent to which individuals are constrained by the job to work hard, while the other attempts to capture discretionary effort. The response scales are termed "Required Effort" and "Discretionary Effort" respectively.

Figure 3.1 and table 3.5 show that work intensity continued to increase during the 1990s. This conclusion is consistent with that of Edwards et al. (1998), but is based here on large representative samples and is not dependent on respondents' recall judgments. The proportion strongly agreeing that they worked under a "great deal of tension" rose

**TABLE 3.5.**
Work Effort in Britain, 1992, 1997, 2000, and 2001

*Working Under a Great Deal of Tension*[†]

|  | All | | Private Sector | | Public Sector | |
| --- | --- | --- | --- | --- | --- | --- |
|  | *1992* | *2001* | *1992* | *2001* | *1992* | *2001* |
| Strongly agree | 15.1 | 20.9 | 13.5 | 19.5 | 18.4 | 24.9 |
| Agree | 33.3 | 37.5 | 32.3 | 37.4 | 35.7 | 37.8 |
| Disagree | 43.2 | 36.6 | 44.9 | 37.7 | 39.8 | 33.2 |
| Strongly disagree | 8.3 | 5.1 | 9.4 | 5.4 | 6.1 | 4.1 |

*Working at Very High Speed* [†]

|  | All | | Private Sector | | Public Sector | |
| --- | --- | --- | --- | --- | --- | --- |
|  | *1992* | *2001* | *1992* | *2001* | *1992* | *2001* |
| All the time | 7.2 | 9.1 | 7.8 | 9.3 | 5.4 | 8.3 |
| Almost all the time | 10.1 | 16.5 | 10.9 | 15.9 | 8.5 | 18.0 |
| Around three-quarters of time | 5.5 | 12.2 | 5.6 | 12.1 | 5.4 | 12.8 |
| Around half the time | 11.7 | 21.1 | 12.6 | 21.6 | 10.2 | 20.0 |
| Around quarter the time | 15.8 | 17.7 | 16.5 | 18.4 | 14.6 | 15.8 |
| Almost never | 24.5 | 16.8 | 22.5 | 16.3 | 29.0 | 18.1 |
| Never | 25.2 | 6.7 | 24.1 | 6.4 | 27.0 | 7.0 |

*Required Effort* [†]

|  | All | | | | Private Sector | | | | Public Sector | | | |
| --- | --- | --- | --- | --- | --- | --- | --- | --- | --- | --- | --- | --- |
|  | *1992* | *1997* | *2000* | *2001* | *1992* | *1997* | *2000* | *2001* | *1992* | *1997* | *2000* | *2001* |
| Strongly agree | 31.7 | 39.9 | 41.6 | 38.3 | 31.7 | 38.3 | 37.4 | 36.7 | 31.9 | 44.4 | 44.8 | 43.2 |
| Agree | 57.3 | 49.4 | 48.1 | 51.9 | 58.1 | 50.4 | 52.1 | 52.8 | 55.4 | 46.8 | 44.3 | 49.1 |
| Disagree | 10.0 | 9.9 | 9.9 | 9.5 | 9.1 | 10.8 | 10.1 | 10.2 | 11.8 | 7.5 | 10.5 | 7.6 |
| Strongly disagree | 1.1 | 0.7 | 0.4 | 0.3 | 1.1 | 0.5 | 0.5 | 0.4 | 0.9 | 1.3 | 0.4 | 0.1 |

*Discretionary Effort* [†]

|  | All | | | Private Sector | | | Public Sector | | |
| --- | --- | --- | --- | --- | --- | --- | --- | --- | --- |
|  | *1992* | *1997* | *2001* | *1992* | *1997* | *2001* | *1992* | *1997* | *2001* |
| A lot | 68.8 | 71.9 | 70.3 | 69.5 | 70.6 | 70.1 | 67.7 | 72.6 | 71.1 |
| Some | 22.7 | 21.1 | 24.1 | 22.4 | 20.6 | 23.8 | 23.5 | 22.7 | 24.6 |
| Little | 5.3 | 4.9 | 3.9 | 4.7 | 5.5 | 4.2 | 5.9 | 3.1 | 3.0 |
| None | 3.3 | 2.1 | 1.7 | 3.3 | 2.3 | 1.9 | 3.0 | 1.6 | 1.3 |

*Source*: EIB, the 1997 and 2001 Skills Surveys, and Working in Britain, 2000.
  [†] For question asked, see text. All figures are percentages of workers.

**Percent**

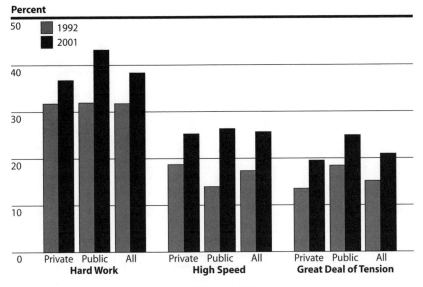

Figure 3.1. Hard Work in Britain, 1992 and 2001
*Source*: See table 3.5.
*Note*: Percentage of workers whose job requires hard work (strong agreement), proportion working at very high speed (all or almost all the time), and proportion working under a great deal of tension (strong agreement).

from 15 percent to 21 percent between 1992 and 2001; while the proportion who never or almost never worked "at very high speed" fell from 50 percent to 24 percent.[25] The picture of the trend in Required Effort is consistent: 40 percent of workers in 1997 strongly agreed that they were in a job that "requires them to work hard," compared with 32 percent in 1992. However, this indicator, which has the advantage of being measured at four data points, suggests that intensification had run its course by 1997: the proportions changed little thereafter up to 2000 and 2001.

An industry-level breakdown shows that this sequence of work intensification followed by stability of work effort appears to have been broadly followed across all industries. Yet it is worth noting that, for two of the measures, effort intensification in the 1990s was greatest in the public sector. Thus, the proportions working at very high speed all or almost all of the time rose by 6.5 and 12.4 percentage points respectively in the private and public sectors. Moreover, from 1992 to 2001 the public sector saw an 11-percentage-point rise in the "strongly agree" category of the Required Effort Index, while the private sector only experienced a 5-point rise.

TABLE 3.6.
Effort Change, 1993–1998

|  | Worker Reps' Perceptions (% of establishments) | Managers' Perceptions (% of establishments) |
|---|---|---|
| Gone up a lot | 60 | 39 |
| Gone up a little | 20 | 37 |
| No change | 14 | 21 |
| Gone down a little | 4 | 2 |
| Gone down a lot | 1 | 0 |
| Base | 922 | 1,965 |

Source: WERS98.

With respect to discretionary effort, the only significant increase took place in the case of public-sector workers between 1992 and 1997, and this was only a small increase. This stability in discretionary effort suggests that overall the work intensification was mainly linked to the pressures of the job rather than individuals pushing themselves beyond requirements.

Further evidence supporting the view that work continued to intensify in the 1990s comes from the 1998 Workplace Employment Relations Survey (WERS98),[26] a nationally representative survey of 2,191 British establishments with ten or more workers. Both the responding manager and (where one existed) a workers' representative in each establishment were asked whether, over the previous five years, there had been "any change in how hard people work." The responses, given in table 3.6, show a substantial number, from both types of respondent, reporting work intensification over the period, though the workers' representatives were more likely than the managers to perceive the work intensification as considerable.

### Changing Sources of Effort Pressure

Since the 1990s were, following 1991, a period of gradual emergence from recession in Britain, it remains possible that work intensification in this period could have been part of a cyclical process. To increase confidence that the changes in work effort in the 1990s are not merely cyclical swings, it will be helpful to have further evidence spanning the 1991 recession that is not dependent on respondents' recall. This can be found in some striking changes in reported sources of effort pressure in 1986, 1992, 1997, and 2001.

Respondents to all four surveys were asked: "Which, if any, of the things on this card are important in determining how hard you work in

**TABLE 3.7.**
Trends in Effort Pressures on Employees, 1986–2001

| Percentage subject to work pressure from: | 1986 | 1992 | 1997 | 2001 |
|---|---|---|---|---|
| Machine or assembly line | 7.1 | 5.3 | 10.2 | 5.8 |
| Clients or customers | 37.2 | 50.4 | 53.9 | 56.7 |
| Supervisor or boss | 26.7 | 37.7 | 41.0 | 42.4 |
| Fellow workers or colleagues | 28.7 | 36.1 | 57.0 | 49.6 |
| Own discretion | 61.5 | 65.1 | 67.6 | 61.9 |
| Pay incentives | 15.3 | 19.4 | 29.8 | 26.4 |
| Reports and appraisals | 15.3 | 27.4 | 23.5 | 30.4 |
| *Effort Pressure Index* [†] | | | | |
| All | 1.91 | 2.41 | 2.83 | 2.73 |
| Private Sector | 1.94 | 2.37 | 2.78 | 2.69 |
| Public Sector | 1.86 | 2.52 | 2.96 | 2.84 |

*Source*: SCELI, EIB, and the 1997 and 2001 Skills Surveys.

[†] Number of influences; see text.

your job?" The card included seven possible sources of effort pressure as follows: a machine or assembly line, clients or customers, supervisor or boss, fellow workers or colleagues, one's own discretion, pay incentives, reports and appraisals. Respondents could check off as many effort pressure sources as they wished, including none. The Effort Pressure Index (EPI) is defined to be the number of pressure sources, which accordingly ranged from 0 (no sources) to 7 (maximum pressure).[27]

To establish the relevance of this evidence as a quantifiable proxy for work intensity, consider first their relationship with the direct measures of effort. For example, in 2001 the proportion of respondents who cited clients or customers as a source of work pressure was 60 percent among those individuals who separately agreed or strongly agreed that their job required them to work very hard, compared with 44 percent among those who disagreed or strongly disagreed. The other sources of work pressure are also positively linked to one or more of the direct measures of work effort. It is thus valid to use responses to the effort pressure questions as proxies for effort itself, and thereby obtain a picture of change over more than a decade of workplace change.

Table 3.7 tells a compelling story. For all possible sources of effort pressure, there is an increase between 1986 and 1997. Most remarkable is the increased impact of colleagues: whereas in 1986 only 29 percent of employees cited colleagues as affecting how hard they work, by 1992 this proportion rose to 36 percent, and by 1997 to 57 percent. It seems that peer pressure had come into its own as a source of labor intensification.

By 2001, peer pressure had eased off somewhat, as had the proportion of workers citing their own discretion. But, the pressure coming from bosses and from clients or customers, and through reports and appraisals, continued to increase. The summary measure of effort pressure is given in the bottom three lines of table 3.7: the EPI increased from 1.91 to 2.73 over the period, a substantial and significant change. The index rose slightly more in the public than in the private sector.[28] Consistent with the story arising from the direct measures of effort, the EPI showed no continued rise after 1997, even having a slight fall.

## Work Intensification in Europe, Australia, and the United States

Less comprehensive but nevertheless representative evidence of work intensification during the 1990s can also be found in other industrialized countries. One can be most confident about changes in effort across the European Union, because evidence is available using the preferred methodology of comparing representative surveys at different time points. Respondents to surveys in 1991, 1996, and 2000, carried out by the European Foundation for the Improvement of Living and Working Conditions, were asked to state how often they were subject to working at very high speed, and how often they had to work to tight deadlines, with responses on a 7-point scale. Responses to the two variables are highly correlated, and a summary effort index can be computed by averaging the scale responses to the two questions. According to this index, work intensification was a widespread phenomenon in Europe during the 1990s, though not ubiquitous (see figure 3.2). Work intensity rose faster over 1991 to 1996 in Britain than in all other EU countries (Green and McIntosh, 2001). Table 3.8 reveals that work intensification persisted in the later period in Belgium, France, Germany, Greece, Ireland, Italy, Luxembourg, the Netherlands, and Sweden; in Denmark and Spain there was little change in work effort; while declines in work effort occurred in Austria, Britain, Finland, and Portugal. The small decrease in Britain over 1996 to 2000 is consistent with the picture afforded by table 3.5, covering the overlapping period 1997 to 2001. In the whole European Union, work intensification in Europe continued but at a much slower pace in the latter half of the 1990s.[29]

According to table 3.8, France experienced a relatively high rate of work intensification in the 1990s. Other evidence, derived from the second (1984), third (1991), and fourth (1998) Enquêtes Conditions de Travail, suggest that this increase was a continuation of a longer-term change. These surveys show rises in the proportions of employees whose pace of work was constrained by organizational factors (such as colleagues), tech-

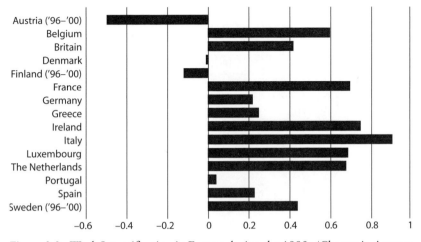

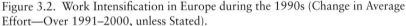

Figure 3.2. Work Intensification in Europe during the 1990s (Change in Average Effort—Over 1991–2000, unless Stated).

*Source*: First European Survey on the Work Environment 1991–1992; Second and Third European Surveys on Working Conditions.

*Note*: See note to table 3.8 for key to scale.

nical factors (such as machine-pacing, assembly line, or automation), and by customers and clients. The increases affected all age groups, and were fastest in the 1984 to 1991 period but persisted through the 1990s (Bué et Rougérie, 1999; Valeyre, 2001; Pailhé, 2002).[30] From 1991 to 1998 there were also increases in the extent to which workers reported being interrupted to carry out unforeseen tasks, having to work at speed, and perceiving that they had insufficient time to carry out their allocated tasks. In the late 1990s there were rises in work intensity following the introduction of successive pieces of legislation, reducing the working week to 35 hours for most of the workforce.

In Australia, the 1994 Workplace Bargaining Survey questioned the employees of a representative sample of establishments about changes over the previous year. A substantial proportion (more than three-fifths) of workers reported that they were working harder than a year before. As table 3.9 shows, perceptions of work intensification were most widely found among managers and professional workers. Unfortunately, figures like these based only on recall are not sufficient on their own to be confident that this is a fair picture of Australian workplaces at that time. Nevertheless, the picture of intensification is well supported by similar surveys using recall methods (Morehead et al., 1997), and by case studies in the fast food and wholesale industries (Reeder, 1989; Wright and Lund, 1998). For both Australia and New Zealand there is also large-scale

**TABLE 3.8.**
Work Effort in Europe in 1991, 1996, and 2000, by Country

| Country | Average Effort Level* | | | Change in Effort Level |
|---|---|---|---|---|
| | 1991 | 1996 | 2000 | 1991–2000 |
| Austria | n.a. | 4.26 | 3.76 | n.a. |
| Belgium | 2.63 | 2.89 | 3.23 | 0.60 |
| Britain | 3.34 | 3.91 | 3.76 | 0.42 |
| Denmark | 3.43 | 3.49 | 3.42 | −0.01 |
| Finland | n.a. | 4.18 | 4.06 | n.a. |
| France | 2.72 | 3.19 | 3.42 | 0.70 |
| Germany | 3.49 | 3.53 | 3.71 | 0.22 |
| Greece | 3.55 | 3.59 | 3.80 | 0.25 |
| Ireland | 2.89 | 3.38 | 3.54 | 0.75 |
| Italy | 2.45 | 2.87 | 3.36 | 0.91 |
| Luxembourg | 2.63 | 2.81 | 3.32 | 0.69 |
| Netherlands | 3.18 | 3.60 | 3.86 | 0.68 |
| Portugal | 2.87 | 3.21 | 2.91 | 0.04 |
| Spain | 2.75 | 2.94 | 2.98 | 0.23 |
| Sweden | n.a. | 3.74 | 4.18 | n.a. |
| All 15 EU countries | n.a. | 3.45 | 3.58 | n.a. |
| All except Austria, Finland, and Sweden | 3.08 | 3.40 | 3.46 | 0.38 |

*Source*: First European Survey on the Work Environment 1991–1992; Second and Third European Surveys on Working Conditions.

* Average effort is the average score on the "high speed" and "tight deadlines" questions. It is thus measured on a scale of 1–7.

survey evidence of companies' use of work intensification strategies, such as through nonreplacement of staff or through incentive schemes (Allan et al., 1999). Formal evidence for work intensification in the United States utilizes the same Required Effort Index that comprised part of the British evidence. Kalleberg (forthcoming) reports a substantial and significant rise in the Required Effort Index between 1992 and 2002. However, there was little change in this index between the 1970s and 1992. In a pattern similar to Britain's, the rise in required effort during the 1990s was not matched by an increase in discretionary effort. Indeed, between 1989 and 1998 there was a small decline in an indicator of discretionary effort (Handel, 2005). Reports of excessive workloads mirror those to be found in Europe and Australia. The evidence is most direct in studies of the lower-paid sections of the American labor market (Appelbaum et al., 2003), though this does not mean that higher-paid workers

**TABLE 3.9.**
Effort Change in Australia, 1993–1994

|  | Percentage of workers reporting higher effort in 1994 compared with a year before |
| --- | --- |
| Laborers and related workers | 54.8 |
| Plant and machine operators and drivers | 57.2 |
| Sales and personal service workers | 63.7 |
| Clerks | 61.1 |
| Tradespeople and apprentices | 58.8 |
| Paraprofessionals | 63.8 |
| Professionals | 64.6 |
| Managers | 66.3 |
| ALL | 61.5 |
| Base | 10,978 |

*Source*: Workplace Bargaining Survey, 1994.

have not also had their work intensified. Case studies of the clothing industry (Taplin, 1995) and of the hotel industry (Bernhardt et al., 2003) include clear indications of work intensification. There is indirect evidence from the consequences of more workers being subject to work overload, shown in rapidly increasing figures for workplace-related illnesses during the 1980s, particularly repetitive motion syndrome (Cappelli et al., 1997). There is also some further indirect evidence. American workers in "new" or "transformed" workplaces—those that have introduced various high-performance work practices, which are said to be becoming more common—tend to suffer from increases in cumulative trauma disorders (Fairris and Brenner, 2001). None of these pieces of evidence are strong on their own, but together the picture of effort intensification during the 1990s is consistent with the similar story in Europe.

### Any Objections?

Though a consistent picture of work intensification has been obtained from multiple methodologies, data sources, and instruments, any common objections to all the approaches would cast doubt on the veracity of the story. One possible objection arises from potential ambiguity over the meaning of work effort: survey respondents might interpret higher effort as longer working hours rather than working with a more intensive work effort. This objection is softened by the use of several instruments and variable wording to capture aspects of work effort, and by the consistency of the trend across instruments. Further checks also revealed that the measures of work effort showed an increase even after controlling for hours by grouping workers into limited hours bands (Green, 2001). Besides this, average work hours have not been rising over the period in which work intensification is recorded. So the story of work intensification cannot easily be construed as a displaced perception of changing work hours.

A second, possibly more telling, objection is that changes in effort levels may be sensitive to the business cycle. If so, recorded changes between particular years could reflect that cycle, not a medium- or long-term trend. The theoretical impact is ambiguous. In times of high unemployment, workers may feel more threatened, and hence work harder. Yet employers also tend to hoard labor during recessions, deciding not to reduce employment as much as demand: this could lead to lower effort in the bad times. Either way, there is (as yet) no empirical evidence to suggest that effort is strongly and significantly affected by the state of the economic cycle. Green and McIntosh (2001) could find no evidence that variable effort intensification across European Union countries was explicable by cyclical variables. Effort is not strongly affected by regional unemployment variations. The effort intensification picture in Britain covers more than a decade and a half. Nevertheless, the influence of cyclical demand changes on effort remains a potential source of distortion to the trends reported above.

A third possible objection concerns effort norms. The survey-based evidence assumes these remain unchanged on average across the population, but over time workers might become accustomed to different norms, which could prompt different responses to at least some of the effort questions. This objection has greater force the longer the time period in question. Over any period, the effect is to bias downward the estimated extent of any changes (up or down). If effort norms are gradually rising (as a result of a long process of work intensification), then the recorded subjective changes in effort would understate the extent of the underlying rise in work effort; and vice versa. The implication is that, if anything, the recorded work intensification in tables 3.5 and 3.8 is downward biased.

Objections can also be countered by reference to the content validity of the effort measures. In other parts of this book, it is found that the effort measures are associated both with well-being and with potential antecedents in ways that would be predicted by plausible models of work organization (chapters 4 and 8). The effort intensification measures used in this chapter are also associated in the expected way with indicators of increased workplace stress, and with sectoral rankings of labor productivity growth (Green, 2001). This chapter closes with some evidence of con-

TABLE 3.10.
Pay Premia for Hard Work

|  | Percentage pay premium for job with high required effort[1] | Percentage pay premium associated with working at high speed and high tension[2] | Percentage pay premium from a unit increase in the Effort Pressure Index[3] |
|---|---|---|---|
| 1986 | — | — | 0.030** |
| 1992 | 0.025* | 0.058** | 0.040** |
| 1997 | 0.040** | — | 0.020** |
| 2001 | 0.048** | 0.033** | 0.025** |

Source: SCELI, EIB, and the 1997 and 2001 Skills Surveys.

Notes: The pay premia are computed as the estimated coefficients of the various effort measures in pay regressions. The dependent variable is log hourly pay, and controls are: 5 education level dummies, a quadratic in work experience, a gender dummy, 17 industry dummies, and 11 regional dummies.

The estimated premia are significantly different from zero at the 5% level (**) or 10% level (*).

[1] See table 3.5; 0/1 dummy representing "strong agreement."

[2] See table 3.5; factor score using standardized indicators of "working under a great deal of tension," and "working at very high speed."

[3] See table 3.7.

tent validity for the effort measures, as derived from a conventional economic perspective.[31]

### Effort and Pay

Economic theory predicts that jobs with high effort requirements will be rewarded with higher pay, for a given level of skill. It is an example of a classic compensating differential. The evidence for compensating differentials in general is, however, quite mixed. Where empirical support is lacking, this could be because labor markets are deeply uncompetitive, or it could be owing to biases in estimates resulting from errors in measuring job characteristics or from omitting other relevant variables. In a dynamic setting, greater effort is also likely to be associated with higher future rewards. The return from working hard may derive from future promotion or better job prospects, rather than current pay, but this element of the compensating differential would only be adequately revealed in a longitudinal survey that follows workers through time.

A straightforward test for static compensating differentials is feasible for the four British surveys in 1986, 1992, 1997, and 2001. Table 3.10 shows pay premia associated with each of the indices of work effort that had been increasing in Britain in the 1990s, as estimated from a conventional augmented earnings equation. In all cases the index has a significant positive association with pay. Being subject to one more source of work pressure is associated with between 2 percent and 4 percent more pay, while holding education and work experience unchanged. For two indices the premium may have fallen somewhat over the period, while for the Required Effort Index the premium appears to have risen. The existence of the positive pay premium is additional support for the validity of the subjective effort data.

## Conclusion: A Summary of Effort Trends

Work effort is a central variable in a range of social sciences, and the maintenance and control of work effort, including the management of the labor process, are integral to the functioning of economies and to the quality of work life. And yet, its measurement poses severe difficulties. This juxtaposition of importance with difficulty of quantification remains a persistent dilemma: the topic ought not to be ignored, but economists prefer not to deal with anything other than "hard" data. It cannot be avoided if one wants to know about the quality of work life.

This chapter has addressed this dilemma by attempting to derive sensible quantitative indicators of changing work effort, in the context of late twentieth-century industrial capitalism. It has tried to assess the real story underlying popular expressions of rising work pressure. The main findings are:

1. Those industrial relations writers who claimed, largely on the basis of reviews of workplace agreements in the 1980s, that work in Britain was being intensified, especially in manufacturing, in the 1980s, were right: their conclusions are confirmed by a reexamination and synthesis of contemporary social surveys.

2. More recent survey evidence supports extant case and sectoral studies showing that work intensification continued in Britain through the first part of the 1990s. At least some of this new evidence uses the best available method for measuring effort trends, namely the comparison of questions in successive surveys. Across Britain from 1992 to 1997, there was a modest increase in "discretionary effort" and a substantial rise in "required effort." Across the whole period, more workers were operating at high speeds and to tight deadlines. By the end of the decade, however, work intensification had apparently reached the point of satiation: there were no further increases in work effort over the 1997 to 2001 period.

3. Just as striking, between 1986 and 1992 and again between 1992 and 1997, there were substantial increases in the number of factors inducing hard

work from employees in Britain. The most notable source of increased pressure for hard work came from colleagues: this was as much the age of peer pressure as of the hard-driving supervisor. These pressures eased off a little between 1997 and 2001.

4. Work intensification was also experienced by workers in almost all European Union countries during the 1990s, though to a varying extent and with different timing. Exceptions are Denmark and Portugal, where over the decade little change in work effort is found, and Austria, where effort fell after 1996. For France, the work intensification that took place in the 1990s was a continuation of change that was already taking place in the 1980s.

5. Almost certainly intensification also took place in Australia and in the United States, though in these cases the evidence is thinner. In Australia, workers in the mid-1990s reported increases in their pace of work. In the United States, formal evidence from one index of work effort and case studies afford the inference that work intensification was present during the 1990s, though what happened during the 1980s is less clear.

To many economic and social commentators, these findings will not be surprising. Nevertheless, given the importance and simultaneously the difficulty of gauging trends in work effort, compiling this albeit incomplete statistical picture has been a necessary first step toward understanding these changes in working life. The next step is to consider explanations: why did this widespread process of work intensification in late twentieth century advanced industrial capitalism take place?

# *Four*

## Accounting for Work Intensification

### The Paradox of Work Intensification in the Affluent Economy

In the 1970s there was reason to expect that in the coming decades the quality of work life might improve, and in particular that for many people throughout the noncommunist industrialized world their work might become more fulfilling, less intense, less onerous, and of shorter duration. For two decades or more, hours of work had been decreasing and workers were getting more holidays; manual work had been steadily giving way to the traditionally more highly regarded nonmanual jobs; women were becoming more completely integrated into the paid workforce, leading to many households no longer being reliant on a male "breadwinner's wage"; and the maturing profession of occupational psychologists, having learned a great deal about the successful enrichment of jobs, were arguably becoming increasingly influential. The Scandinavian countries, in particular, were at the forefront of policy development for improvements in the quality of work life (Gallie, 2003). The problems of the 1970s surrounded accelerating inflation and emergent unemployment, each linked to the crises of the floundering international monetary system and successive oil price hikes; but these were essentially macroeconomic issues, with only indirect implications for the quality of work life. If future macroeconomic stability could be delivered, preventing a return to mass unemployment and job insecurity, a simple extrapolation of the previous two decades might have presented nothing but an optimistic prognosis for the future of work, from the point of view of the worker.

Yet, as was discussed in the previous chapter, in many countries there followed some substantive and significant periods of work intensification, and in a few major countries even the long-term decline in work hours came to a halt during the 1980s and 1990s. These developments alone call into question whether an improvement in the quality of work life since the 1970s has taken place. For those who have suffered significant stress from the extra pace of work, the reality is one of deteriorating work quality. Any policies to improve the quality of work life in this dimension need to be based on an adequate understanding of underlying causes. So: why did this work intensification occur?

The paradox is that work intensification seems to have taken place in an era when, for the most part, material life has improved for workers in Western capitalism. In most countries—the United States being the main exception—real wages have continued to increase over recent decades (see chapter 6). One might have expected that increasing affluence (in both wealth and income) would result in a declining supply of work effort, as they had done in many previous decades, and that this would be reflected also in a more relaxed pace of work.[1] Or, to put the question the other way around, if the rising pressures of work brought on by increased competitiveness and the changing balance of power between capital and labor are behind the intensification of work and the cessation in the decline of work hours, why is this not also reflected in declining real wages?

Any resolution to this paradox must account for the evidence that work intensification in this era has been widespread. This chapter considers several explanations for why work intensification has been taking place. Distinction may first be made between explanations which see the origin of change on the supply side of the labor market, and those which locate the source in factors affecting employers' demand for high effort. There are also other aspects of potential importance, which cannot be neatly partitioned in this way: these include changes in the way that work is monitored, changes in the balance of power, and a changing approach to human resource management. In the sections that follow, each of these explanations is examined for consistency with the social survey evidence and other existing evidence.

Although no single explanation will suffice, a connecting theme is the nature of technological change in this era, which has structured the changes in employers' demands for high effort and in their ability to monitor the labor process, and which has helped to facilitate some of the changes in the balance of power between capital and labor (Green, 2004a). It will be maintained that technical change and work re-organizations in this era have together been the major proximate determinant of work intensification.

## The Supply of Effort

It is conceivable that exogenous shifts on the supply side might have prompted an intensification of work effort. If workers' aversion to high-effort jobs were reduced, they would choose jobs requiring higher effort than before.[2] The relative cost of high-effort workers would be reduced by the excess supply. In a competitive labor market, firms would respond by offering more jobs that require a high level of effort. Some weak, circumstantial, support for such an explanation is available. For example, Gallie et al. (1998) report an increase in "employment commitment," which might be loosely interpreted in economists' terms as a rising preference for work.

Yet, an exogenous increase in the supply of work effort is an unlikely explanation for work intensification in the current period. There are two pieces of evidence that serve to cast doubt. First, if work really was becoming more fulfilling, it would be expected to show up in increased job satisfaction, unless some other significant negative influence was also abroad. As will be seen in chapter 8, there is no indication of such an upward shift in satisfaction. Second, if increased willingness to work hard were the exogenous factor driving intensification, one would expect to see a decline in the compensating differential attached to effort. As noted in the previous chapter, there are no good estimates of the dynamic returns to high effort (as reflected in future promotion and pay raises). The contemporaneous premium attached to effort, though positive, has increased according to one measure but decreased according to two others (see table 3.10). This evidence is hardly decisive either way. Without further support it is tempting to leave this explanation aside, at least until more adequate and relevant evidence is forthcoming.

An alternative supply-side explanation for work intensification derives from a systemwide perspective, in which consumerism, as driven by the imperatives of large corporations, creates an increasing need for consumer goods and services. The craving for more, fueled by relative income effects,[3] and by the advertising and marketing apparatchiks, is translated into a need for more wages, and hence harder and longer work. Using a systemwide framework, Schor (1991) explains the long-term increase in average work hours of Americans, who, she argues, are caught on a "work and spend" treadmill. Workers are choosing to supply more hours, but this choice is constrained and shifted by the increasing and manipulated wants of the affluent, materialist society. Perhaps a similar argument applies to work intensification, with workers straining harder to gain more pay in order to buy the new goods and services they want.

Assessment of such an explanation is not easy. Whether employees work more to get more income and therefore are able to spend more is hard to distinguish empirically from the opposite chain of causation suggested by Schor, where the pressure to increase spending drives the requirement for more wages. A more complex story is also available in which workers gain increases in income and thence spend more, but after each income rise get locked into the higher spending levels by their changed habits or their long-term debts; in this story, effort levels are ratcheted up along with the materialist wants. There is ample support in the savings literature for the relative income theory (Green, 1979). Nevertheless, consumerism is hardly a strong and plausible explanation for work intensification in the current period. There is no obvious reason why consumerism should have taken a greater hold of workers in recent decades than in earlier times. Although "work and spend" *might* explain recent work intensification, it remains an ad hoc explanation without an additional tale that could rationalize the timing, and it is hard to devise an appropriate test.

### "Amber Lights" and Effort-Biased Technological Change

A more appealing account for why intensification has occurred, and why on so broad a front, lies in technological change, which structures the demand side of the labor market. The term "technological change" includes both new techniques and new ways of organizing work—the two can be indistinguishable, though new techniques are normally embodied in new equipment. A major factor is the prevalence of a particular aspect of technological change in the current era, where the gain lies in the increased efficiency with which it is possible to deliver work to the worker.

To better understand this process of matching work to worker, it is useful to consider briefly the allocation of a worker's tasks. The experience of work effort will depend on the number and complexity of the tasks that must be undertaken at any one moment, and on the frequency and duration of gaps between tasks in which recuperation and relaxation can take place. Work effort is limited on the supply side by what employees are able and willing to perform. On the demand side, effort is constrained by the complexities and uncertainties of work flows, which means that the match between the flow of work and the worker's availability for more tasks is imperfect. By improving this match, either by increasing the average number of tasks that can be done at a time or by reducing the frequency and duration of the gaps between active work, productivity can be increased. To achieve this, however, workers must be able and willing to devote more intensive effort. In this way, technological change can be associated with work intensification. This "effort-biased technological change" is analogous to the widely discussed "skill-biased technological change" in its effect on the demand for labor. Effort-biased technological change differentially increases the productivity of workers who are prepared to, or who can be persuaded to, devote high effort levels.[4] For those workers who are unwilling to comply with the greater effort levels, productivity is not enhanced by this aspect of technological change.

Here are some examples to illustrate the argument. Delbridge et al. (1992) cite the case of a Japanese automotive plant, which had been suffering from bottlenecks whereby work piled up at one work station, leaving workers elsewhere with unavoidable idle time. To address this matching inefficiency, managers installed a system of traffic lights at each workstation. Amber lights meant that the worker at that station was bordering on full capacity, while red indicated a bottleneck and green meant idle time. The lights made it possible for line managers to adjust work flows toward the optimum, by aiming for amber lights at all stations. Gaps in the working day were thereby closed up and the productivity of the line enhanced.

The story of how work was intensified in a British clothing factory bears a striking resemblance to the case of the Japanese automotive plant. According to Boggis (2001), the major proximate source of work intensification in the denim jeans plant she examined was the introduction of a computerized, numerically controlled automated handling system. This system optimized the flow of work to the machinists, cut inventories of work-in-progress, and reduced workers' ability to take breaks—thereby eradicating their "leisure in work." The system also enabled managers to exercise much more detailed control of the labor process. Workers' discretion was thus reduced at the same time as their work was intensified—a classic Fordist/Taylorist development taking place in very recent times. The response of workers was complex, but the new handling system almost certainly stimulated an increase in labor turnover. According to managers, those leaving were the ones not willing to put in the greater effort required in the new system and no longer able to hide in the new monitoring environment. Managers also claimed the system would lead to increased pay for the remaining workers who were now working harder.

An example of work intensification in the services is found in the rapid growth of the call center, which has been described as the "twentieth-century sweatshop" (Wazir, 1999). A ubiquitous feature of call centers is the superior monitoring capability afforded to managers. For some writers the main consequence is taken to be the increased ability to prevent shirking, that is, to ensure the labor contract is honored by the worker (Fernie and Metcalf, 1998). But this attribute of call center technology may be less significant than the facility it affords for delivering work instantaneously to workers: as soon as one call is finished, another is routed immediately to the operator. Different types of calls can be efficiently routed to appropriate departments and to workers with the knowledge and skills needed to serve customers. It is this ability to achieve optimal use of employee time at work, for millions of workers across the industrialized world, which marks the contribution of this relatively new type of workplace to the intensification of labor in the modern world.

Computer and communications technologies, involved in the preceding examples, also enable faster delivery of work to workers in many jobs with high degrees of autonomy and discretion. Cellular phones, for example, have made work more flexible for countless workers who travel for work, but also enable managers and customers to reach workers and call on their services at times when they would otherwise relax. Cell phones make it easier for fixed-place workers to keep working as they travel home or when they get there.[5] A variety of electronic devices are available to enable employees to work effectively from home. Modern technologies thereby drive a potential wedge through the traditional psychological and physical barrier between work and nonwork activities (Felstead et al., 2005). However, effort-biased technological change is not solely associated with the information and communication technology revolution. There are other prominent and recent technological changes, some complementary with the introduction of computing technology, which may deliver improved matching of worker to work. These include Just-In-Time methods of inventory control, Total Quality Management and "Quality Circles," the spread of teamworking, and manifold other reorganizations of work that take different forms across different organizations.

The facility with which management can increase the productivity of workers who devote high effort is enhanced by the spread of flexible production systems and the associated multi-skilling of workers. The development of flexible production systems and multi-skilling was part of the steady dismantling of the stand-off that had, earlier in the twentieth century, accompanied the growth of scientific management, in which unions had accepted management's prerogatives to set a narrow division of labor in their search for maximum control, in return for rising wages and some job security. With a flexible production system, managers can more easily switch production lines to match changing demand, and thereby keep the workforce more fully occupied. With multi-skilling—the development of workers' abilities to carry out many tasks—workers can be re-allocated more easily among required tasks. For example, by being able to carry out repair and maintenance tasks, workers can be kept busy even when machines go down, rather than awaiting the arrival of specialist maintenance engineers. They can also perform routine maintenance at times when the flow of work is slack, and they can be re-allocated to other tasks when fluctuations in demand cause bottlenecks elsewhere.

In service industries, where the service is consumed at the same time it is generated, the flow of work is especially dependent on the flow of customer demand. Here, functional flexibility can keep workers fully occupied during the time that work is paid for. Functional flexibility thus complements labor market flexibility, which also intensifies work in a similar way. By arranging flexible work hours, employers can roster their workforce to be at work when customers need them; through multi-skilling and functional flexibility they can be redeployed within their paid work time to the required tasks. In both cases, the employer is able to economize on the idle time of workers, while meeting the customers' demand. Multi-skilling in services is also apt to involve a hierarchical expansion of tasks. Nurses, for example, have found themselves required to take on expanded supervisory and managerial functions while retaining responsibility for covering basic nursing tasks (Adams et al., 2000). Thus is found in the same group simultaneous extra demands on the workers—for both greater effort and increased skill.

These arguments, it should be said, are not meant to carry a Newtonian certainty. That technological change should be effort-biased is neither necessary nor universal—after all, many changes in the past have been such as to remove the physical burden of work. Nevertheless, the conjecture is that the predominant form technological change has taken in this era has been oriented to demanding higher effort levels from workers.[6] To support this account it is necessary to draw on the survey evidence of work intensification.

A first hint that recent technological change might be effort-biased as well as skill-biased arose from analysis of the Employment in Britain survey (Gallie et al., 1998). Looking at individuals' reports of how their jobs were changing, Gallie and colleagues observed a strong association between experiences of increased skill requirements and reports of work intensification. This association is robustly found in other data sets. In a number of cases, surveys also offer general indicators of the presence of technological changes in establishments. Inevitably, any such generic indicators do not capture the specific characters of the technologies used by each establishment; nevertheless, managers' reports of workplace change have been validated and are now utilized as evidence in a number of studies (e.g., Caroli and Van Reenen, 2001). The hypothesis being tested is that effort is increased where workplaces have experienced technological change. Supportive evidence, based on five data sets and a range of methodologies, is as follows:

   1. In two studies, high effort levels have been robustly linked with computer usage (Green and McIntosh, 2001; Gallie, 2002). The inference is that expanding computer usage, itself a proxy for technological change, is associated with work intensification. However, in addition to the looseness of this proxy, there are two further qualifications to the finding. First, the magnitude of the effect of computer usage on effort, together with the expansion of computer usage, is not sufficient to account for more than a small proportion of the work intensification across Europe. Second, it derives from cross-section

regressions which cannot exclude that the estimated relationship of computer usage to worker effort could be biased, owing to some unobserved causal variable that is related to both computer usage and effort. Any such variable is quite likely to be a "fixed effect," that is, a constant for each individual case over time.

2. To try to get around this problem of potential bias, table A4.5 in the appendix to this chapter uses a pseudo-cohort analysis to examine the link between effort and computerization. The Employment in Britain survey and the 2001 Skills Survey are combined, and aggregated into seventy-two cohorts defined by occupation and age band. The advantage of these data sets is that several effort indicators can be investigated, to check for robustness. The table gives estimates of the determinants of the change in effort level over 1992 to 2001 for each cohort. The advantage of this method is that, by looking at changes within cohorts one can eliminate "fixed effects," as in a conventional panel analysis. When looking at changes in effort over time, the fixed effect cancels out, leaving only the causal role of the explanatory variables that also change.

In this analysis, technology is again proxied by the extent of usage of computerized or automated equipment within each cohort. Table A4.5 confirms that there is an association between technology and work effort. For three out of four measures, work effort is greater where the usage of computerized or automated equipment is higher. In two of these cases, this effect is not very robust: it becomes insignificant when cohort age is introduced as a control. In the case of the Effort Pressure Index (EPI), however, the effect remains positive, statistically significant, and reasonably substantial. The magnitude of the coefficient (0.69), together with the rise in the proportion using computerized or automated equipment (0.18), yields a predicted rise of 0.13 in the average EPI during 1992–2001: this compares with an actual rise of 0.32 (see table 3.7).

3. In tables 4.1 to 4.4, direct measures of work intensification are examined for their relationship with measures of technological change.

Only 23 percent of establishments where, according to managers, there had been neither technical nor organizational change nor increased task flexibility between 1993 and 1998 experienced "a lot higher" work intensity (table 4.1). By contrast, in establishments where all of these changes had occurred: "a lot higher" work intensity was reported in 51 percent of cases. In a fuller analysis that controls for other factors, technical and organizational changes and new functional flexibility are each robustly associated with work intensification in this period, though the impact of each varies between small and large establishments and between the production and service sectors; the collective effect of these changes is substantial (Green, 2004a; also see appendix table A4.1).

TABLE 4.1

Effort Intensification in Britain, 1993–1998, by Technical/Organizational
Change

| Proportion of establishments experiencing *"a lot higher" work intensity** | (%) |
| --- | --- |
| *Technological Change* | |
| Establishments with: | |
| Neither technical nor organizational | |
| change nor increased task flexibility | 22.9 |
| New technology, and new work techniques or procedures | 44.2 |
| Change in work organization | 45.3 |
| Increased task flexibility | 48.0 |
| New technology, new work techniques | |
| or procedures, change in work organization, | |
| *and* increased task flexibility | 51.2 |
| *Commitment* | |
| Establishments with: | |
| No new involvement initiative | 30.5 |
| New involvement initiative | 48.0 |
| *Incentives* | |
| Establishments with: | |
| No extra use of performance-related pay | 37.9 |
| More use of performance-related pay | 44.3 |

*Source*: WERS98.

* See notes to table A4.1. Proportions calculated using sample probability weights.

Table 4.2 gives some further confirmation of effort-biased technological change from earlier data. For both manual and nonmanual workers, effort intensification between 1987 and 1990 was substantially greater where establishments had experienced either technological change or organizational change or both, compared with where no changes had taken place. Among establishments with no changes for manual workers, just 22 percent experienced "a lot higher" work effort, compared with 36 percent where there was either some technical or some organizational change. Among nonmanual workers, 33 percent report a lot higher effort when there are no changes, compared with 49 percent when there is technical or organizational change. This relationship holds after controlling for other possible determinants (appendix table A4.2).

Table 4.3 shows the same link between work intensification and technological change, here for the case of Australia over 1993 to 1994. Where neither technical nor organizational change had occurred, 48 percent of workers

**TABLE 4.2.**
Effort Intensification in Britain, 1987–1990, by Technical/Organizational Change

| Proportion of establishments experiencing "a lot higher" work intensity* among establishments with: | Manual Workers (%) | Nonmanual Workers (%) |
|---|---|---|
| No technical or organizational change | 21.6 | 33.0 |
| Either technical or organizational change or both | 36.4 | 49.2 |

*Source*: WIRS90.

* See notes to table A4.2 and appendix text. Proportions calculated using sample probability weights.

reported intensification; where, for example, there had been technical change, the figure rose to 68 percent. Table A4.3 confirms that either technical change or change in work organization, or both, raise work intensification, after controlling for other factors and distinguishing between small and large establishments.

Table 4.4 uses data from the 2001 Skills Survey in Britain. A limitation is that, in order to match data on technological change with worker outcomes in a survey of individuals, the analysis has to be confined to those who remained with the same employer for five years—less than half the full sample. Yet it has the advantage of offering four possible measures of technological change.

**TABLE 4.3.**
Effort Intensification in Australia, 1993–1994, by Technical/Organizational Change

| Proportion experiencing higher work effort compared with to one year Previously among establishments with: | All Bargaining Regimes (%) | Workplace Bargaining | |
|---|---|---|---|
| | | No (%) | Yes (%) |
| No technical[1] or organizational[2] change | 48.1 | 49.5 | 46.8 |
| Technical change over last 12 months | 67.7 | 70.6 | 66.8 |
| Organizational change over last 12 months | 70.1 | 73.9 | 69.0 |
| No incentive or bonus system introduced | 57.4 | 58.8 | 56.8 |
| Incentive or bonus system introduced in last 12 months | 67.8 | 70.9 | 67.0 |

*Source*: Workplace Bargaining Survey.
*Notes*:
[1] "New technology or equipment which affects my work."
[2] Change in way that work is organised.

TABLE 4.4.
Effort Intensification in Britain, 1996–2001, by Technical/Organizational Change

| Proportion experiencing higher work effort in 2001 than in 1996 among establishments with:* | | (%) |
|---|---|---|
| Organizational Change? | | |
| | Yes | 56.0 |
| | No | 32.0 |
| New Computerized or Automated Equipment? | | |
| | Yes | 50.3 |
| | No | 36.3 |
| New Communications Technology Equipment? | | |
| | Yes | 49.8 |
| | No | 38.4 |
| Other New Equipment? | | |
| | Yes | 53.2 |
| | No | 38.2 |

Source: The 2001 Skills Survey.

* Proportion of jobs where the job-holder reports an increase in work effort since 5 years previously.

For all these measures, work intensification is significantly higher in the presence of technological change. Table A4.4 confirms that work intensification is significantly associated with changes in work organization, and with the introduction of new equipment other than computerization and communications equipment, after controlling for other factors.

Taken together, these findings, drawn from Australia, Britain, and elsewhere in Europe, support the conjecture that the effort intensification reported in recent decades has on average been associated with technological change—that is, either with the introduction of new production techniques or with changes in the organization of work. The consistency of findings from different data sets and approaches offers a certain level of confidence. Yet, though supportive, the evidence does not prove incontrovertibly the hypothesis that technological change in this era has been effort-biased. The measures of technological change are generic, and inevitably only loosely proxy the changes that occur in diverse ways across workplaces. Computerization is often chosen to represent technological change because of its pervasive nature, and because it is relatively easily measured, but this measure masks considerable variations in the complexity of the technology involved. The measures of change in work organization are also open to the flexible interpretation of survey respondents. Moreover, technological change might well have different effects at different times: there is no reason why it should always be effort-biased.

The role of technological change in generating work intensification also goes beyond the changes in the efficiency of production flows discussed so far. Technological change frequently accompanies changes in the management of labor and an alteration of the balance of power between workers and employers, developments which yield additional or alternative reasons for the intensification of effort. These additional explanations must now be explored.

## Big Brother

A significant explanation for work intensification focuses on the increased capacity of employers to monitor conformity with employment contracts. One effect of Total Quality Management and Just-In-Time systems is to make work much more visible (Sewell and Wilkinson, 1992; Delbridge et al., 1992). A system that enables managers to trace quality deficiencies back to specific points in the production process also facilitates accountability for individual workers. While permitting genuine improvement by correcting faults along the line (an efficiency gain), managers are also able to detect instances of low effort by individual workers who are therefore less likely to risk shirking their work duties. Information technology is intimately involved in this "electronic panopticon." Automating the flow of work enables management to measure work rate with great accuracy (Miozzo and Ramirez, 2003; Boggis, 2001). In the typical call center work can be observed virtually perfectly. More use of staff appraisal, and improvements through training in appraisal practices, also increase an employer's ability to monitor workers' conformity with their labor contracts over a medium-term horizon. In an economic framework, these developments could be characterized as an upward shift in the marginal impact of monitoring resources on work effort. In a conventional efficiency wage model with a continuum of effort (where workers choose how hard to work given the chances and the cost of being caught working too slowly), improved monitoring would result in less shirking and greater effort.

This association of the increased facility to monitor workers' performance with new information technology and new ways of organizing work is also consistent with the above-cited evidence that work intensification is associated with forms of technological change. This evidence does not distinguish between the channels through which work has been intensified through technological change.

Nevertheless, it would be a mistake to place too much emphasis on the role of the "worker discipline effect" in this context. It seems unlikely that in reality asymmetric information is the major factor constraining higher work effort in most cases. Extensive monitoring of work tasks can be as much or more for quality control purposes as for surveillance of recalcitrant workers. For certain technologies the facility afforded for monitoring effort more closely may be a by-product, and accordingly underutilized for that purpose. This can happen where effort is reasonably well observed through other pre-existing means (Lankshear et al., 2001), or where the surveillance technology is incompatible with professional norms of conduct (Timmons, 2003). Moreover, the extent to which new technologies for monitoring effort deliver increased work intensification is constrained by forms of employee resistance, which vary according to the workplace social context. Perfect monitoring capability does not imply absolute control and subordination of labor as a factor of production. Workers can overtly assert their preference for less hard work through absenteeism, high turnover, and union organization (Bain and Taylor, 2000).[7]

## The Changing Balance of Power

The declining power of unions, and increased competitive pressures on employers, have also been responsible for work intensification (Burchell et al., 1999; Bacon, 1999). Under pressure to lower their costs and to raise the quality of their products, firms have found it necessary to attempt to forward the pressure onto their employees. As unions' power has declined (in Britain's case with considerable assistance from the state), collective resistance to work intensification has diminished. Tactics like downsizing and union de-recognition are used to make a radical break with established effort norms and to reduce payroll costs. Downsizing tactics do not necessarily succeed in improving financial performance, but usually result in increased workloads (e.g., deVries and Balazs, 1997). This approach of "lean and mean" production can also be associated with technological changes. For example, Just-In-Time and Total Quality Management systems reduce the ability of workers to hide their performance behind production buffers, or to evade constant measurement of their performance, reducing the extent to which they can organize formal or informal resistance to speeding up the work process.

One problem with this explanation of increasing work effort is that it does not address the paradoxical fact that work intensification has occurred while, in most parts of the industrialized world, real wages have continued to rise. If effort is rising because workers are becoming more oppressed, as their bosses get the upper hand in the contest for workplace control, one might expect a reduction in wages alongside work intensification.

Many cases do, however, conform more closely to such a model. For example, Taplin (1995) showed how, in the face of immensely increased competition, workers in the American apparel industry experienced intensified work effort and lower wages. The case of public-sector workers in Britain can also be cited. Public-sector wages declined, relative to those in the private sector, during the 1992 to 1997 period by about six percentage points (Green, 2004a). This was also a period in which effort pressures were rising faster in the public than the private sector (see figure 3.1). During this period, the public sector was under a continuous strong fiscal constraint, extending the influence of Margaret Thatcher's policies long after she had ceased serving as Prime Minister. Providers in the public sector were under increasing pressure to meet customer demands, whether for rising health needs or to expand education. Managers' powers were extended. Reinforced by technological changes, managers could increase the flows of work to work stations, and at the same time ensure reasonable compliance on the part of workers.

Ackroyd and Bolton (1999) describe how the workloads of nurses working for the British National Health Service were increased in this period. They found no systematic attempt to re-assert Tayloristic control over what nurses do. While not encroaching on nurses' professional autonomy, the reorganization of wards and of the inflow and outflow of patients was used to maintain the service provided with fewer nurses. Nurses' commitment to their patients meant that there was little resistance to the provision of the necessary extra effort. Dissatisfaction increased, but as much because of the inability to provide the desired service as because of the increased work effort. Foster and Hoggett (1999) tell a similar story about workers in the Benefits Agency (responsible for payment of social security to qualifying members of the public). Higher service requirements had necessitated reforms in the methods of delivery of benefits to clients, a concomitant restructuring of work organization, and a substantial intensification of labor.[8]

There is some formal evidence of an association between work intensification and the decline of union power. For example, in the early 1990s there was a link at the national level across the European Union: in countries where union power had decreased the most, there were higher rates of work intensification (Green and McIntosh, 2001). Gallie (2002) finds a link between trade union membership and lower effort levels across individual European economies. Green and McIntosh (1998) find an indirect association in Britain, in that union power reduces the impact of the cost of job loss on effort. The evidence from Australia also suggests that intensification was less where workplace bargaining was taking place, although trade union membership per se had no inhibiting effect. For example, as table 4.3 shows, among establishments experiencing technical change, work intensification was experienced in 67 percent of cases when workplace bargaining was taking place, compared with 71 percent elsewhere. The link is robustly confirmed in the multivariate analysis shown in the appendix (Table A4.3). Yet, this impact of bargaining is modest and it only partially offsets any effect from the experience of organizational change.

Overall, not much of the increase in work effort in Britain or elsewhere is directly attributable to the declining power of unions. Effort intensification in British establishments over the period 1993–98 was strongly associated with reductions in bargaining (appendix table A4.1 and Green 2004a), but in that period reductions took place only in a very small number of establishments and could not possibly explain more than a fraction of the widespread experience of work intensification. Evidence from the 2001 Skills Survey does not suggest that workers in establishments covered by trade union bargaining were less likely to encounter work intensification than those in uncovered workplaces. Workers in nonunion establishments reported no more work intensification than those covered by union bargaining.

Of course, the effect of the changed balance of power on work effort may not be adequately reflected in such findings. The timing of any decline in the power of unions to affect workplace regulation cannot be investigated with the limited survey data available. Arguably, the power of unions to decrease effort may have already diminished to a considerable extent before the 1990s. Declining union power also affects the timing and the form taken by technological changes. Moreover, the changed balance of power in the workplace is a broader political phenomenon, not confined to the labor market. The diminished scope of unions to constrain management's prerogatives at the workplace is associated both with their declining membership and coverage and, especially in Britain's case, with the changed legislative and political environment since the early 1980s. The changing fortunes of public-sector workers are also linked to the political constraints placed upon the fiscal balance.

Politics is also linked to regulation of the workplace. Incremental improvements in health and safety regulations may have been responsible for some diminution in excessive work intensity over recent decades, though not enough to prevent the general level of work effort from rising. Moreover, the work hazard that has risen the most, across many countries, is stress and its related manifestations of ill health. In excessive cases, this hazard is manifest in large damage suits by employees. As yet, there is no major attempt to regulate intensive work effort, because of the difficulties of enforcement and the preference of Western governments to stay clear of what is not generally considered a legitimate domain for interference. Nevertheless, one area of intervention has had an intriguing indirect impact on effort: the French government's legislation limiting weekly work hours to thirty-five hours (the Aubry law) went far beyond the provision of the European Directive on Working Time. The main objective of the French legislation was to provide more jobs by dividing work hours more evenly among the workforce. Whether or not that objective has been achieved, the weekly productivity of workers did not diminish by nearly as much as the decline in work hours, largely owing to increased work intensity. Survey evidence shows that there are very many workers who must perform the same tasks as before the working time reduction, but in less time (Askenazy, 2002). Such a finding is testimony to the sustained power of employers to dictate terms within the workplace, even if their political power to influence the course of legislation is at times proscribed.

### The Stick, the Carrot, and the Smooth Sell

One aspect of the declining power of organized labor might be a heightened sense of insecurity. As will be seen in chapter 7, there is some evidence of a temporary increase in perceptions of insecurity relative to the unemployment environment during the early part of the 1990s in both Britain and the United States. In some other countries there is evidence of a considerable increase in the deployment of temporary labor in a number of fields. The Australian economy is a notable case where temporary labor has become widespread, and there is evidence, as has been seen, of simultaneous and substantial work intensification in that country. Whether increased job insecurity would raise work effort is, however, by no means inevitable. On the one hand, workers might work harder if they think it will help them to keep their jobs, perhaps by improving their employers' likelihood of surviving the pressures of competition; or perhaps in the case of temporary workers hard work would be seen as a way of ensuring that their contracts were renewed, or made permanent. On the other hand, insecure workers are also typically demoralized; they may lose a sense of commitment to their employers, perceiving that nothing they do can make a difference in an uncertain market and might reduce their work effort as a result.

The popular perception is sometimes that job insecurity is at the heart of work intensification (e.g., London Hazards Centre, 1994). In Green (2004a), some evidence is reported of an association between establishments' introduction of temporary labor contracts and work intensification. Gallie (2002) also finds a cross-sectional association between perceptions of job insecurity and work effort. However, as an overall explanation of work intensification in the 1990s, job insecurity is a nonstarter in the case of Britain and probably also in most European countries. The fear of losing one's job has small and insignificant links with the level of work effort (see Green, 2000a). For the most part, job insecurity in Britain has decreased over the 1990s, in response to the considerable decline in the unemployment rate; and temporary work contracts remain the province of only a small part of the workforce.

Though the discipline of the market, as expressed in the possibility of job loss, has relatively little bearing on the explanation of work intensification, the carrot of better rewards at work could be a different story. Though there is nothing new in the idea that identifiable rewards stimulate work effort (this, after all, is the essence of the labor contract), it could be argued that the use of incentive structures more explicitly relating reward to effort has been driving up the intensity of effort. Effort-related pay structures may have been stimulated by the decline in union and other regulatory constraints on pay setting. Linking effort more closely to reward may also have been made easier by some of the new technologies themselves: improving the measurability of individual outputs makes it easier to design contracts more explicitly based on those outputs. It is also possible that more complex production processes lead employers to rely more on trusting their workers and on arms-length monitoring.

Where employers have successfully introduced systems of effort-related pay, they have normally been successful in raising effort levels. For example, over the 1993 to 1998 period, work intensification was present in 44 percent of establishments that increased their use of performance-related pay, compared with only 38 percent of establishments that did not increase their use of this incentive (see table 4.1 and appendix table A4.1). Table 4.3 and appendix table A4.3 provide similar evidence in the context of Australia in 1994. Work intensification is reported in 68 percent of establishments that had introduced incentives or bonuses but in only 57 percent of other establishments. There is also recent evidence that U.S. companies introducing systems of piece rates are generally able to increase productivity (Lazear, 2000), from which one may infer with certain assumptions that the effect of piece rates was to raise work effort.

This evidence is not surprising, in that offering rewards for effort would be a loss-making strategy if it did not result in increases in effort. Yet, piece rate systems of work reward are hardly new. Their advantages for employers are constrained by the difficulties of measuring outputs in many fields. These difficulties are increased by continual technological changes, which also reinforce the need to change reward structures that are themselves contested and affected by the extent to which workers can exercise collective control over effort. The use of piece rate systems has varied over the years and across industries, and remains the province of only a minority of workplaces. More recently, systems of Performance Related Pay have been introduced where outputs are measured through supervisor evaluations, often with the aid of new technology. Yet, in Britain there is no evidence that incentive-pay schemes of various kinds have become more prevalent during the 1990s (Millward et al., 2000). It is doubtful therefore whether any considerable part of effort intensification can be laid at the door of explicit incentive-pay systems. A more intriguing possibility is that effort intensification could be associated in part with rising inequality of pay. If hard work is rewarded by improved chances of promotion and of pay hikes, and if those pay hikes become greater, the result would be increased work effort. But this possibility is hard to evaluate. None of the current data sources can furnish good estimates of the extent of such an effect.[9]

Another way of generating more intensive work effort from employees is to try to alter their perceptions and attitudes, and hence their behavior, so as to align employees' objectives more closely with those of the organization. In the private sector the objective of the organization is to make profits, while that of the worker is to obtain wages and other rewards. Bringing the two together is a challenge to the powers of the company to sell itself to the worker as something to which he or she should be emotionally committed. There has been an attempt to meet that challenge in recent decades through the development of the soft side of Human Resource Management (HRM). Techniques like mentoring, empowerment, forms of training, and consultation and information meetings between management and employees, designed to foster the commitment of employees to company objectives, have become more common. Such practices are often part of the "psychological contract" between employer and workers, in which security and trust are implicitly traded for commitment. Redesigning jobs to make them more fulfilling is one way to try to call forth increased effort from employees (Ichniowski et al., 1996). Practices designed to engender commitment are also likely to increase the supply of effort to companies: the theoretical consequences include lower equilibrium unemployment and an incentive for employers to invest in general training (Green, 2000b). In some areas, especially in the public sector, employees' and the organizations' objectives are more naturally aligned in at least some respects: both nurses and their employers want their patients to get better. As was shown in the study of nurses by Ackroyd and Bolton (1999), the commitment of nurses to their patients was the rock upon which work intensification was built by management, by the simple expedient of imposing higher service requirements through increased patient flows. Nurses have retained their professional autonomy, but cannot control the hospital environment that delivers their workloads. Similar considerations apply in many areas of public service.

Most evidence about whether high commitment policies are effective has pertained to their effect on the economic performance of the organisation (Huselid, 1995). Not much is known yet about their impact on individuals. Only some sorts of communication channels designed to foster employee involvement tend to be associated with greater effort levels. Godard (2001) finds that high workloads are associated with Total Quality Management, re-engineering, teams, quality circles, use of regular workplace committees, and profit-sharing schemes. Downward communication through use of the management chain and through newsletters are linked to above-average effort, according to Green and McIntosh (1998). There is weak evidence, too, that downward communication channels were linked to work intensification during the period from 1987 to 1990 (see appendix table A4.2). Upward communication channels, by contrast, like suggestion schemes or two-way channels such as consultation meetings with workers, had no association with effort. Initiatives to encourage more involvement were associated with work intensification over 1993 to 1998 (see table 4.1): in the absence of such an initiative, work intensification occurred in 31 percent of establishments, compared with 48 percent where there was some employee involvement initiative. As appendix table A4.1 implies, the initiatives appear to have been effective only in generating work intensification in smaller establishments (Green, 2004a). Fairris and Brenner (2001) review evidence in the United States that employees in modern or "transformed" workplaces (which normally include the use of high-commitment human resource policies) tend to have a greater experience of health hazards associated with work intensification. By contrast, Appelbaum et al. (2000) found no evidence that role overload went along with high-performance work systems when used in the steel, apparel, and medical electronic instruments and imaging industries in the United States.

## Conclusion: The Role of Technological Change

The intensification of work effort in many countries during the 1990s and before has been a considerable blow to hopes of increasing the quality of work life in the current era of affluence in the Western industrialized world. One resolution to the paradox of rising work effort in the affluent economy lies in the nature of technical and organizational change during this recent era. Technological change, it has been argued, may have been predominantly "effort-biased," in the sense that it leads employers to value ever more greatly the contribution of compliant workers who are able to provide high effort. However, technological change is by no means an exogenous factor, a *deus ex machina* descending upon the modern workplace. Rather, it is associated with the rise of competitive practices, and of the global economy. Technological change can facilitate and be enabled by institutional change.

Another major factor has been the rise of the "lean and mean" system, in all its guises and across many industries. The changing balance of power enables managers to reduce the share of any rents that workers have traditionally obtained from their work.[10] One area where the employers' hand has been strengthened is the public sector, in countries where a fiscal squeeze has restricted resources. Yet, on the whole the expansion of the lean and mean approach, and the changing balance of power in the labor market, do not adequately explain why employers should widely be demanding more effort and paying more wages. This combination is an unlikely one in conventional economic models of labor supply. Although one can always rationalize this combination by a suitable choice of utility function and of bargaining model (Andrews and Simmons, 1995), a more general explanation is preferable.

Technological change is important not only because much of it has been effort-biased, but also because it has helped to facilitate some of the changes in the balance of labour market power. The evidence reviewed above provided some considerable support. In addition, an attraction of technological change as an explanation for work intensification is that it implies that work intensification will be a widespread phenomenon, not localized in particular economies—a prediction that is verified by the trends described in chapter 3. Other explanations may also be valid: perhaps workers are choosing to work harder because they have more fully absorbed a protestant work ethic, or because work has become inherently a more pleasurable or less distasteful activity than before. Yet these kinds of explanations are ad hoc: there is no compelling reason for them to apply in the current period, and no strong evidence to distinguish them. Two further explanations, though superficially plausible, have seemed in the light of the evidence to have been especially unlikely: the ideas that work intensification is caused by increased job insecurity, or that it is the result of modern human resource practices.

Work intensification may be a source of economic growth for firms and nations, as well as a negative influence on the quality of work life. If work intensification is associated with technological change, might there be no end to it? For three reasons, it is likely that work intensification will not be a sustainable mode for growth.

First, the achievement of a more efficient match between work flows and workers' readiness to work is self-limiting: once an optimal match is gained, further efficiency increases have to be sought elsewhere. At the extreme, if all the gaps in working time have been closed up, the day is then full. Second, the piling on of tasks and responsibilities is constrained by the physical and mental limitations of the human frame. However, these limitations are known to be elastic, especially over the short term under extreme conditions, so one should not rest the case for unsustainability on just this naturalistic argument.

A third reason is the resistance of workers to excessive intensification. Collective resistance, whether organized through trade unions or informally in work groups, remains in place to constrain the boundaries of managers' powers. There is also the informal resistance of individual workers, who practice selective absenteeism and exercise their choices to quit. Periods of work intensification are also followed by workers learning new ways to prevent or limit the process. A notable example is the way workers have been learning to use email selectively and more efficiently as a means of communication, while limiting the pressure it brings. Workers can also learn to manage their time, and to keep stress at bay—as testified by the proliferation of self-help manuals to be found in popular bookshops. Responsible employers consider the use of stress management policies so as to avoid extremes of high work pressure and to minimize the risks of legal action by disgruntled employees. These forms of resistance to high or increasing work effort, which are of varying and uncertain effectiveness, are in their turn supplemented and conditioned by public policies. "Health and Safety" is conventional terrain for state intervention in the nature of the work contract. This criterion has driven public regulation in Europe on the duration of work (the European Directive on Working Time). While interventions explicitly on work intensification are generally infeasible, owing to the difficulty of providing external criteria suitable for legal assessment, many of the standard health and safety regulations contribute to putting limits and restrictions on the pace of work. There was a cessation of work intensification in Britain between 1997 and 2001: could this be a first indication of the power of individual and collective resistance to excessive workloads, or is it rather a reflection of the satiation of the processes leading to work intensification and of the limitations of the human frame?

### Appendix: Multivariate Analyses

This appendix summarizes findings from multivariate analyses, using broadly similar approaches, based on four data sets.

Table A4.1 shows that the predicted probability of work intensification in the establishment over the five-year period is increased if there has been:

- an introduction of new technology and changes in work techniques or procedures
- an increase in the ability of managers to re-deploy employees among tasks, that is, greater task flexibility
- a change in work organization; in large establishments this effect is associated mainly with the introduction of greater task flexibility
- an increase in the proportion of nonmanagerial pay that is linked to performance
- in small establishments, initiatives to involve employees
- a reduction in collective bargaining
- an increase in the usage of temporary agency employees

These effects vary somewhat between sectors. For a full analysis and extensions, see Green (2004a).

In WIRS90, managers were asked: "During the past 3 years have there been here any of the following types of change, directly affecting the jobs or working practices of any section or sections of the manual/nonmanual workforce: (a) . . . the introduction of new plant, machinery, or equipment (excluding routine replacement)?; (b) . . . substantial changes in work organization or working practices not involving new plant, machinery, or equipment?" There is a substantial association between these indicators of technical or organizational change and the effort change independently reported by workers' representatives. Table A4.2 presents ordinal probit analyses where the dependent variable is the effort change for manual workers (column 1) and for nonmanual workers (column 2). The dummy variable Technical or Organizational Change captures whether there has been technical or organizational change affecting the relevant group of workers. Several control variables were included, as follows. Downward Communication captures whether there are channels for downward communication at the establishment (newsletters, systematic use of the management chain of communication). Upward Communication captures whether there are company surveys or suggestion schemes, either of which permits upward communication. Two-way Communication captures whether there are regular consultation meetings between management and other sections of the workforce. Lastly, there are controls for establishment size and union density.

The findings are as follows:

- They support the hypothesis that effort intensification is linked to technological change; thus, organizational or technical change over the past three years is significantly associated with effort intensification, after controlling for other possible explanatory factors. (The presence or absence of the

**TABLE A4.1.**
Determinants of Effort Intensification in Britain, 1993–1998

|  | Small Establishment | | Large Establishment | |
| --- | --- | --- | --- | --- |
| *Technological Change* | | | | |
| Technical innovation | 0.158* | 0.113 | 0.312*** | 0.272*** |
|  | (0.086) | (0.085) | (0.086) | (0.087) |
| New work organization | 0.289*** | 0.199** | 0.101 | 0.053 |
|  | (0.091) | (0.094) | (0.097) | (0.100) |
| Greater task flexibility |  | 0.494*** |  | 0.401*** |
|  |  | (0.087) |  | (0.090) |
| *High Commitment* | | | | |
| Involvement initiatives | 0.289*** | 0.275*** | 0.018 | 0.005 |
|  | (0.088) | (0.089) | (0.080) | (0.081) |
| More use of performance-related pay | 0.267*** | 0.196** | 0.150* | 0.118 |
|  | (0.090) | (0.090) | (0.080) | (0.080) |
| *Workforce Structures* | | | | |
| Less collective bargaining | 0.247* | 0.222 | 0.211* | 0.194* |
|  | (0.146) | (0.148) | (0.114) | (0.113) |
| *Increases in use of:* | | | | |
| Fixed-term workers | −0.037 | −0.011 | 0.023 | 0.024 |
|  | (0.109) | (0.108) | (0.089) | (0.089) |
| Temporary workers | 0.198* | 0.195* | 0.189** | 0.196** |
|  | (0.116) | (0.117) | (0.088) | (0.089) |
| Contractors | −0.008 | −0.039 | 0.321*** | 0.309*** |
|  | (0.093) | (0.094) | (0.085) | (0.086) |
| *Observations* | 857 | 856 | 951 | 951 |
| Pseudo-$R^2$ | 0.059 | 0.076 | 0.049 | 0.059 |
| Wald chi2 | 113.32 | 143.62 | 93.85 | 123.73 |

*Source*: Extract from table 3 in Green (2004a). © 2004, the Regents of the University of California.

*Notes*: Dependent variable is managers' report of effort change over 1993–98 on a 5-point scale from "gone down a lot" (0) to "increased a lot" (4). All covariates shown are 0/1 dummy variables indicating changes over the 5 years. Estimation is by ordinal probit. Other included controls are: sectoral dummies, change in use of part-time workers, recent privatization. Robust standard errors are in parentheses; significance levels, *** = 1%, ** = 5%, * = 10%. "Small" establishments have fewer than 100 employees.

controls does not alter the sign or significance of the impact attributable to organizational or technical change.)

- Of those other factors, there are positive coefficients on Downward Communication for both manual and nonmanual workers, and for manual workers the coefficient is on the margin of statistical significance ($p = 0.101$). This would be consistent with the view that good downward communication can help to elicit increases in effort, though the causation could easily be reversed, with effort intensification affecting the use of the policies. However, upward communication and two-way communication have only small and very insignificant links to effort change.
- Effort intensification for nonmanual workers appears to be greater in larger establishments.
- The coefficient on trade union density is insignificant in both cases; however, it should be recalled that the sample is restricted to those (mainly unionized) establishments where worker representatives have responded, so no comparison is possible with non-union establishments.

**TABLE A4.2.**

Determinants of Effort Intensification in Britain, 1987–1990 (Ordinal Probit Estimates)

|  | Manual Workers | Nonmanual Workers |
| --- | --- | --- |
| Technical or Organizational Change | 0.31 | 0.29 |
|  | (0.10)** | (0.12)** |
| Downward Communication[1] | 0.22 | 0.17 |
|  | (0.14) | (0.18) |
| Upward Communication[2] | −0.04 | −0.00 |
|  | (0.09) | (0.10) |
| Two-Way Communication[3] | 0.04 | 0.04 |
|  | (0.11) | (0.13) |
| Establishment Size (*1000s of employees*) | 0.044 | 0.091 |
|  | (0.048) | (0.048)* |
| Union Density (*manual/nonmanual*) (%) | −0.014 | 0.20 |
|  | (0.018) | (0.17) |
| Pseudo-$R^2$ | 0.01 | 0.01 |
| Observations | 548 | 622 |

*Source*: WIRS90.

*Notes*: Dependent variable is effort change over 1987 to 1990 on a 5-point scale from "a lot lower" (0) to "a lot higher" (4).

Standard errors in parentheses; significance levels: * = 10%, ** = 5%.

[1] Newsletters, systematic use of the management chain of communication.

[2] Company surveys or suggestions schemes.

[3] Regular consultation meetings with workforce.

**TABLE A4.3.**
Determinants of Work Intensification in Australia, 1993–1994 (Ordinal Probit Estimates)

|  | All Establishments | Small and Medium-Sized Establishments (up to 200 workers) | Large Establishments (more than 200 workers) |
|---|---|---|---|
| *Changes since 1 Year Ago* | | | |
| Technical Change[1] | 0.117 | 0.146 | 0.096 |
|  | (0.040)*** | (0.054)*** | (0.059) |
| Change in | 0.316 | 0.285 | 0.327 |
|   Work Organization[2] | (0.037)*** | (0.051)*** | (0.052)*** |
| Newly Involved in | 0.101 | 0.166 | 0.054 |
|   Appraisal System | (0.063) | (0.098)* | (0.083) |
| New Incentives or Bonuses | 0.211 | 0.272 | 0.168 |
|  | (0.037)*** | (0.053)*** | (0.052)*** |
| *Other Characteristics* | | | |
| Workplace Bargaining | −0.112 | −0.097 | −0.180 |
|  | (0.038)*** | (0.049)* | (0.060)*** |
| Union Member | −0.055 | | |
|  | (0.038) | — | — |
| Public Sector | −0.056 | −0.048 | −0.076 |
|  | (0.039) | (0.051) | (0.057) |
| Job Tenure (months) | 0.00031 | 0.00024 | 0.00031 |
|  | (0.00018)* | (0.00027) | (0.00024) |
| Male | 0.045 | 0.073 | 0.019 |
|  | (0.037) | (0.053) | (0.050) |
| Pseudo-$R^2$ | 0.023 | 0.026 | 0.021 |
| Observations | 5615 | 2869 | 2803 |

*Source*: Workplace Bargaining Survey 1994.

*Notes*: Dependent variable is individual effort change on 3-point scale: "lower" (0), "no change" (1), "higher" (2).

Robust standard errors, adjusted to allow for correlation within establishments, are given in parentheses; significance levels: * = 10%, ** = 5%, *** = 1%.

[1] "New technology or equipment which affects my work."

[2] Change in way that work is organized.

Table A4.3 uses a sample of Australian establishments in 1994. It shows that the probability that employees experienced an intensification of their work effort over the previous year:

- is raised if new technology or equipment affecting their work had been introduced in that year.

- is raised if they had experienced a change in the way their work was organized.
- is raised if they had become subject to a new system of incentives or bonuses.
- is raised if they had become involved with an appraisal system (small establishments only).
- is lowered if workplace bargaining took place in the establishment.

In extensions to this analysis (not shown):

- the pattern of the estimates is not substantially changed if the study also controls for hours change (this helps to counter the possibility that respondents may be conflating rises in work intensity with rises in work hours).

**TABLE A4.4.**
Determinants of Effort Intensification in Britain, 1996–2001: A Cohort Analysis (Ordinal Probit Estimates)

|  | *(1)* | *(2)* |
|---|---|---|
| *Changes Since 5 Years Ago* | | |
| New Computerized or Automated Equipment | 0.050 | 0.052 |
|  | (0.070) | (0.071) |
| New Communications Technology Equipment | 0.062 | 0.063 |
|  | (0.068) | (0.069) |
| Other New Equipment | 0.190 | 0.181 |
|  | (0.060)*** | (0.060)*** |
| Change in Work Organization | 0.358 | 0.369 |
|  | (0.057)*** | (0.058)*** |
| Change in Hours |  | 0.029 |
|  |  | (0.004)*** |
| *Other Characteristics* | | |
| Public Sector | 0.140 | 0.124 |
|  | (0.062)** | (0.062)** |
| 25 or More in Establishment | −0.076 | −0.076 |
|  | (0.056) | (0.057) |
| Age | −0.006 | −0.006 |
|  | (0.003)** | (0.003)** |
| Male | −0.187 | −0.189 |
|  | (0.056)*** | (0.057)*** |
| Pseudo-$R^2$ | 0.0333 | 0.0518 |
| Observations | 1965 | 1965 |

*Source*: The 2001 Skills Survey.
*Notes*: The dependent variable is individual effort change on a 3-point scale (fall, stay the same, increase).
Robust standard errors are given in parentheses; significance levels: * = 10%, ** = 5%, *** = 1%.

- the impact of organizational or technical change is not significantly altered by whether the change had been the result of workplace bargaining.

Table A4.4 examines the link between work intensification and technological change using individual-based data. Work intensification is measured through workers' recall of effort change over the previous five years. Only those who remained in the same job over this period are included, so there could be some selection bias: those most dissatisfied by work intensification would be more likely to have quit and therefore be excluded. Table A4.4 shows that the probability that employees experienced an intensification of their work effort over the previous year is raised if:

- they had experienced a change in the way their work was organized.
- new equipment had been introduced (other than IT and communications equipment).
- they were in the public sector.
- they were female.
- they were young.

Table A4.5 presents a set of pseudo-panel analyses with just two periods. Fixed effects are eliminated by conventional panel estimators (in this case the same as a first-difference estimator). However, pseudo-panel analyses require cohorts of a reasonable size, and there remains the possibility that small cohorts can generate biases (Deaton, 1985). The mean cell size is 49. To minimize any such biases, the estimates were weighted by cell size; however, the pattern of findings here is not substantially altered by whether or not weights are used.

The findings are:

- More complex or skilled jobs engender higher effort, using three out of the four effort measures.
- When measured in terms of high work speed or of high required effort, the intensification of work was greater in the public sector.
- Cohorts whose jobs become more intensive in the use of computers or automated equipment also experience higher work effort, according to three measures out of the four, but for two of these the effect becomes insignificant, once age is controlled for.

**TABLE A4.5.**
Determinants of Effort Intensification in Britain, 1992–2001: A Cohort Analysis

| | (1) | (2) | (3) | (4) | (5) | (6) | (7) | (8) |
|---|---|---|---|---|---|---|---|---|
| | High Tension | High Tension | High Speed | High Speed | Required Effort | Required Effort | Effort Pressure Index | Effort Pressure Index |
| Public sector | −0.363 (0.234) | −0.083 (0.243) | −0.937 (0.625) | −0.539 (0.678) | −0.268 (0.147) * | −0.319 (0.161) * | 0.059 (0.331) | 0.262 (0.359) |
| Public sector in 2001 | 0.084 (0.098) | −0.163 (0.127) | 1.594 (0.263) *** | 1.242 (0.356) *** | 0.126 (0.062) ** | 0.171 (0.084) ** | 0.042 (0.139) | −0.138 (0.188) |
| Required learning | 0.113 (0.065) * | 0.080 (0.063) | 0.428 (0.175) ** | 0.381 (0.177) ** | 0.086 (0.041) ** | 0.092 (0.042) ** | 0.025 (0.093) | 0.001 (0.094) |
| Uses computers or automated equipment | 0.396 (0.224) * | 0.089 (0.239) | 1.285 (0.600) ** | 0.848 (0.667) | −0.108 (0.141) | −0.052 (0.158) | 0.916 (0.317) *** | 0.693 (0.353) * |
| Age | | 0.018 (0.006) *** | | 0.025 (0.017) | | −0.003 (0.004) | | 0.013 (0.009) |
| Constant | 2.125 (0.295) *** | 1.695 (0.318) *** | 1.309 (0.788) | 0.697 (0.888) | 3.078 (0.185) *** | 3.157 (0.211) *** | 1.795 (0.417) *** | 1.483 (0.470) *** |
| n | 144 | 144 | 144 | 144 | 144 | 144 | 144 | 144 |
| $R^2$ | 0.83 | 0.85 | 0.80 | 0.80 | 0.84 | 0.84 | 0.89 | 0.89 |

*Notes*: The samples from the Employment in Britain Survey (1992) and the 2001 Skills Survey were divided into eight birth cohorts, each of which were grouped in nine 1-digit occupations, giving 72 cells, and 144 observations over the two periods.

Dependent variables: High tension is the average within-cell score on agreement with phrase "I work under a great deal of tension" (range 1 to 4); High Speed is the average within-cell score on frequency of working at very high speed (range 1 to 7); Required Effort is the average within-cell score on agreement with phrase "My job requires that I work very hard" (range 1 to 4); Effort Pressure is the average within-cell score on the Effort Pressure Index, the sum of sources of effort pressure (range 0 to 7). See chapter 3.

The Required Learning Index is an indicator of the length of time taken to learn to do the job well, hence a proxy for the complexity or skill of the job; see chapter 2. Both this and the "uses computers" dummy are entered as the average within-cell score.

Estimates are fixed-effects weighted regression panel estimates, where the cases are weighted by the number of cases in the cell.

# *Five*

## The Workers' Discretion

### The Importance of Influence

One of the distinctive aspects of job contracts is that they are imprecise. In settlement of a contract, wages or other remuneration are exchanged for work; but how much work, and exactly what kind, is usually complex, uncertain, and subject to contestable norms. This imprecision means that employers must manage the labor process: they must instruct their employees what to do and try to ensure compliance. Yet there always remains part of the work planning to which each individual employee contributes, and part of its execution which the employee can influence. This latitude over the manner of performance of work, which has varied from one era to another in the history of capitalism, is a matter of the greatest importance to workers. It is the space in which they participate in the creative and collective act of production. If there were no discretion left, one might as well be a machine. From the most fulfilling to even the most alienating and tightly controlled lines of work, to have some remaining discretion in the performance of the job is to retain that element of humanity.

The exercise of a high level of discretion requires a correspondingly high level of personal skill.[1] To make decisions about task performance, workers must be able to solve problems, make judgments, and take responsibilities, all of which also require knowledge and ability. This necessary condition for high discretion and autonomy underpins the empirical correlation between discretion and skill. But the possession and exercise of skill do not constitute a sufficient condition for being granted high levels of discretion. That license depends also on the balance of power between workers and their bosses and on the extent to which the management of employee relations is conducted on the basis of trust. Where there is relatively low trust, and workers have limited market power to resist, it is possible to have low levels of discretion—and hence a low quality of work life—even when the work is highly skilled.

Unfortunately, the impact of discretion on the quality of work life has not been of central concern to economists. Traditional neoclassical economics discretion begins, not with freedom inside the labor process, but with the "freedom to choose," which has figured most prominently in

support of the market as a means of regulating consumption and production decisions. As a defense of liberalism in the economic sphere, the
cry of freedom has been a powerful stimulant for the opposition to private monopoly power, to state industry or services, and to most forms of
regulation except those in defense of private property rights (Friedman
and Friedman, 1980).[2] Yet, the argument for freedom to choose is not
often extended into the workplace. According to traditional economics,
the firm is the place where market relations cease and where compliance
with the employer's plan begins. Inside the firm, once a work contract is
entered into, the most significant remaining freedom is whether or not to
quit.

In recent years, economic theory has nevertheless investigated a second
freedom, concerning the extent to which the worker complies with the
employer's plan. The worker is seen in this light as the employer's agent.
Workers may "shirk" their duties, because their performance is imperfectly monitored; they also may withhold valuable information about
how to raise productivity, if the changes are not in their interests. Special
wage contracts can be devised to make the best of the situation that arises
from the problem of incomplete compliance, such as agreed seniority
wages and compulsory retirement ages; and managers can devise the optimal extent to which they communicate with workers. In this view of the
workplace, the decision latitude afforded to workers can be seen as having both advantages and disadvantages. It has advantages because the
costs of specifying and regulating what the worker should do in all even-
tualities are prohibitive; trusting and utilizing the workers' judgments
economizes on these costs. But decision latitude also has disadvantages
because it permits potentially opportunistic workers to act in their own,
not the employers', interests and this can generate inefficiency and unemployment of workers who would otherwise want to work at the going
wage (e.g., Shapiro and Stiglitz, 1984). Workers allowed more decision
latitude need not, in this framework, be better off—that would depend
on the particular configuration of the resulting "equilibrium" work contract. The study of optimal work contracts has been developed over the
last two decades and used to extend the explanatory power of economics
into the field of human resource management. This foray outside the traditional sphere was incorporated as part of a new subdiscipline, called
"personnel economics."

It could also be held that the experience of choice and discretion is a
directly valued aspect of a job for the worker, if conceived in the same
way as any other working condition. Economics takes no prior view on
the value of discretion per se for workers, just as it does not take a prior
view on the value of, say, a clean environment. Its value is to be determined on the market, as a compensating differential. If workers prefer

high levels of discretion, jobs that afford more decision latitude should be able—all else being equal—to attract workers with a lower wage rate. Lower wage costs would be an added advantage for employers.

Yet, reliance on the theory of compensating differentials perspective as a means to identify valued job aspects is problematic. Apart from the fact that labor markets are often imperfectly competitive, it has been empirically difficult to observe, and hence to gauge accurately, the market's valuation of particular job characteristics. Typically, heterogeneous working conditions are found to have at most quite modest impacts on pay, often because they are poorly measured or are correlated with other characteristics that are not observed or are badly measured. This issue becomes acute when the working condition in question is discretion, because discretion is so closely related to skill, which itself is expected to have a positive return on the labor market. Few surveys even come close to approximations of the idea of discretion. Where approximate measures do exist, the negative impact on wages that discretion might be expected to have, in a reasonably competitive labor market, is likely to be obscured by the positive impact of unobserved skill.[3] The net effect is that the potential value to workers of having high levels of discretion in their jobs has been missed. There have been few hints in the large empirical literature of estimates of earnings functions; and the idea of assigning value to discretion or choice per se does not enter the prior assumptions of economic thought,[4] except in the rather different perspective of Amartya Sen's capabilities approach (see chapter 1).

Notwithstanding the agnostic approach in economic theory, to understand the evolution of the quality of work life in the modern era, it is important to gauge more about how the extent of discretion is changing. Variations in the extent of task discretion may be having substantial impacts on the trend in workers' job satisfaction—a measure which only sporadically impinges upon the economist's work. Another smoking gun is the finding, by those who have examined the trends in self-employment in modern industrialized countries, that there is evidence of substantial unrealized demand to become self-employed: many more than the typical one in ten workers who are self-employed would like to be so. That they do not actually become self-employed may be due to risk aversion, but the evidence suggests it is also because of constraints on their access to credit (Blanchflower et al., 2001). That they want to do so is testimony to the high value placed on the scope for personal initiative and on the quality of the work itself that self-employment permits (Taylor, 1996). Those who do become self-employed express greater job satisfaction.

In contrast to economics, sociology and social psychology have attributed a high value to discretion. Sociology has seen it as one of the two pillars of skill, while psychology has through its empirical work seen discretion and autonomy as essential to high work quality.

Sociology's concern with workers' discretion and autonomy stems in part from its analysis of the decline of the comparative freedom traditionally afforded to craft workers (Friedmann, 1946) and in part from its origins in the works of Marx and Weber. In all occupations, the extent to which work becomes alienated—separated from the human subject—is fundamental to the analysis of job quality; the extent to which workers can influence their work duties, requirements, and organization is, then, of central importance. In this tradition, Braverman's *Labor and Monopoly Capital* was particularly influential in the English-speaking world in pressing a pessimistic view of job quality in late twentieth century industrial capitalism, and in inspiring the "labor process" school of sociologists.

Psychology arrived at the conclusion that work discretion was of fundamental importance through many small-scale studies of job satisfaction in particular settings. Though "economic" variables like pay were seen as determinants of job satisfaction, much emphasis was placed in these studies on the importance of the content of the job. Job design theorists saw job satisfaction and effective performance as following "mainly from the intrinsic content of the job" (e.g., Cooper, 1973: 4, who emphasizes both discretion and variety). Worker satisfaction, it was argued, could be enhanced by designing into jobs a combination of responsibility and autonomy (Davis, 1966). These ideas were simultaneously developed, through the work of the Tavistock Institute of Human Relations in Britain and others elsewhere, into a normative framework in which theories of job design and of sociotechnical systems implied certain characteristics of ideal job requirements, and the injunction to design jobs that give job-holders some facility to regulate and control their own work. There was a movement toward the re-design of jobs in order to enrich them, which found its strongest expression in the quality of work-life policies adopted from the 1970s onward in Sweden and, to a lesser extent, elsewhere in Scandinavia. The movement was instigated both by unions and by some employers. Many writers in that period anticipated and advocated a trend toward greater employee influence and discretion in jobs, though neither the prognosis nor the optimism escaped cogent criticisms (Kelly, 1982). A subsequent elaboration was the argument that the role of decision latitude has a particular importance for job quality in situations with a high and demanding workload (Karasek and Theorell, 1990; Karasek, 1979). A low decision latitude and high work demands interact to produce the greatest levels of stress.

Given the emphasis accorded to workers' discretion in sociology and psychology, and despite the comparative neglect of this aspect of job quality within economics, the aim of this chapter is to examine what the social survey evidence can reveal about secular trends in the extent of decision latitude in modern industrialized economies. First, a distinction is made between the discretion afforded to individuals about their job tasks, and the wider opportunities they may or may not enjoy for participating in organization-wide decision-making. Then, the stage is set with a brief outline of how work theorists have envisaged the development of task discretion in the modern era. There follows an analysis of trends in the two countries for which suitable data exist (Britain and Finland), and a preliminary picture of shorter-term movements in several other countries.[5] The chapter closes with a discussion of alternative explanations for change in the extent of task discretion and examines in particular the association of changes in discretion with technological change.

## The Workers' Voice

Influence and discretion within an individual's job are not the same as having influence over an organization's decision-making overall. Nevertheless, the wider participation and involvement of employees in such decision-making is for obvious reasons relevant in the long term to what happens in the employees' jobs. Employees who enjoy more autonomy in their own job tend to have a greater preference for participation than those doing closely controlled, low-skilled, and alienating work (Gardell, 1977).

Wider participation and influence can take many forms and can vary according to the character of relations between managers and employees. Traditional influence of employees has been exercised through trade union representation. Unions represented workers' interests in wage bargaining and provided a voice for their grievances (Freeman and Medoff, 1984). The effectiveness of this communication channel depended on the bargaining powers of unions and management. With the decline of union coverage in many countries during the 1980s and 1990s, new types of communication formed to replace the union voice with other forms of representation—such as works committees, regular meetings to consult with or simply to inform the workforce, and suggestion schemes. Millward et al. (2000) judge that the overall extent to which British workers had a voice in the organization did not change substantially. Thus, among establishments with twenty-five or more workers, the proportion affording neither a union nor a non-union voice to their workers was 16 percent in 1984, 19 percent in 1990, and 17 percent in 1998.

Yet, tracing an overall account of how the extent to which workers have the opportunity to participate in organization-level decision-making is difficult. Not only are there many forms that participation can take, but their effectiveness can vary from the kinds of superficial participation that carry no influence to those that enable genuine employee involvement. This variability in the form and effectiveness of wider participation is one reason why no attempt is made here to draw up a statistical picture of changing employee voice.

A second reason for not doing so is that the chief value to workers of organization-level representation or participation may be largely instrumental: they are possible means toward improvement in job quality, rather than something to be valued for themselves. If union jobs are seen as good jobs, this is mainly because and insofar as they deliver better wages and conditions. If participation through works committees or other channels improves the intrinsic quality of jobs, the effects should be seen directly in indicators of that quality. For some workers there may also be a direct value in being able to participate in organization-level decision-making, beyond the instrumental value. But it is to be expected that such valuations are of the second order of magnitude compared to the importance of the job itself, which individuals experience every day. Moreover, if there is a direct value in the opportunity to participate, this would be as much gauged by, say, the freedom to join a union, or to stand for election on a works committee, as by the actual decision to join or stand.

For the purposes of the rest of this chapter, therefore the decision latitude to be examined concerns the opportunity for individuals to have some discretion and influence over their work tasks.

### Theory about How Discretion Is Changing

Just as the value of discretion rarely has been discussed within economics, so economists have not developed particular views about how discretion and decision latitude would change over time in the affluent economy. By contrast, the direction of change has been central to diverse schools of sociology. According to Braverman's pessimistic perspective, workers' discretion was the casualty of a creeping tendency in modern industrial life toward closer control of the labor process by management. It was held that "Taylorism" (or "scientific management") was the dominant tendency in twentieth-century industrial capitalism, and that this involved managers deliberately de-skilling work by pursuing a horizontal and hierarchical division of labor: employees would have little need for brain work since management would have taken on the planning of all work tasks. "Fordism" constituted an extension of this strategy, involving a systematic deployment of technology to control the flow of work. In this perspective, the secular tendency for workers to experience a decline in discretion over their work tasks is the other side of the coin of work intensification.

A more sophisticated perspective recognized the importance also of bureaucratic forms of control of the labor process (Edwards, 1979; Edwards et al., 1982). Sociological writers in the tradition of Weber saw the creeping extension of this form of control in more complex labor processes. In short, this school of sociology foresaw a decline in the quality of work life as gauged by the workers' discretion, though there was disagreement as to whether this was attributable to the ascendancy of capital in its struggle with labor, or to the nature of modern technology as it has evolved over the last half century. The two in combination are still emphasized in more popular neo-Taylorist accounts of the modern workplace in the era of information technology (e.g., Head, 2003).

There also arose a less pessimistic perspective, in which it was hypothesized that the progressive automation of the more routine jobs would begin to leave industry with those complex forms of work that required employees to exercise more discretion in their daily tasks (Blauner, 1964). Even within the Marxian critique of capitalist control, the contradictions of a managerial strategy of extreme direct control of workers were recognized (Friedman, 1977). The alternative strategy of "Responsible Autonomy" entailed giving workers leeway and co-opting them so that they would act in the interests of the firm, but in so doing satisfy in part their need for commitment and for doing interesting and creative work. The "Responsible Autonomy" strategy for management, which relieves worker dissatisfaction but without being able to remove their alienation in the capitalist labor process, began as far back as the era of monopoly capitalism (early twentieth century).

Still more optimistic was the new paradigm among management writers that took root in the 1980s, urging the development of workers' commitment to the organization (Mowday et al., 1982; Walton, 1985). The advantages of workers' sharing at least some values with their managers and also being lured by incentives to the good performance of the firm were that workers exercising discretion were better suited to efficiently navigate the many and unforeseeable requirements of production schedules. Though some of this "post-Fordist" outlook on the labor process was often seen as merely management rhetoric—especially when accompanied by widespread downsizing of firms in the early 1990s—the modern legacy of the more optimistic perspective on employee discretion is the vision of the "high performance work organization." In such an organization there is said to be a high degree of employee involvement through granting workers various performance incentives, more discretion and influence on their everyday work practices, and more of a say in organizational decisions.

Evidence of the effectiveness of organizations that foster high employee involvement has been adduced (Ichniowski et al., 1996; Huselid, 1995; Huselid and Becker, 1996; Appelbaum et al., 2000). The reason many firms have not adopted high-performance work practices is claimed to be the substantial initial costs of introducing them. The costs of change are a short-term obstacle to something that presumably would be beneficial for all parties. In this scenario, one could only expect that with the gradual removal or surmounting of barriers, more firms would adopt high-performance human resource practices as they realize their superiority. Assuming workers share in this bounty of increased productivity, it seems likely that the quality of work life would only improve. Unsurprisingly, this perspective has attracted some skeptical critics who suggest that high-performance work practices might only be improving firms' financial performance at the expense of greater risk to health, or lower wages, for workers (Fairris and Brenner, 2001), or that all the gains are being captured by employers (Osterman, 2000). This debate remains unresolved.

In this age of affluence there are, in short, contrasting expectations about workers' freedom to influence everyday work practices and gain a sense of achievement. Moreover, there is a further school of thought that emphasizes the diversity in the quality of work life that arises from variation in managerial strategy (e.g., Kochan et al., 1986). In this view, there is no discoverable unique optimal solution to the configuration of the labor process. The direction of change, therefore, depends on the beliefs of management and on the extent to which they have the power to install different regimes of control. Managers' influence depends on the countervailing power of trade unions, on the interplay of labor and capital market institutions, and on the state of the labor market. According to Hall and Soskice (2001), managerial strategies matter greatly, but need to be seen in the context of national institutions and cultures which define "varieties of capitalism." Variation also results from an "employment systems" perspective, which stresses the interrelated logics of management strategies, skill formation and bargaining institutions, and unemployment systems. Dobbin and Boychuk (1999) use this perspective to account for their finding that, during the 1980s, there were distinct cross-national differences in the level of worker autonomy, with the Nordic countries showing significantly greater autonomy than Canada, the United States, and Australia. The varying beliefs of management allow the possibility that employees' decision latitude can vary across countries and regions and indeed may be influenced by the social and economic policies of governments (Gallie, 2003). In a similar vein, Rubery and Grimshaw (2001), while emphasizing that the impact of new technologies on employment relationships (including autonomy) is open-ended and subject to institutional pressure and to political choice, are quite pessimistic in their judgment about the prospects for job quality in the current era. In particular, they suggest that political pressures exist toward a new bifurcation of job quality in the knowledge economy between full-time and part-time jobs, with the latter increasingly confined to lower-level, tightly defined jobs.

## Trends in Discretion

Even though decision latitude is a major dimension of the quality of work life, not a great deal of solid empirical evidence is available at the national level about how it has been changing over time in modern workplaces. What there is shows a mixed picture, with contrasting trends in Finland and Britain where there exists relevant data spanning at least a decade, and similarly contrasting changes elsewhere in Europe over a short period.

Evidence is scarce because research effort has not focused on the extent to which individuals can influence their daily work tasks. Nor has proper distinction always been made between this personal influence over the workers' tasks and the broader question of the extent of participation in an organization's decision-making. In some cases, surveys have asked vague questions such as "Do you agree with the statement 'I can work independently'?" whose interpretation is unclear to both researcher and survey respondent.

The workers' decision latitude is captured much more precisely in the Finnish Quality of Work Life Surveys. Respondents were asked, "Are you able to influence a lot, quite a lot, a little or not at all," with respect to various aspects of their work. Figure 5.1 shows the changes in four central aspects. Over the period 1984 to 1997 there was a distinct improvement in the extent of influence over the content of tasks: the proportion of employees answering "a lot" or "quite a lot" rose from 25 percent to 40 percent. There was also a modest increase in influence over working methods. These changes are consistent with the more optimistic prognoses discussed above, though note that most of the increase occurred during the 1980s, before the crisis in the Finnish economy occasioned by the collapse of the Soviet Union, a major trading partner up to that point. Other facets of decision latitude changed little over the period.

In Britain, a similar approach to measuring decision latitude presents a dramatically different picture over the 1992 to 2001 period. As in Finland, respondents were asked to state how much influence they personally had over aspects of their job. The proportions answering at the top of the four-point scale—indicating "a great deal" of influence—are shown

**Percent**

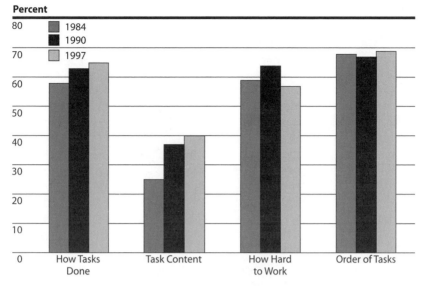

Figure 5.1. Task Discretion in Finland, 1984, 1990, and 1997

*Source*: Estimates reported by Lehto and Sutela (1999).

*Note*: Percentage of employees who can influence aspects of task performance a lot or quite a lot.

in figure 5.2. Along each of four dimensions a substantial decline of decision latitude is recorded. Thus, the proportion with a great deal of influence over what tasks are to be done fell from 42 percent to 30 percent in just nine years; with respect to influence over how to do the tasks, the proportions fell from 57 percent to 43 percent.

It is worth noting that most other aspects of work display considerable stability over time, usually with only a few percentage-point changes even over a decade. So the changes shown in figure 5.2 are likely indicators of a substantial trend in British workplaces. Does this picture withstand further scrutiny, and can it be explained? Panel A of table 5.1 looks at the changes in task discretion in Britain in more detail. It presents, for each occupation, the average Task Discretion Score, being the mean response to the four aspects of task influence shown in figure 5.2. For individuals, the Task Discretion Score ranges in principle from 1 (no influence over any aspect) to 4 (a great deal of influence over all aspects). The table shows that, as expected, the average score was substantially higher in the more skilled occupations, such as managers and professionals, than it is for the low-skilled occupations. Discretion is also greater as expected in full-time jobs, relative to part-time jobs. The Task Discretion Score is

**Percent**

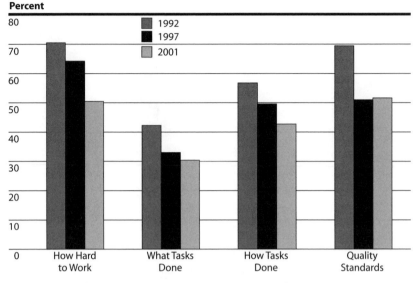

Figure 5.2. Task Discretion in Britain, 1992, 1997, and 2001

*Source*: EIB and Skills Surveys, 1997and 2001.

*Note*: Percentage of employees with "a great deal" of influence over aspects of task performance.

also strongly positively correlated with other indicators of skill. For example, with the Composite Skill Index, a measure of the education, training, and on-the-job learning requirements of the job (see chapter 2), the correlation coefficient of the Task Discretion Score was 0.254 in 2001. This association affords some degree of content validity to this index of discretion.

Looking across Panel A, one can see a decline in task discretion between 1992 and 2001 among all occupational groups in Britain, least so for managers. Consistent with the conjecture of Rubery and Grimshaw (2001) that in Britain there is a growing full-time/part-time divide in job quality, female workers in part-time jobs are the group for whom discretion has fallen most rapidly.

Some further confirmation of this trend is given in Panel B. A quite separate question was asked: "How much choice do you have over the way in which you do your job?" Although "choice" is not the same as "influence," it is closely related; this question is therefore similar to the previous question about influence over how tasks are done. The similarity is useful: first, because it confirms a decline between 1997 and 2001 in choice over working methods; second, because the available survey data permit extension of the picture backward to 1986. As can be seen, the

**TABLE 5.1.**

Employees' Discretion and Choice in Britain's Workplaces, 1986–2001, by Occupation

| Occupation[1] | Panel A Task Discretion Score[2] | | | | Panel B % with a great deal of choice | | | |
|---|---|---|---|---|---|---|---|---|
| | 1992 | 1997 | 2001 | Change 1992 to 2001 | 1986 | 1997 | 2001 | Change 1986 to 2001 |
| ALL | 2.43 | 2.25 | 2.18 | −0.25 | 51.8 | 44.3 | 38.6 | −13.2 |
| Male, full-time | 2.43 | 2.26 | 2.19 | −0.24 | 56.0 | 48.9 | 42.4 | −13.6 |
| Female, full-time | 2.48 | 2.32 | 2.25 | −0.23 | 47.9 | 41.4 | 37.0 | −10.9 |
| Female, part-time | 2.40 | 2.13 | 2.06 | −0.36 | 43.9 | 35.8 | 30.1 | −13.8 |
| Managers | 2.71 | 2.61 | 2.58 | −0.13 | 79.8 | 60.9 | 62.9 | −16.9 |
| Professionals | 2.54 | 2.48 | 2.23 | −0.31 | 71.7 | 56.9 | 38.3 | −33.4 |
| Associate professionals | 2.60 | 2.38 | 2.30 | −0.30 | 51.6 | 43.9 | 37.8 | −13.8 |
| Administrative and secretarial | 2.45 | 2.25 | 2.15 | −0.30 | 47.3 | 41.1 | 35.2 | −12.1 |
| Skilled trades | 2.37 | 2.29 | 2.18 | −0.19 | 49.4 | 49.5 | 43.3 | −6.1 |
| Personal service | 2.57 | 2.24 | 2.24 | −0.33 | 49.7 | 34.3 | 30.4 | −19.3 |
| Sales | 2.28 | 2.06 | 1.94 | −0.34 | 45.6 | 32.0 | 30.0 | −15.6 |
| Plant and machine operatives | 2.16 | 1.90 | 1.86 | −0.30 | 37.0 | 38.9 | 28.7 | −8.3 |
| Elementary | 2.24 | 2.04 | 1.92 | −0.32 | 44.6 | 37.3 | 29.5 | −15.1 |

*Source*: SCELI, EIB, 1997 and 2001 Skills Surveys.

*Notes*:

[1] Occupations are classified by SOC2000 Major Groups.

[2] The Task Discretion Score, ranging from 1 to 4, is here the simple average score of the scaled responses to the four questions regarding influence over what tasks are done, how they are done, how hard to work at those tasks, and the quality standards to which they are performed. In 2001, the mean score was 2.184 with a standard error of 0.011. All change estimates differ significantly from zero ($p = 0.00$).

1990s drop in task discretion was part of a longer-term decline. Most remarkable is the fall in the extent to which professional workers were experiencing choice in their working methods. Whereas in 1986, professional workers were, as a group, comparable with managers in the discretion they enjoyed over working methods, by 2001 they enjoyed less choice than skilled craft workers and very much less than managers. In this respect, professional workers in Britain appear to have experienced a substantial decline in the quality of their work life.

A broader picture of change in task discretion across Europe is given in table 5.2, based on surveys by the European Foundation for Living and Working Conditions. For this particular purpose, the data in the table are

**TABLE 5.2.**
Changes in Discretion in Europe's Workplaces, 1996–2000

|  | Change in Task Discretion Score[1] | Change in Percentage Able to Choose Order of Tasks | Change in Percentage Able to Choose Methods of Work | Change in Percentage Able to Choose Speed or Rate of Work |
|---|---|---|---|---|
| Austria | 0.033* | 3.6 | 5.1** | 1.8 |
| Belgium | −0.087** | −2.9 | −11.9** | −10.4** |
| Britain | −0.052** | −3.4 | −3.7* | −8.2** |
| Denmark | −0.029* | −2.7 | −4.1** | −1.3 |
| Finland | −0.015 | 0.5 | −3 | −2.4 |
| France | −0.019 | 0.1 | −4.8** | −1.5 |
| Germany | 0.054** | 3.7* | 8.1** | 3.8* |
| Greece | −0.028 | −2.6 | −5.9** | 0.1 |
| Ireland | −0.045** | −4.4* | −4.2* | −4.4* |
| Italy | −0.033* | −2.7 | −3.7* | −3.5* |
| Luxembourg | −0.028 | −5.4 | −1.4 | −1.6 |
| Netherlands | 0.004 | −2 | 1.8 | 0.8 |
| Portugal | −0.111** | −7.2** | −12.8** | −13.0** |
| Spain | −0.031 | −1.1 | −4.9** | −2.7 |
| Sweden | 0.0013 | −1.9 | 1 | 1.2 |
| ALL | −0.009 | −0.2 | −0.5 | −1.5* |

*Source*: Second and Third European Surveys on Working Conditions.
*Notes*:
Asterisks indicate significantly different from zero at the 10% level (*) or 5% level (**).
Data are weighted to reflect population sampling probabilities.

[1] The Task Discretion Score is here defined as the simple average of responses to the three questions: ability to influence the order of tasks, the methods of working, and the speed or rate of work, each of which has a dichotomous response scale (0/1). In 2001 the score across Europe had an average of 0.685, and a standard error of 0.0044.

less satisfactory than the Finnish and British surveys. The surveys only covered three aspects of decision latitude (work methods, task order, and pace of work), and only dichotomous responses were elicited ("can you influence (each one) or not?"). Moreover, there is only a short period of valid change data to consider, and, although discretion is unlikely to be a highly cyclical variable, changes are likely to be modest over only short periods, making it hard to confidently identify longer-term trends.[6] Nevertheless, given the general scarcity of data on this major aspect of work quality, and because these surveys constitute an excellent benchmark for evaluating change after 2000, the picture of change that they represent can be seen as suggestive, though not definitive. The table confirms the decline in discretion in Britain in the late 1990s, as indicated by the different sources used for figure 5.2. It also shows a decline in this period in Belgium, Denmark, Italy, Ireland, and Portugal. In Austria and in Germany, by contrast, workers were experiencing increases in influence over their work tasks. Finally, there were no significant overall changes in Finland (extending the 1990s stability shown in figure 5.1), Greece, Spain, France, Luxembourg, the Netherlands, and Sweden; however, among these Greece, Spain, and France did show statistically significant, if modest, declines in the proportions of workers able to influence their methods of work.

## Conclusion: An Incomplete Account

Deconstructing and extending this picture of the changes in workers' discretion is now a substantial task confronting the community of social and economic researchers. The decline in discretion experienced by individuals in British workplaces, representing a notable fall in the quality of their work life, is at first sight consistent with a neo-Taylorist perspective. Reduced discretion is apparently the other side of the coin from the work intensification examined in previous chapters. As managers acquire the power and the facility to control ever more closely the various production processes, so they are able to intensify work, and the employee's freedom within work is diminished.

Yet closer examination suggests that such a story would be too great a simplification. First, the "Big Brother" hypothesis is not adequate as a general explanation for work intensification (see chapter 4): it does not account for the fact that workers on average were enjoying increased real wages during the period of intensification of their work. Second, whereas in Britain work intensification ceased after 1997, the decline in discretion continued unabated. Third, it may be noted that, although discretion and skill are highly correlated aspects of jobs, these aspects were moving in opposite directions in Britain. The neo-Taylorist perspective calls for a secular de-skilling of the workforce, yet there is no general evidence to support this, and indeed the trend in job skill has inched modestly upward (see chapter 2). The proximate origins of the changes in task discretion in Britain remain, unfortunately, unexplained. In a comprehensive examination, Gallie et al. (2004) show that, just as the skill trend does not account for the discretion trend, so also other observable factors associated with discretion do not change in ways that would predict a decline in workers' discretion. For example, the organization of work in quality circles (continuous improvement groups), which is linked to higher individual discretion, has been increasing in Britain during the 1990s.

TABLE 5.3.
Discretion and Advanced Technology within Cohorts, 1992–2001

|  | Discretion 1992 | Discretion 2001 | Intra-Cohort Change in Discretion, 1992–2002 |
|---|---|---|---|
| Advanced Technology 1992 | 0.342 (0.00) |  |  |
| Advanced Technology 2001 |  | 0.269 (0.02) |  |
| Intra-Cohort Change in Advanced Technology 1992–2001 |  |  | −0.240 (0.04) |

Source: EIB and the 2001 Skills Survey.
The reported figures are correlation coefficients across the cohorts, with p-values in parentheses. For a definition of the cohorts, see table A4.5. "Advanced Technology" is the proportion of workers in each cohort using computers or automated equipment; "Discretion" is the mean Task Discretion Score in each cohort.

The potential role of technology is perhaps the most intriguing. If new technologies are skill-biased, and skill is positively associated with discretion, the Task Discretion Score would be higher for those workers using new technologies. If, on the other hand, new technologies permit greater control of work—and if managers choose to use the technologies in this way—there would instead be a negative association between the Task Discretion Score and use of new technologies. In the event, Gallie et al. (2004) find no significant cross-sectional association between discretion and the use of advanced technology, after controlling for other variables. This is no prima facie evidence for the neo-Taylorist explanation for a decline in discretion over time.

An alternative analysis is, however, more supportive of the view that new technologies are at least part of the story. If the samples are grouped into occupation-cohorts in 1992, one can trace how each cohort experienced changes in its Task Discretion Score between 1992 and 2001. Table 5.3 does just this. The first two elements in the leading diagonal show that, across the cohorts, there is a positive association with the use of new computers or automated equipment in both 1992 and 2001. This positive association probably reflects other factors associated both with technology and discretion, such as skill. More telling is what happens when the advanced technology is introduced. In the third element of the diagonal, a negative correlation coefficient is shown between the *change* in use of computers or automated equipment and the *change* in the Task Discretion Score. Thus, occupation-cohorts that were more subject to increased use of new technologies experienced greater declines in their average Task Discretion Score.[7] This finding is consistent with the view that new technologies are part of the reason for declining discretion, as implied by, for example, the neo-Taylorist analysis of declining discretion in the British clothing industry discussed in the previous chapter; but since the connections between discretion and automation, and between discretion and skill, are loose, the finding is not inconsistent with an average upskilling of the workforce.

In the absence of other longitudinal databases, further explanation of the decline in discretion has to rely more on theory, on a small amount of case study research, and on informed speculation. A plausible interpretation of the findings concerning professional workers in Britain attributes their declining discretion to the increasing extent that this group has been subject to public scrutiny and accountability (Gallie et al., 2004). Target setting, and the inculcation of an "audit culture," have been used by successive British governments to attempt to improve public services even while subject to considerable fiscal constraints, but these have narrowed and distorted the choices of many public-sector workers. Across both private and public spheres, workers have felt the controlling impact of health and safety regulation. And while the rise of the subcontracting industry might, at first glance, be seen as an extension of market relations allowing increased freedom, the consequence of subcontracting services is the need to codify and specify work requirements more precisely than when the work is done in house. Case study research suggests that subcontracting accounts for some of the experienced decline in the discretion of professional workers (Grimshaw et al., 2002). The wider decline in discretion is consistent also with an increasing bureaucratization of work life. Raising the extent to which individuals conform to good and efficient practice—in whatever field—constitutes the beneficial impact of bureaucratic control. However, in a bureaucratic culture, the negative impact of reduced trust and limited freedoms at work typically are not properly valued, because these costs are hidden and usually not borne by the groups of workers making the rules.

The different experience of Finland supports the view that trends in the quality of work life are not subject to a deterministic law, and is consistent with the argument that discretion is in part a matter of managerial strategy, potentially amenable to public influence. Though not such a strong and early adherent of the Scandinavian model for improving the quality of work life as Sweden and Norway, the Finnish government nevertheless passed legislation in 1979 enabling matters concerning work organization to become an area for negotiation.[8] The detailed effects of such legislation on workers' discretion have yet to be traced. The origins of the improvements in workers' discretion in Finland also remain inadequately explained. The diversity in the picture of change across other European countries, though covering too short a period to be confident that these are longer term trends, also reinforces the need to avoid deterministic explanations about autonomy at work.

The freedom for workers to influence the scope and the manner of performance of the tasks which make up their daily work is something of great value in itself, and a major dimension of the quality of work life. Yet, its value appears to have been missed twice over. It has largely failed to enter the domain of economic analysis, because economic theory does not point in this direction, because discretion and freedom are hard to measure, and because the framework of compensating differentials is not well suited to permit the value of such a concept to become obvious in quantitative labor market analyses. The value of discretion appears also to have been missed by many in the ranks of the armies of bureaucrats, across many sectors of industry, who impose detailed rules for the conduct of work, with little care for the well-being of workers. The understanding of workers' discretion—its dependence on managerial culture, its relationship to modern technologies, and its importance to workers— needs further development across all the social sciences.

# Six

## The Wages of Nations

### Wages and the Fairness of Wages

Are the jobs being generated and sustained in modern industrial capitalism paying better wages than they used to? To an economist, it is obvious that the wage rate is a key indication of a job's quality. Surprisingly, some of the discourse among social scientists and policy makers about the quality of work life takes place without even a passing reference to pay. The mystery of the missing wage rate in this debate might have a mundane origin in semantics—perhaps some prefer to use the phrase "quality of work life" to refer just to its intrinsic aspects. Of greater concern is the possibility that the omission stems from an idealistic and false vision in which the need for fulfilling and creative work overrides material needs. Or, perhaps, it stems from conflating the quality of work life with the quality of the workers' output. As exemplified in the deliberations of the European Commission (see chapter 1), there is a propensity for the representatives of governments to assert that all parties would gain from quality improvements. In the "knowledge economy" this assertion can be persuasive when the aspect of job quality at issue is, for example, skill. It is problematic when the talk is of wages. The unpleasant political consequences of signaling pay raises as indicators of quality improvements would be contentious in any polity where business interests are robustly represented; consequently, wages get left off the menu.

Higher wages might not always be regarded as beneficial beyond doubt for all employees. Just as critics question the benefits of economic growth for already-rich nations, citing both environmental fragility and artificial creation of consumer wants,[1] so one might query the benefits of further increasing the pay of the already well-heeled employee. Nevertheless, a rising wage rate is a sign of improving job quality, a fall a strong indication of deterioration if there is nothing in compensation.

Whether the wage rate is considered fair is also a significant part of the quality of jobs. Fairness is hard to define, but one aspect is known to be important to how workers judge job quality: to be perceived as fair, pay should be related to a worker's contribution to the performance of the organization. The invocation of "a fair day's pay for a fair day's work" is widely respected, and dissatisfaction follows when the rule is perceived to be flouted by employers or by other employees (Adams, 1965; Akerlof, 1982). A common source of public disillusion concerns expansions in boardroom pay that are not matched by company performance (Gregg et al., 1993). However, assessment of "fair pay" and of productive performance is imprecise and subjective. Typically, pay is compared with an expected norm, which is historically determined and likely to be adapted only gradually. If actual pay falls short of this norm, workers report job dissatisfaction, while if they are "surprised" to find themselves receiving higher pay than they expected, they feel more than usually satisfied (Hamermesh, 2001).

There are no accepted broad indicators of fairness available over time to provide a picture of how the industrialized world is changing. There is, however, a clear picture of what has been happening to the dispersion of wages within many nations. Rising wage dispersion can be unambiguously regarded as signaling declining quality of work life, if it is not "justified" by an increasing dispersion of the productive contributions of workers. A major concern of economists has been to estimate the extent to which changes in pay inequality are attributable to the changing distribution of skills (and hence, by assumption, productivity). Discrimination is a particular instance of unfairness, as is picking on unprotected weak labor market groups (often the same thing). Leaving fairness aside, rising wage dispersion can also be a special problem if it means that significant minorities of low-paid workers are suffering decreases in wages.

This chapter will first review the extent to which economic growth has in practice been delivering real wage growth for the average worker over recent decades. For these purposes, the book diverges at this point from its reliance on social survey series. It turns to official data on wages which are collected directly from employers' surveys and records, which yield a picture of wage change in a broad range of industrialized countries. Unfortunately, the reliability of wage series within many countries is hindered by frequent changes in methodology. Given the centrality of this statistic for the welfare of the majority of the population, it is regrettable that more resources have not been devoted to generating more highly reliable, internationally comparable information on wages. Some wages, especially those at the extremes, are apt to be hidden from view in the informal economy. Internationally comparable data are scarce, in part owing to practical difficulties over exactly what is included in the wage package. Political ambivalence over whether high or low wages are deemed desirable may have played a role in limiting the research effort devoted to resolving the data consistency problems more comprehensively.

## The Growth of Average Wages

As far back as the eighteenth century, there was a definite but subtle link between the wages of ordinary jobs and the "wealth of nations." Adam

Smith maintained that the wages of nations would be high in a thriving economy—one whose wealth was growing rapidly. In a stationary economy, even one that had become wealthy, wages were regulated at subsistence level by population growth, chiefly through their effect on the death rate. In fact, Smith seemed quite bullish about the prospects for wages in his day, inspired in part by the example of the American economy. But his followers, the classical economists of the nineteenth century, were notoriously glum about the prospects for improving the quality of jobs over the long term. For Malthus, the issue for all societies was the rapid population growth rate if wages rose above subsistence level. He forecast that population would grow multiplicatively while food production, he maintained, could only be expanded as an arithmetic series. Sooner or later wages would be forced down to subsistence level or below by market forces. This mechanistic and pessimistic outlook earned for political economy, courtesy of contemporary historian Thomas Carlyle, the epithet from which it barely ever recovered: the "dismal science." For Marx, writing a half century later, it was the periodic and deepening capitalist economic crises which presaged the "immiseration of the proletariat." Wages were being held down, in Marx's view, not by a universal law of nature but by the character of the economic system at the time (which could be transformed).

The hindsight of the twentieth century turned these perspectives around. It became recognized that, with sufficient ongoing technological progress, there could be sustainable long-term increases in the average person's income even within a capitalist economic system. With the development of national statistical offices, these increases came to be computed as the growth of per capita Gross Domestic Product (GDP). With per capita GDP growth, it could be expected that at least in the long term there would also be growth in the real wage rate. Wages in the industrialized countries are now enormously higher than they had been in the nineteenth century; most would see this affluence as a refutation of classical pessimism, though such a conclusion is colored by the stagnation of living standards in many parts of the developing world. And, since most industrialized nations have in recent decades kept up a positive if fluctuating rate of growth of per capita GDP, it might be expected that the growing affluence would be reflected in an increasing quality of jobs, at least as gauged by their wages.

The problem with this supposition, however, is that per capita GDP growth need not be reflected in wage rate growth, if at the same time either the share of the aggregate wage bill in national income, or the proportion of the population gainfully employed (the "participation rate") is changing. If the wage bill share is falling during a period of economic growth, this means that workers are receiving less than their proportionate share of the rising affluence; if the participation rate is rising, the wage bill is being distributed among a larger number of jobs.[2] The share of wages could decline if there is a shift in the balance of power between capital and labor. The participation rate could increase for political and economic reasons, though it has a mathematical ceiling of 100 percent and a practical one well below that, if child labor is proscribed and retirement is accepted. Though neither the wage share nor the participation rate is likely to fall or grow indefinitely, it remains possible for wage growth to deviate substantially from general economic growth for many years.

Figure 6.1 gives the big picture of real wage growth in practice.[3] The graphs show real wages relative to the base year 1970 in each country. In most nations, average wages have increased over the last three decades. There is a sharp contrast, however, between European nations and elsewhere. In the larger European nations real wages increased steadily after 1970, though they stabilized in Italy in the mid-1980s. In the Scandinavian nations the mid-1980s marked the end of a decade of stability; from then on wages rose substantially. Throughout Europe, Spain stands out with the highest increase in wages, starting from a low base in 1970, when Spain was still ruled by the dictator Franco. Outside Europe, however, the picture is different: wages remained fairly stable in Canada, New Zealand, and Australia after 1974, and in the United States after 1970.[4] Among the non-European nations shown, Japan is the only country in which wages have continued to increase.

Table 6.1 uses a different source to give wage changes in the private sectors of a wider range of countries.[5] A similar overall picture emerges of comparative stagnation in wages in the United States, Canada, New Zealand, and Australia. Elsewhere the wages of the average job rose everywhere between 1975 and 2002, with the single exception of Turkey, where high inflation exceeded wage increases for many of the early years. After 1986, real wages also rose in Turkey. The most striking improvement among OECD countries was in the Republic of Korea, which during this period was experiencing its growth "miracle": starting from a low base, wages for the average private-sector job grew by nearly 5 percent per year between 1975 and 2002.

As expected, for the most part those national economies that have had the greatest growth in GDP per head over the last three decades rendered the greatest increases in wage rates (figure 6.2a). Similarly, countries with high productivity growth in the business sector had high wage growth in that sector (figure 6.2b). Thus, whatever the source of the high productivity growth in the Republic of Korea, or the low productivity growth in Switzerland, the difference accounts for much of the large variation between these two countries in the growth of wages.

In most countries, wages did not grow as fast as productivity. One reason is that the share of wages in output was falling. For the OECD countries as a whole, the share of wages fell roughly 5 percentage points

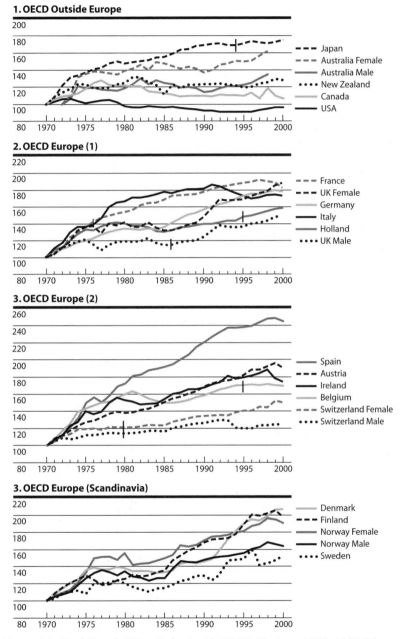

**1. OECD Outside Europe**

- – – Japan
- – – Australia Female
- —— Australia Male
- •••• New Zealand
- —— Canada
- —— USA

**2. OECD Europe (1)**

- – – France
- – – UK Female
- —— Germany
- —— Italy
- —— Holland
- •••• UK Male

**3. OECD Europe (2)**

- —— Spain
- – – Austria
- —— Ireland
- —— Belgium
- – – Switzerland Female
- •••• Switzerland Male

**3. OECD Europe (Scandinavia)**

- —— Denmark
- – – Finland
- —— Norway Female
- —— Norway Male
- •••• Sweden

Figure 6.1.  Real Hourly Wage Index in 18 OECD Nations, 1970–2000 (Non-Agricultural Workers unless stated; see notes)

Figure 6.1 (*continued*)

*Source*: International Labor Office, *Yearbook of Labour Statistics*, various issues 1970 to 2000.

*Notes*:

1. Base year: 1970.

2. Where there occurs a substantial break in a country's wage series owing to changes in sample design, sufficient to generate a significant series shift, the series before and after the break have been spliced together to generate a continuous series. The splice is marked by a I in the diagram. This method arbitrarily imposes a zero change in real wages in the year in which the break occurs. The method has been used for six countries: Japan (from 1994), the Netherlands (HOL) (from 1994), Italy (from 1975), U.K. (from 1986), Belgium (from 1994), and Switzerland (from 1980). "Germany" (GER) means the Federal Republic of Germany until 1992. Other minor changes in design, which were not the occasion for noticeable or significant shifts in the series, are noted as follows:

OECD Outside Europe

| United States | 1988 | New industrial classification |
| Canada | 1987 | Sample design revised |
| Australia | 1972 | Scope of series enlarged |
| | 1982 | Series replacing former series prior to 1982 |
| New Zealand | Prior to 1982 | F/T employees  and half or P/T employees |
| Japan | 1973, 1979, 1986 | Sampling design revised |

OECD Europe[1]

| United Kingdom | 1983 | New industrial classification |
| France | 1994 | New industrial classification |
| Germany | 1973 | Sampling design revised |
| Italy | 1978 | Scope of series revised |

OECD Europe[2]

| Ireland | 1980–98 | Wages in Manufacturing Sector |
| Belgium | 1972 | New industrial classification |
| Switzerland | 1995, 1997 | Data missing |
| Austria | 1971 | Scope of series enlarged |
| | 1971–83 | Excluding Major Division 6 (Trade and Restaurants) |
| | 1984–99 | Wages in Manufacturing, Mining, and Quarrying |

OECD Europe (Scandinavia)

| Norway | 1976–98 | Wages in Manufacturing Sector |
| Finland | 1977–85 | Wages in Manufacturing Sector |
| Sweden | 1971 | New industrial classification, |
| | 1974 | Sampling design revised |
| | 1976–2000 | Wages in Manufacturing Sector |
| | 1970–1997 | Including holidays and sick-leave payments and the value of payments in kind |

**TABLE 6.1.**
Growth of Real Compensation per Employee in the Business Sector in
24 OECD Nations, 1975–2002.

| | Percentage Growth of Real Wages | | |
|---|---|---|---|
| | *1975–1985* | *1985–2002* | *1975–2002* |
| Australia | −4.7 | 4.4 | −0.4 |
| Austria | 23.4 | 28.4 | 58.5 |
| Belgium | 21.8 | 26.6 | 54.1 |
| Canada | 3.1 | 17.9 | 21.6 |
| Denmark | 2.8 | 33.8 | 37.5 |
| Finland | 19.5 | 39.9 | 67.2 |
| France | 18.6 | 9.1 | 29.4 |
| Germany | 15.8 | 19.0 | 37.7 |
| Greece | 36.1 | 4.7 | 42.5 |
| Ireland | 20.3 | 39.8 | 68.2 |
| Italy | 22.6 | 12.9 | 38.5 |
| Japan | 15.2 | 7.1 | 23.4 |
| Korea | 78.7 | 117.1 | 288.1 |
| Luxembourg | −5.0 | 37.5 | 30.6 |
| Netherlands | 4.1 | 18.0 | 22.9 |
| New Zealand | −11.9 | −3.7 | −15.2 |
| Norway | 0.5 | 38.3 | 38.9 |
| Portugal | −27.2 | 60.3 | 16.8 |
| Spain | 26.2 | 29.8 | 63.8 |
| Sweden | 8.5 | 49.8 | 62.5 |
| Switzerland | 18.8 | 23.1 | 46.2 |
| Turkey | −48.5 | 20.2 | −38.1 |
| United Kingdom | 11.8 | 37.1 | 53.3 |
| United States | 0.5 | 11.8 | 12.4 |

*Source*: Author's calculation from *OECD Economic Outlook* 73, June 2003, Annex, tables 12 and 19.

Business-sector employees are defined as total employees less public-sector employees. Real compensation includes pay and nonwage labor costs paid by employers such as unemployment insurance, social security and pensions, all deflated by the consumer price index. See also: *OECD Economic Outlook Sources and Methods* (http://www.oecd.org/eco/sources-and-methods).

during the 1980s, and then the fall continued at a slower pace during the 1990s.[6] In most countries, also, the participation rate was rising.[7] In both diagrams the deviations from the regression line (which gives the expected wage growth rate for each GDP per capita growth rate) are in principle due to changes in the wage share or changes in the participation rate that differ from the average changes experienced by all the countries shown.[8]

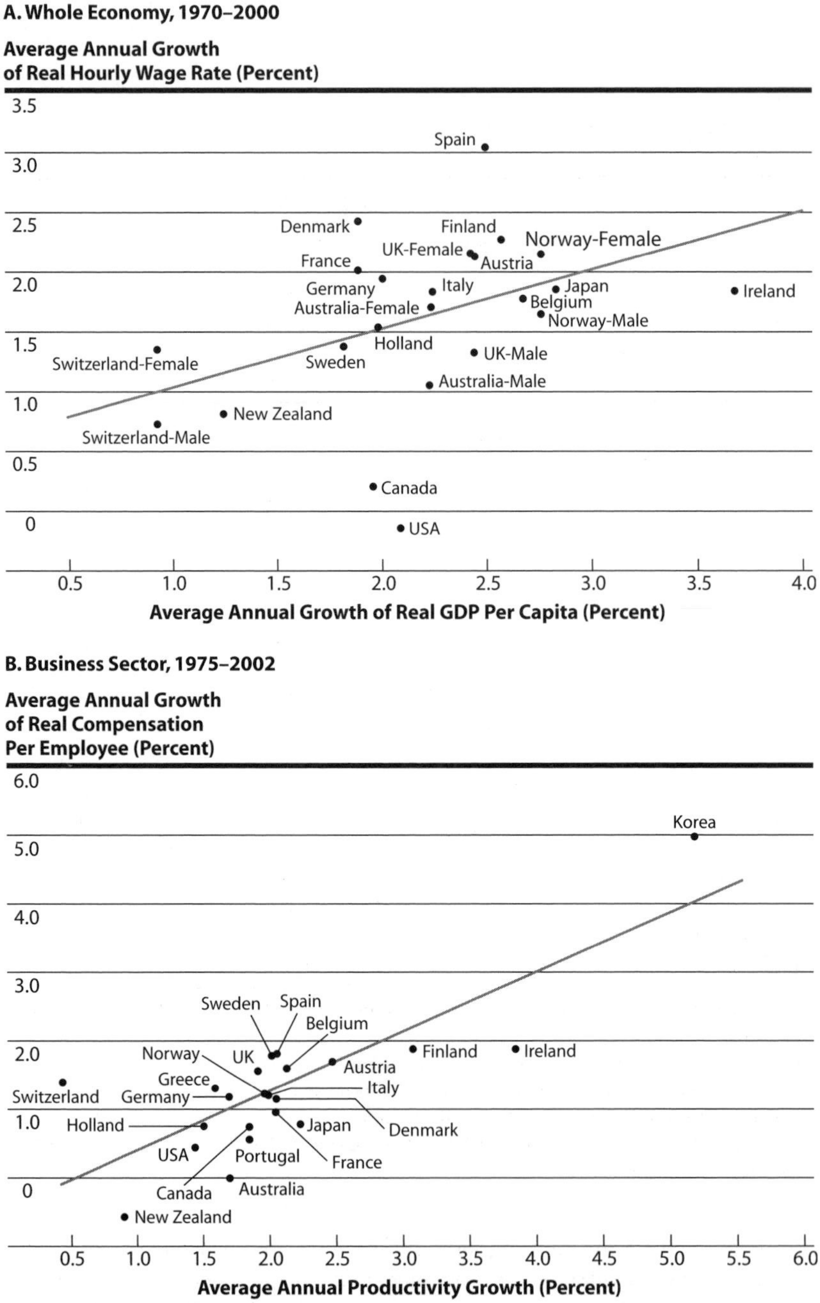

## A. Whole Economy, 1970–2000

**Average Annual Growth
of Real Hourly Wage Rate (Percent)**

**Average Annual Growth of Real GDP Per Capita (Percent)**

## B. Business Sector, 1975–2002

**Average Annual Growth
of Real Compensation
Per Employee (Percent)**

**Average Annual Productivity Growth (Percent)**

Figure 6.2. Economic Growth and Real Wages Growth in OECD Nations
   a. Whole Economy, 1970–2000
   *Source*: http://www.imf.org/external/pubs/ft/weo/2003/01/data/index.htm and figure 6.1.
   M—male; F—female; data for Australia (AUS) refer to 1972–2000.
   b. Business Sector, 1975–2002
   *Source*: Author's calculation from *OECD Economic Outlook* 73, June 2003, Annex: tables 12, 13, and 19.

The slow growth of wages in Switzerland appears, in this light, as largely a reflection of relatively low economic growth overall. But Switzerland's business sector workers did not fare as badly as they might have done, given the low productivity growth rate, owing to the increased wage share there. In contrast, New Zealand, Canada, and the United States are outliers on the down side. Their economic growth was quite slow relative to other countries during this era; their wage growth was even slower than could be accounted for simply by that slow growth. In each of these countries the wage share fell by more than the average; and, in the United States, the participation rate rose by 8 percentage points between 1980 and 2000.[9] At the other end of the spectrum, workers in Ireland enjoyed rapid wage growth but again substantially less than might be expected given Ireland's productivity growth. There, the wage share fell a great deal during both the 1980s and 1990s, while the participation rate soared by 13 percentage points during the 1990s.

Evident in this description of wages rising at a varying pace across nations is a process of convergence: in 1970 the average job in the United States paid more than in other countries, and the stagnation of wages in the United States allowed jobs elsewhere to start to catch up. To say how far convergence has reached requires international comparisons of wage levels. These comparisons are difficult because what is included in wages differs according to national tax and social insurance regimes. They also require estimates of differential purchasing power parities, in order to make wages denominated in national currencies commensurate. The Economic Policy Institute in Washington, D.C., has, nevertheless, drawn up the big picture, and table 6.2 gives their main findings (Mishel et al., 2003). They confirm the catch-up story, with regard to hourly earnings in the manufacturing sectors of nations.[10] In 1970, by a considerable margin the average manufacturing job in the United States was better paid than the equivalent in all other countries. By 2000 this was no longer so. In Belgium, (West) Germany, and the Netherlands, pay for the average manufacturing job had easily overtaken that in the United States; in all other countries the pay was a lot closer.

## The Fairness of Wages

Unlike the average wage, there are no specifically economic reasons to look forward to long-term improvements or any other trend in the perceived fairness of material rewards. In the analysis of the process of development, there was in the mid-twentieth century a "Kuznets curve," whereby countries in the early stages of growing from a mainly agricultural economy toward industrialization would experience a long swing of rising inequality, followed by a later equalizing trend as economies

TABLE 6.2.
Relative Hourly Compensation of Manufacturing Production Workers in
20 OECD Nations, 1979, 1989, 2000 (Percentage of U.S. Manufacturing
Production Workers' Hourly Compensation)

|  | 1979 | 1989 | 2000 |
| --- | --- | --- | --- |
| Australia | 71 | 79 | 94 |
| Austria | 72 | 92 | 108 |
| Belgium | 91 | 107 | 126 |
| Canada | 81 | 92 | 102 |
| Denmark | 71 | 78 | 96 |
| Finland | 59 | 80 | 102 |
| France | 66 | 86 | 89 |
| Germany* | 86 | 111 | 127 |
| Ireland | 50 | 65 | 72 |
| Italy | 87 | 100 | 97 |
| Japan | 49 | 61 | 79 |
| Netherlands | 87 | 101 | 114 |
| New Zealand | 55 | 56 | 61 |
| Norway | 70 | 90 | 91 |
| Portugal | 31 | 34 | 40 |
| Spain | 58 | 70 | 75 |
| Sweden | 78 | 88 | 96 |
| Switzerland | 75 | 87 | 96 |
| United Kingdom | 62 | 76 | 81 |
| United States | 100 | 100 | 100 |

Source: Mishel et al. (2003), 405.

Notes: International comparisons using purchasing-power parities.

* Old Federal States.

matured into modernity with rising services, more broad-based wealth, and educational achievement among the population.[11] A number of countries experienced declining income inequality for most of the twentieth century, attributable in part to falls in wage inequality. But, with the experience of the 1970s and after, the vision of reduced inequality in many industrialized capitalist economies was dimmed (Atkinson, 2002).

Figure 6.3 encapsulates this modern disappointment. For the majority of countries there has been a trend toward increased wage inequality, as measured by the ratio of the wages of the ninetieth percentile in the pay rankings to that of the tenth percentile.[12] In the United States, the growing inequality was especially marked at the top end: the wage ratio of the ninety-fifth percentile to the tenth percentile rose from 4.6 in 1973 to 5.3 in 1989, and to 5.5 in 2001.[13] It is striking that wage inequality increased quite markedly in two of the outside-Europe countries with stagnating

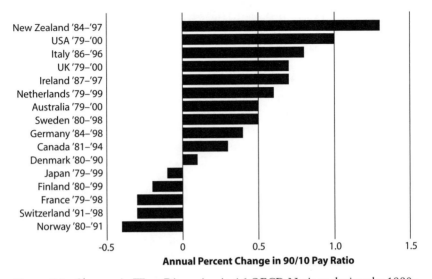

Figure 6.3. Changes in Wage Dispersion in 16 OECD Nations during the 1980s and 1990s
   *Source*: Glyn (2001), table 1.

average wages—the United States and New Zealand. The flip side of the coin is that the real wages of the lower paid groups have declined for long periods: between 1973 and 1989 real wages fell for all groups of workers in the lower half of the U.S. wage distribution.[14]

It is self-evident that a rising dispersion of wages implies that job quality is becoming more unequal (unless balanced by an egalitarian trend in the other elements of work). Whether increased dispersion also portends a rising experience of unfair treatment is another matter. There is no direct evidence about this trend from the surveys used in this book. However, it is possible to examine the extent to which the changes in wage inequality appear to be "justified" by changes in economic conditions.

Three economic sources of change have been identified and widely investigated: the rapid growth of manufacturing sites in low-wage developing nations (especially China) and simultaneous extension of trade, the widespread diffusion of information and communication technologies (identified as a burst of skill-biased technological change), and in the case of the United States a deceleration in the growth of college-educated labor. From each of these sources, to various extents, stem observed rises in the wage premium attached to skilled labor, which is a substantive part of the rising wage dispersion.[15] In addition, increases in wage dispersion within observed skill groups are often linked to increases in the premiums for unobserved skills, though this attribution is largely an ad hoc response to residual ignorance. If these sources were accepted as the only reason for rising wage inequality, the fairness of the wages in the industrialized world would nevertheless be impaired if workers are prevented from gaining access to the higher and different skills needed to become more productive in the modern economy.

It has come to be recognized, however, that changes in labor market institutions and in the general tenor of labor market policies over recent decades may be an important source of distributional changes, potentially more significant than fluctuations in the supply and demand for skill. In the U.S. case, the weakness of the skill-biased technological change argument is that it does not explain the timing of the most rapid change in wage dispersion, namely, the first part of the 1980s. Moreover, automation has not reduced the demand for relatively low-skilled *nonroutine* jobs (Autor et al., 2003b; Goos and Manning, 2003). Rather, a substantial part of increasing inequality can be attributed to declines in the real value of the minimum wage, which were a feature of that era in the time of President Reagan; other sources of rising inequality are the diminishing powers of trade unions (which in most countries tend to negotiate more equal wages), and reductions in the wage floor provided by state benefit systems (Card and DiNardo, 2002; Lee, 1999; Mishel et al., 2003). Institutional differences are also seen as the source of the variation in inequality trends across countries that are shown in figure 6.3 (e.g., Blau and Kahn, 1996; Fostin and Lemieux, 1997). The fact that in some countries there has been little or no rise in wage inequality over two decades suggests that the global demand pressures arising from expanding world trade and ubiquitous technological progress are not decisive. In this circumstance increasing wage inequality is not easily attributed to increased dispersion of productive contributions. Where the relative wages of the lower-paid workers were reduced because the minimum wage was lowered in real terms (or, in the case of Britain in the early 1990s, abolished for many workers), the quality of these jobs was diminished by the unfairness.

There is, in short, a strong sense of loss in the rising dispersion of wages in several industrialized nations in recent decades, even if the extent of the loss of fairness is impossible to quantify. Set against this trend, however, are other aspects of wage fairness that have shown a long-term progressive change in recent decades. Of these the most striking is differential treatment of men and women. Discrimination constitutes a partial break in the link between productivity and pay. When employees of equal productive power are paid differently according to their sex or race, the unfairness is blatant.[16] Historically, sex and race discrimination in recruitment, pay, and most other work matters has been the normal practice. Since the 1970s, antidiscriminatory legislation and concomitant progressive cultural change have successfully reduced the extent of gender discrimination.

One simple though not ideal measure of discrimination is the gender-pay ratio, the ratio of the average hourly pay for women and men. The ratio varies considerably between countries. For example, in 1998 the gender-wage ratios in the United States and Britain were among the lowest, at 78 percent and 75 percent respectively; the ratio was at its highest in Portugal, at 95 percent. Everywhere, the ratio had been increasing. In the United States, for example, the ratio was just 63 percent in 1979, indicating that women's pay was chasing men's pay quite rapidly in the 1980s and 1990s. This narrowing of differences occurred despite generally rising wage dispersion, partly because women were converging on men in their achievement of qualifications (Blau and Kahn, 1997). Thus, not all of the improvement is due to explicit antidiscriminatory policies in the labor market. Equal opportunity policies and changing attitudes in other spheres, especially in schools, also contributed to less differentiation in the labor market. Other regulatory policies that were not explicitly framed to counter discrimination did so implicitly: a recent example is the introduction of national minimum pay in Britain (Robinson, 2003). However, labor market discrimination remains in all countries. The most important factor underlying the gap between men's and women's pay is the segregation of the sexes among occupations, industries, and workplaces (Grimshaw and Rubery, 2001).

## Conclusion: Alright for Some

Across the world there is a large variation in the extent to which wages are rising and so lifting the quality of jobs—from the stagnation and decline witnessed widely in many Latin American countries (Weeks, 1999) and across Sub-Saharan Africa to the transformations experienced in the newly industrialized economies of East Asia, such as Taiwan, Singapore, Malaysia, and the Republic of Korea. In the large majority of industrialized nations that have been examined in this chapter, however, the story of wages in the modern era is largely a positive one: in real terms hourly wage rates have been increasing, reflecting and embodying the rising affluence of nations. It is a good-news story that is often taken for granted and rarely iterated. Reconstructing it serves to illustrate again the apparent paradox of rising affluence coexisting with declining job quality in other significant dimensions.

Yet the story also contains a major exception, namely the United States. During the "golden years" of capitalism after the Second World War, workers shared in the economic prosperity of the whole economy. Wages grew by around 3 percent per annum during the 1950s, and still by 2½ percent during the 1960s (Schmidt, 2001). But thereafter things changed.

For the two decades through to the late 1990s wages on average made no further substantive gains; the poorer sectors of the labor market experienced real wage falls. This stagnation occurred despite the fact that the economy continued to grow. Only in the boom years following 1995 did the quality of jobs, as measured by their wages, start again to improve for the poorer half of the American labor force. This poorer half comprised some 68 million workers at the millennium, or roughly one in seven of all the workers in the industrialized world. Though American workers began the recent thirty-year period much more affluent on average than their counterparts elsewhere, by the millennium many in the lower segments were earning less than similar workers in several European nations.

Low pay has, in fact, become an increasingly important aspect of American poverty. Nearly a quarter of American workers earned less than $8.70 an hour in 2001, which for a full-time worker translates roughly to income at the low official American poverty line for a family of four (Appelbaum et al., 2003). Low-paid American workers cannot achieve a reasonable living standard on their own. To get by, they rely on pooled family resources. Dependence on the volatile family unit is, then, an integral aspect of the fragility that pervades many people's working lives. The declining pay of millions of jobs has rightly highlighted the question of economic survival: how do the poor make ends meet? The answer, for one group of low-paid workers, is to take two or more jobs—to survive by working inordinately long hours, extending the misery of low-quality work life for the entirely instrumental purpose of survival. Generally, responses are complex and not well understood; they depend greatly on the family and local social environment. One way of examining survival strategies, inspired by Orwell's *Down and Out in Paris and London*, has been for investigators to live as low-wage workers and record their ordeals. Examples include Ehrenreich (2002) for the United States and Toynbee (2003) for Britain. This approach brings to life the experience of low-wage poverty, including the hard work and drudgery, though it is not designed to deliver a systematic understanding of attitudes and behavior. For an example of a formal study in a small town setting, see Nelson and Smith (1999).

The broadly positive perspective on the quality of work life, as measured by wage rates in the modern industrialized world, therefore needs to be tempered with the American experience, which may yet be a harbinger for lagging economies elsewhere in the industrialized world. The stagnating average wage, accompanied by the widening distribution of pay, was manifested in falling wages for the lower half of the American workforce. In many other countries, although wages have risen, the fruits of economic growth have been distributed increasingly unequally among employees, particularly in the liberal market economies. And there is a further modern twist to the tale that applies with varying force in many countries: the potential undoing of the link between high-quality jobs and the "deferred wage" in retirement. With some pension systems said to be in a critical state, a successful reform, one that does not place an increasing burden on future workers, is required to sustain the advances made in this aspect of job quality.

Finally, there is the security of the wage to be considered. The receipt of a high wage in one year is important, but job quality is also determined by the risks entailed in the work, whether it brings a chance of accident or illness with accompanying wage loss, and whether in any case it is overshadowed by the prospect of redundancy and unemployment. The uncertainty surrounding work is the theme of the next chapter.

# *Seven*

## Workers' Risk

### Is This an Age of Uncertainty in the Workplace?

Those writers who dress the present and future world of work in the cloak of despair, or even just of pessimism and protest, are apt to underestimate the awfulness of the past. Such is the case with popular perceptions about the risks surrounding modern work life.

There is no doubting the baleful effects of uncertainty. Confidence in the continuity of and progress of employment is a core element in the quality of work life. For most workers, a job is neither a daily tradable commodity, nor a comprehensive detailed labor contract, but a peculiar exchange relationship of variable and uncertain duration and loosely defined content. The fear of redundancy or of occupational injury, uncertainty over how and where the employer will choose to deploy the workers' labor, or over whether existing wages will be maintained, can all reduce employees' welfare.[1]

Yet can it be maintained, as some have argued, that the quality of work life has been systematically undermined in the modern capitalist era by rising uncertainty (e.g., Elliott and Atkinson, 1998)? From 1990, the issue of job security and insecurity was increasingly the subject of media interest and political debate (see figure 7.1). In the mid-1990s, the phrase "job security" or "job insecurity" occurred on average one and a half times a day in the U.K. national press. Is this explosion of concern with insecurity a reflection of a real change in the way that the capitalist system is operating? On the face of it, this concern is surprising in both its extent and timing, considering that insecurity is an endemic feature of economic life in a capitalist economy, and that the recent era of mass unemployment began more than a decade earlier. In the late 1960s, industrialized countries tended to have unemployment rates of approximately 3 percent, with a few exceptions, like Germany, where rates were even lower. Unemployment edged up in the 1970s, then erupted in the early 1980s to peaks of 9.7 percent (United States), 11.9 percent (United Kingdom), and 12.2 percent (the Netherlands); then after some prolonged periods at high levels, unemployment in these countries came down in the 1990s, returning by 2001 to 4.8 percent (both the United States and the United Kingdom), and 2.7 percent (the Netherlands).[2] So why were the British and

**Number of References**

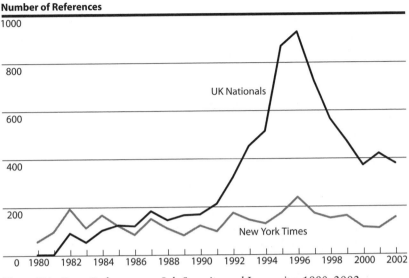

Figure 7.1. Press References to Job Security and Insecurity, 1980–2002.
*Source*: http://80-web.lexis.com.chain.ukc.ac.uk/professional/

American press not more vocal on workers' fears for their jobs during the 1980s when real insecurity was worse than in the 1990s? What, if anything, was different about the 1990s? On the face of it, insecurity would appear to have become more problematic in Germany where the unemployment rate rose to 9.9 percent in 1997 but less serious in Britain and the United States.

The links between uncertainty and the quality of work life have also been the focus of considerable independent research in recent years, especially from psychologists investigating the consequences for employees, and from socioeconomists examining the changing labor market. The research stems from the view that product and labor markets are each undergoing a sea change in the modern era, driven by a combination of pervasive developments in the economic and institutional structures of modern capitalism: the progressive globalization and intensification of competition, the arrival and ubiquitous diffusion of radical information and communication technologies, and a deep transformation and subversion of the ideologies of the postwar Keynesian state. The transformation encompasses *inter alia* the fiscal squeeze and the commercialization of public sectors, the political acceptance of mass unemployment in the 1980s, a widespread decline of trade union influence coupled with some retrenchment in employment protection regulations and reforms to benefit systems. These widespread developments have affected different countries and the various types of capitalism in different ways (Hall and Soskice, 2001). In the United States new uncertainties in the workplace are attributed to competition from foreign models of capitalism, to the government's relaxation of employment protection, to increasingly volatile product markets that demand in turn a numerically flexible labor market, and to a tranche of new management ideologies (Cappelli et al., 1997). These changes are thought to have severely undermined the internal labor markets upon which part of the postwar U.S. economy was constructed (Osterman, 1999). Similar pressures are recounted in the case of Britain (Gallie et al., 1998), but in addition labor market change is attributed to the commercialization of the public sector (driven by fiscal constraints), the growth in stock market influence on managers' choices, reforms to the benefit system, and the decline of trade unions from their previous position of considerable influence (Ladipo and Wilkinson, 2002; Heery and Salmon, 2000). In Germany after unification, institutional reforms have been less widespread, but unemployment rates have soared. Though they have not converged on a liberal model of firm-level wage bargaining, other coordinated market economies have adapted their institutions of wage bargaining and have accommodated demands for flexibility in various ways (Thelen, 2001).

One prominent argument among economists about the source of labor market change attributes it directly to the arrival of new technologies. Another emphasizes exposure to increased competition. A subset of the latter hypothesis is that the culprit is competition from low-wage economies. In this view, insecurity would derive from fear of commercial failure owing to intensified competition from cheap imports, or from fear of plant relocation to a low-cost area. In every case, the implication would be that lower-skilled workers are more likely to be subject to increased insecurity. There is a parallel here to debate about the reasons for decline in the relative economic fortunes of lower-skilled workers in industrialized countries. According to one side of the debate, the opening up of world manufacturing trade to low-wage economies triggered a substantive decline in the demand for low-skilled workers, as economies moved from autarky to open trade (Wood, 1995). According to the other side of the argument, the primary shock derives from the accelerated introduction of new technologies that are skill-biased—ICT and biotechnology are the usual named causes. A consequence of both perspectives is that job security is thought to be less attainable in the industrialized world than in the 1950s, 1960s, and early 1970s, when most economies experienced a "golden age" of stable growth, with high employment rates and low inflation. It is held, moreover, that the process is ongoing—that even by the 1990s and beyond job insecurity was continuing to figure ever more strongly as a feature of modern capitalism. For some commentators upon the times in the mid-1990s, the decline in security came to epitomize the weakening of social democracy and the ascendance of liberal capitalism (Elliott and Atkinson, 1998).

In the economic perspective the detrimental impact of uncertainty on the quality of jobs is plain to see, since the pecuniary aspect of the risk lies primarily on the downside.[3] Studies in psychology are consistent with the economics. Uncertainty and ambiguity (a lack of "situational clarity") are found to be theoretically related to stress. Part of the reason for this link is the idea that well-being is related to the workers' ability to foresee, control, and especially to cope with bad events. An immensely important and robust contribution from psychology has been to confirm this relationship empirically. Job insecurity is a substantive source of ill health and job dissatisfaction, has long-lasting impacts on individuals, and extends beyond insecure individuals to their households.[4] In some studies, the effects of insecurity on well-being are found to be at least as great as the impact of becoming unemployed. Nelson and Smith (1999) put a sociological spin on the same process, in examining the coping difficulties of the many households in rural Vermont where family members found themselves, in the mid-1990s, in distinctly unstable jobs.

In order to make the case that the quality of work life has been declining in the modern era because of the effect of insecurity, it would need to be established that there has been a genuine secular increase in job insecurity. And, while it could be legitimate to see the era of high unemployment that overcame many countries in the 1980s and 1990s as part of a long period or stage of capitalism, following the "golden age" of stability of full employment for postwar capitalism, the espoused argument about insecurity goes further than this. It has been held that insecurity is increasingly a feature of work in the modern era, above and beyond unemployment itself. But is it?[5]

To investigate whether the risks workers face are especially threatening in this modern era of capitalism, this chapter addresses the following questions:

- What valid and reliable ways exist for measuring the core elements of job insecurity in a consistent way over time?
- Has there been a secular rise in workers' risks in recent decades?
- Has the distribution of job insecurity changed, and do the distribution and its changes reflect posited technological changes and/or global competition?
- Finally, there is a subsidiary question, relevant as much to the sociology of knowledge as to the understanding of insecurity: do changes in job security or its distribution match the popular interest in this topic?

## The Concept and Measurement of Job Insecurity

Job insecurity is the loss of welfare that comes from uncertainty at work. A sense of job insecurity may derive either from economic aspects of a job or from the content of the work itself. The former, which is more amenable to measurement, is likely to have considerable consequences for life beyond the workplace. Job insecurity derives from uncertainty over the present value[6] of a worker's income stream, which depends on both the current known wage rate and uncertain future income from work or other sources. Because the income stream is uncertain, each worker will form an opinion about the probability of various outcomes. One possible outcome would be the norm as perceived by the worker, on the assumption that employment continues and regular normal wage increases materialize. However, the worker may fear that this norm will not be realized. A loss, that is, a downward deviation from the norm, can occur. The possible outcomes have a subjective distribution in the mind of the worker, which could be characterized by the mean and the variance of the possible loss. Job insecurity is the reduction in well-being that comes from the uncertain loss. It increases with the mean loss, for the straightforward reason that a loss, if realized, causes a reduction in living standards. Job insecurity also increases with the variance of the loss, on the assumption that workers are averse to risk. Thus, a job is more insecure, either if something changes to make the expected loss of income greater, or if something happens to make future income more uncertain.[7]

This fairly general formulation implies that there can be a number of constituents of job insecurity, each of which contribute to poor job quality. Consider first the mean loss. One can divide this into two parts: the economic loss that could occur if the job is ended (through redundancy or occupational hazard), and the loss that could occur if the job continues (through wage cuts, failure to secure expected promotions, and so on). Each of these parts depends on the probability of the event and the severity of its consequences.[8] Most attention has been lavished on the components of the first part: that is, on the risk and the cost of job loss. This emphasis makes sense. The risks and costs of job loss will usually far exceed those associated with wage reductions in the same job. Many commentators on job insecurity consider the risk of job loss to be the most important element in practice, even taken to be synonymous with the concept of job insecurity. Yet it should be remembered that the other elements of the mean loss, and the uncertainty of the loss, contribute also to the worker's loss of welfare, even if these other elements cannot be easily measured and their trends ascertained.

Since the uncertainty surrounding job loss concerns beliefs about the probability of a future event, the conceptually ideal measure is forward looking. Arguably the measure should also be subjective. How workers perceive the security of their own jobs is important for two main reasons: for the privileged information this gives about the objective risks they face and for the predictive value of the perceptions about subsequent behavior or of affective well-being. In practice, objective measures of the *ex ante* risk of job loss would be hard to recover from observations on behavior and hard to collect directly in a survey context. Direct subjective measures of expectations are, therefore, not only valid, but also the only practical measures of *ex ante* risk.

An alternative way to measure the uncertainty is to compute *ex post* the frequency of events and to assume that protagonists compute the probability of experiencing an event using available information. By tracking event frequency one can impute the changing risks they face, on the assumption that *ex ante* the events were equally likely to be experienced by each member of the relevant population. Economists have normally preferred this latter measurement strategy, owing to skepticism about the reliability of subjective data.[9] *Ex post* measures are more easily collected as objective data—that is, data which do not rely on the accuracy of reports of survey respondents' expectations or attitudes, drawing instead on their reports of behavioral events, or else on administrative records. Yet, particularly in the area of job insecurity, measures of event frequency may not always be valid indicators of insecurity. For example, the members of an observed group need not all have an equal chance of job loss.

There is thus a balance of advantages between the closer conceptual validity of subjective measures and the potentially superior reliability of objective indicators. The ideal outcome of the research strategy will be a picture of change that is consistent across measurement approaches. The next two sections use each method, in turn, to address the questions of the trend and distribution of job risk.

## Workers' Perceptions of the Trend and Distribution of Job Risk

### Changes in the Average Risk of Job Loss

To capture how workers perceive the risk of job loss, survey respondents in Britain were first asked: "Do you think there is any chance at all of your losing your job and becoming unemployed in the next twelve months? Those responding yes were then asked: "From this card, how would you rate the likelihood of this happening?" where the card showed a five-point probability scale. The responses are combined into a single variable, the Job Insecurity Scale, ranging from 0 ("no chance") to 5

**TABLE 7.1.**
Job Loss by Prior Fear of Job Loss (Percent Having an Unemployment Spell)

| Perceived Likelihood of Job Loss and Unemployment | All Employed | Employed Men | Employed Women |
|---|---|---|---|
| No chance, very or quite unlikely | 4.9 | 4.9 | 5.0 |
| Evens | 13.4 | 12.2 | 15.7 |
| Quite likely | 19.8 | 16.7 | 22.9 |
| Very likely | 38.1 | 38.6 | 37.5 |

Source: 2001 Skills Survey and postal follow-up.

("very likely"). In the United States, respondents were asked one direct question: "Thinking about the next twelve months, how likely do you think it is that you will lose your job or be laid off—very likely, fairly likely, not too likely, or not at all likely?" In Germany, respondents were asked: "How probable is it in the next two years that you will lose your job?" and could answer on the scale: definitely, probable, probably not, unlikely.[10]

While the validity of these instruments for capturing the risk of job loss is not in question, their reliability might be doubted. The responses could be biased and/or randomized through the psychological state of respondents or their relationship to interviewers, which might generate, for example, a social esteem effect.[11] Accordingly, reliability checks are desirable.

Two sets of findings support the view that responses to these instruments contain reliable information. First, respondents' perceived risks of job loss and unemployment are related, as expected, to objective factors that should inform those perceptions. The fear of unemployment is found to be negatively correlated with industry employment growth, and/or with the local labor market environment, with a worker's previous unemployment experience, and with having a temporary job contract (see Green et al., 2000, and the evidence shown later in table 7.3).

Second, fears of unemployment are correlated, as expected, with subsequent experience. In the case of the 2001 Skills Survey, respondents were re-contacted between twelve and fifteen months after their interview, and asked whether they had experienced a spell of unemployment in that period. Table 7.1 gives the findings. It is unequivocal that the greater the perceived risk, the greater the proportion that became unemployed. Among those perceiving that there was no chance of unemployment or that it was unlikely, just 5 percent subsequently experienced unemployment; by contrast, among those who feared that job loss and unemployment were very likely, the subsequent experience confirmed this

TABLE 7.2.
Job Insecurity Scale in Britain, by Sex, 1986, 1997, and 2001

| Likelihood of Job Loss | All Employed* | | | Employed Men | | | Employed Women | | |
|---|---|---|---|---|---|---|---|---|---|
| | 1986 | 1997 | 2001 | 1986 | 1997 | 2001 | 1986 | 1997 | 2001 |
| No chance | 80.0 | 77.1 | 83.4 | 77.1 | 73.7 | 79.9 | 84.0 | 81.4 | 87.8 |
| Very unlikely | 1.3 | 1.3 | 1.0 | 2.0 | 1.9 | 1.4 | 0.3 | 0.6 | 0.5 |
| Quite unlikely | 3.5 | 5.2 | 3.7 | 4.9 | 6.8 | 5.1 | 1.7 | 3.3 | 1.9 |
| Evens | 6.6 | 9.2 | 5.9 | 7.3 | 10.9 | 7.2 | 5.7 | 7.2 | 4.4 |
| Quite likely | 4.0 | 3.5 | 3.1 | 3.9 | 2.8 | 3.3 | 4.0 | 4.2 | 2.9 |
| Very likely | 4.6 | 3.6 | 2.9 | 4.8 | 3.9 | 3.1 | 4.3 | 3.3 | 2.6 |
| National unemploy-ment rate** | 11.3 | 7.2 | 4.9 | 11.7 | 8.2 | 5.4 | 10.7 | 5.9 | 4.4 |

Source: SCELI and the 1997 and 2001 Skills Surveys; www.statistics.gov.uk/statbase.
* Base is all those in work, aged 20–60; ** Labor Force Survey definition.

fear for 38 percent of respondents. Men and women appear to be equally adept at predicting their chances of job loss. Campbell et al. (2001) report similar findings using the British Household Panel Study (BHPS), based on a similar instrument for perceived risk of job loss. Moreover, the perceived risk of job loss turns out to be a good predictor of future unemployment even after controlling for all objective observable factors. It can reasonably be concluded that, in stating their perceptions of job loss risk, respondents are making use of private information not otherwise revealed to researchers.

Table 7.2 and figure 7.2 show responses on the Job Insecurity Scale at three time points. Over the whole period 1986 to 2001 there was a decline in the perceived risk of job loss in Britain. If the top three response points ("evens" or greater) are designated as "high job insecurity," it can be seen that the proportion of all workers in Britain experiencing high job insecurity fell from 15.2 percent to 11.9 percent. This statistically significant fall matches in direction the decline in aggregate unemployment from 11 percent to 5 percent, and is therefore expected. Moreover, in each year, women's perceived risk of job loss is less than that of men, also consistent with their relative unemployment rates.

The picture in the intervening year, 1997, is notable. Despite the fact that aggregate unemployment in Britain had by then fallen to 7 percent, there was no statistically significant difference between the proportions reporting high job insecurity in 1986 and 1997. In previous work it has therefore been hypothesized that between 1986 and 1997 there was a shift in the relationship between the perceived risk of job loss and the unemployment rate (Green et al., 2000). The subsequent decline in perceived

**Percent**

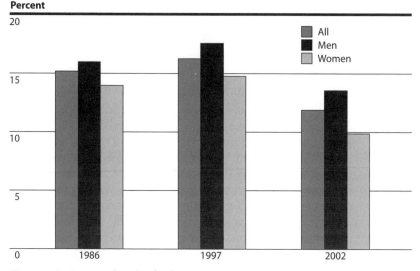

Figure 7.2. Perceived Risk of Job Loss, Britain, 1986, 1997, and 2001
*Source*: SCELI and the 1997 and 2001 Skills Surveys.
Note: Proportion of workers reporting at least an even chance of job loss and unemployment within one year.

insecurity by 2001 casts some doubt on the strength of that conclusion.[12] The relatively high insecurity recorded in 1997 is linked in part to the changing distribution of insecurity (on which, see below), which in turn may have been linked to the shakeout of particular sectors of the economy in the early 1990s (especially finance).

The picture of perceived risk of job loss in the United States, shown in figure 7.3, is somewhat similar but covers a longer period. Those workers responding that they were fairly or very likely to lose their job were categorized as experiencing high job insecurity. The mean proportion of workers reporting high job insecurity was 8 percent in 1978. The subsequent rise and fall of perceived insecurity is approximately synchronized with the cycle of the unemployment rate (the lower line in the diagram). As with Britain, during the mid-1990s the perceived risk of job loss in the United States was relatively high, compared with the aggregate unemployment rate (Schmidt, 1999). One reason for the heightened insecurity may have been the introduction of new high-performance work practices which, according to survey evidence, were being diffused rapidly throughout industry in the early 1990s, and which were the source of increased layoffs among both managerial and nonmanagerial staff (Osterman, 2000). The subsequent fall in job loss fears up until the end of the decade suggests at first that the elevation of insecurity may have

**Percent**

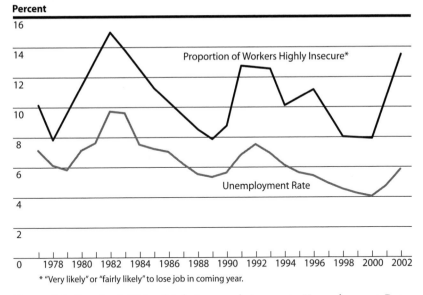

Figure 7.3. Perceived Risk of Job Loss and Aggregate Unemployment Rate, United States, 1977–2002

*Source*: General Social Survey; Bureau of Labor Statistics (www.bls.gov.data).

\* "Very likely" or "fairly likely" to lose job in coming year.

been a temporary phenomenon, rather than a secular change. In 2000, perceived insecurity was back to the low level previously seen in 1989 (when the national unemployment rate among job losers was less than half a percentage point higher). Nevertheless, the effects of the post-"dotcom" collapse of confidence are again reflected in a substantive rise of insecurity in 2002. Taking the 1977–2002 period as a whole, there is a modest downward trend in the aggregate unemployment rate, but no obvious secular trend in the proportions feeling highly insecure.[13]

In Germany, as in the United States and the United Kingdom, fears of job loss have also tracked the unemployment rate for much of the last two decades, as shown in figure 7.4. By the late 1990s, approximately one in ten Germans thought that it was probable or certain that they would lose their job within two years. Thus, despite the very different macroeconomic and institutional circumstances of the British, American, and German labor markets, there are no great differences between them in the proportions of workers who perceive their jobs to be very insecure. One exceptional episode of insecurity in Germany stands out, however. Unsurprisingly, fears of unemployment soared in East Germany following its reunification with the rest of the country. Meanwhile, perceived insecurity in the rest of

**Percent**

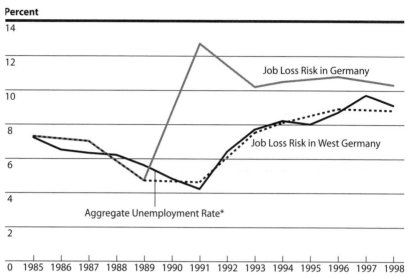

* Standardised ILO unemployment rate; prior to 1993 data refer to West Germany.

Figure 7.4. Perceived Risk of Job Loss and Aggregate Unemployment Rate, Germany, 1985–1998

 *Source*: German Socio-Economic Panel (GSOEP); OECD (2002).

 *Notes*:

 Proportion of workers for whom job loss within 2 years is certain or probable.

 * Standardized ILO unemployment rate; prior to 1993 data refer to West Germany.

the newly unified country remained at normal levels. But, as the general unemployment rate crept steadily upward after 1991, so the insecurity of job-holders in Western Germany rose. Perceptions of insecurity in East Germany had by 1998 converged much closer to that of the rest of the country.

## Changes in the Distribution of Risk of Job Loss

The rises and falls in the perceived risk of job loss have been unevenly experienced among the populations of both Britain and the United States. Blue-collar workers have traditionally experienced the highest levels of insecurity, but during the 1990s certain white-collar groups became more insecure, some possibly for the first time. Professional workers in Britain, in particular, were the most secure group in 1986, the least secure in 1997 (see table 7.3). In the United States, white-collar occupations as a whole reported greater insecurity in the 1990s than in the 1980s, while blue-collar workers recorded a decline, leading therefore to a convergence in the experience of insecurity (Schmidt, 1999).

**TABLE 7.3.**

Indices of Job Insecurity and Difficulty of Re-Employment by Sex, Job Contract, Sector, Industry, and Occupation, 1986–2001

| | Job Insecurity Index | | | Difficulty of Re-Employment Index | | | |
|---|---|---|---|---|---|---|---|
| | 1986 | 1997 | 2001 | 1986 | 1992 | 1997 | 2001 |
| All | 0.67 | 0.71 | 0.53 | 3.14 | 3.11 | 2.90 | 2.70 |
| Men | 0.74 | 0.79 | 0.62 | 3.18 | 3.15 | 3.00 | 2.74 |
| Women | 0.58 | 0.62 | 0.42 | 3.08 | 3.06 | 2.78 | 2.66 |
| Women and Full-Time | 0.57 | 0.57 | 0.46 | 3.11 | — | 2.79 | 2.65 |
| Women and Part-Time | 0.60 | 0.70 | 0.37 | 3.04 | — | 2.77 | 2.67 |
| *Job Contract* | | | | | | | |
| Permanent | — | 0.59 | 0.48 | — | — | 2.92 | 2.72 |
| Temporary | — | 2.27 | 1.63 | — | — | 2.80 | 2.42 |
| *Ownership* | | | | | | | |
| Public | 0.64 | 0.71 | 0.38 | 3.23 | 3.12 | 3.04 | 2.73 |
| Private | 0.68 | 0.72 | 0.59 | 3.09 | 3.10 | 2.86 | 2.69 |
| *Of which:* All UK | — | 0.72 | 0.55 | — | — | 2.81 | 2.66 |
| Part/all non-UK | — | 0.69 | 0.83 | — | — | 3.00 | 2.77 |
| Competing with low-wage economy | — | — | 1.04 | — | — | — | 2.97 |
| *Industry* | | | | | | | |
| Manufacturing | 0.84 | 0.65 | 0.84 | 3.22 | 3.22 | 3.09 | 2.92 |
| Construction | 0.95 | 1.34 | 0.49 | 2.96 | 3.16 | 2.84 | 2.48 |
| Wholesale | 0.53 | 0.53 | 0.38 | 3.07 | 3.17 | 2.77 | 2.71 |
| Hotels | 0.49 | 0.71 | 0.24 | 2.78 | 2.73 | 2.70 | 2.41 |
| Transport | 0.80 | 0.77 | 0.69 | 3.32 | 3.28 | 3.08 | 2.80 |
| Finance | 0.19 | 0.84 | 0.47 | 3.22 | 3.07 | 2.95 | 2.61 |
| Real Estate and Business Services | 0.62 | 0.78 | 0.54 | 2.95 | 3.00 | 2.61 | 2.53 |
| Public Administration | 0.58 | 0.56 | 0.48 | 3.33 | 3.19 | 3.24 | 2.92 |
| Education | 0.47 | 0.67 | 0.43 | 3.18 | 3.08 | 2.98 | 2.65 |
| Health | 0.52 | 0.62 | 0.30 | 3.05 | 2.88 | 2.60 | 2.58 |
| Other Community | 0.54 | 0.83 | 0.64 | 3.07 | 3.03 | 2.88 | 2.70 |
| *Occupation* | | | | | | | |
| Managers and Administrators | 0.51 | 0.64 | 0.57 | 3.12 | 3.08 | 2.93 | 2.74 |
| Professionals | 0.49 | 0.93 | 0.47 | 3.11 | 2.90 | 2.88 | 2.57 |
| Associate Professionals | 0.60 | 0.57 | 0.50 | 3.09 | 2.54 | 2.88 | 2.75 |
| Administrative and Secretarial | 0.57 | 0.72 | 0.42 | 3.19 | 3.20 | 2.96 | 2.74 |
| Skilled Trades | 0.90 | 0.87 | 0.55 | 3.14 | 3.15 | 3.01 | 2.66 |
| Personal Service | 0.58 | 0.43 | 0.48 | 3.10 | 2.99 | 2.57 | 2.57 |
| Sales | 0.56 | 0.46 | 0.46 | 2.94 | 3.21 | 2.84 | 2.61 |
| Plant and Machine Operatives | 1.00 | 0.77 | 0.86 | 3.37 | 3.34 | 3.08 | 2.88 |
| Elementary | 0.71 | 0.82 | 0.50 | 3.06 | 3.21 | 2.79 | 2.74 |

*Source*: SCELI, EIB, and the 1997 and 2001 Skills Surveys.

Base is all those in work, aged 20–60.

The Job Insecurity Index in each group is the average value of the Job Insecurity Scale, where the chance of job loss ranges from 0 ("no chance") to 5 ("very likely"). The Difficulty of Re-Employment Index in each group is the average value of the Difficulty of Re-Employment scale, where the ease of re-employment ranges from 1 ("very easy") to 4 ("very difficult").

The similarity of this picture of change and convergence in Britain and the United States is striking, and this distributional change may account in part for the increased press interest in job insecurity (figure 7.1).[14] When some professional workers became insecure this was news, unlike the fate of blue-collar workers. Perhaps also the reportage of anecdotal evidence is dominated by the experiences of the middle and upper classes. In Britain there remain close links between the City of London and the world of journalism, which tends to highlight the world of finance. That industry endured a considerable shakeout in the early 1990s, a fact that is reflected in residual high insecurity among financial workers in 1997 (see table 7.3). Note, however, that both the professional occupations and the finance industry returned to much lower levels of insecurity by 2001, as did press interest in the topic. Meanwhile, manufacturing workers who, in the mid-1980s, were very insecure and had become significantly less so by 1997, returned to greater levels of insecurity again in 2001, against the average trend for the rest of the economy.

The most recent changes in how insecurity is distributed among the workforce has reflected exposure to competition and ownership of the organization. While public-sector workers felt considerably more secure in 2001 than in 1997, private-sector workers only enjoyed greater security if their workplaces were entirely British-owned. Those that were working in partly or fully foreign-owned establishments became significantly less secure in recent years. In addition, working in an establishment in 2001 that competed with low-wage economies was associated with much greater insecurity.[15] Taken together, these findings are consistent with the view that global competition may be becoming a significant source of insecurity.

Finally, and unsurprisingly, insecurity is much higher for temporary workers and for men, and the pattern of change is similar according to contract status and sex. However, it is notable that women working part time now report feeling more secure than any other group.[16, 17]

### Changes in the Cost of Job Loss

As noted in the previous section, another component of job insecurity is the cost incurred by workers in the event that job loss takes place. The perception of the cost of job loss is partially and imperfectly captured in the British surveys by the following instrument: "If you were looking for work today, how easy or difficult do you think it would be for you to find as good a job as your current one?" with a four-point scale, ranging from "very easy" to "very difficult." The responses on this scale can be averaged to form the Difficulty of Re-employment Index for each group (see notes to table 7.3). In the United States, the General Social Survey uses a similar instrument: "About how easy would it be for you to find a

**Percent**

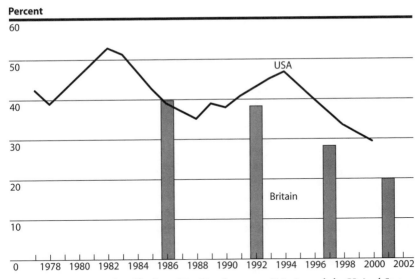

Figure 7.5. Perceived Difficulty of Re-Employment, Britain and the United States
*Source*: SCELI, EIB, 1997 and 2001 Skills Surveys, General Social Survey.
*Notes*: Proportion of workers who would find it "very difficult" (Britain) or "not easy"
(United States) to get an equally good job.
Base is employed people, aged 20–60 (Britain), 18 or over (United States).

job with another employer with approximately the same income and fringe
benefits you now have? Would you say very easy, somewhat easy, or not
easy at all?" Neither instrument picks up all the elements of the cost of job
loss, which include the loss of pay (net of benefits) while unemployed, the
duration of unemployment, and the potentially lower wage in a new post-
displacement job. The latter two elements might be thought of as contributing to the difficulty of reemployment in an equivalent job, which the
instruments try to capture. But the first element, the financial loss while
unemployed, is not addressed in the question. In addition to this issue of
validity, there are no direct ways to check the reliability of the instruments
in measuring difficulty of re-employment. One can only fall back on an
indirect check on the reliability of the responses, which is that they are
correlated as expected with indicators of the labor market environment.
For example, 70 percent of workers in unionized establishments register
that equivalent reemployment would be quite or very difficult, compared
with just 59 percent in non-union jobs. The perceived difficulty of re-
employment is also greater for individuals with a history of unemployment and for those working in declining industries.

Figure 7.5 and table 7.3 show how the perceived difficulty of re-
employment has been changing. Over the longer period of observation

available in the United States, the perceived difficulty of re-employment has broadly risen and fallen with the unemployment cycle. There is a small downward trend taking the 1977–2000 period as a whole. In Britain the difficulty of re-employment remained unchanged from 1986 to 1997 but, as in the United States, decreased substantially in the late 1990s. This pattern of stability, then decline was largely followed by all socioeconomic groups.

Those trends present one unequivocal conclusion for both countries: there is no detectable trend for perceptions of the difficulty of reemployment in an equally good job—a major component of the perceived cost of job loss—to rise over recent years, either absolutely or relative to unemployment.

### Alternative Subjective Instruments for Insecurity

In the International Social Survey Programme (ISSP), respondents in 1989 and 1997 were asked whether they agreed with the statement, "My job is secure," using a five-point scale. This type of question does not specifically link insecurity either to the risk of job loss or to the cost of job loss. Arguably, it may lead respondents to consider the wider implications of insecurity, such as the stability of their employment conditions (Burchell et al., 1999). One might expect that the risk of job loss would be the main consideration in most respondents' minds. The validity of the instrument for measuring insecurity is thus not ideal, because it relies on the respondent's perception coinciding with that of the researcher. Unfortunately, there are also no separate opportunities for checking its reliability. The value of the instrument lies in its availability for a range of countries in representative surveys at two points in time.[18]

A convenient shorthand is to define workers as insecure, from the point of view of this instrument, if they "disagreed" or "strongly disagreed" with the statement that their job was secure. Using this classification, it may be seen that 20.1 percent of British workers viewed their job as being insecure in 1989, while in 1997 this proportion had increased to 28.2 percent (figure 7.6). In the United States, the proportion of insecure workers also increased significantly, from 10.9 percent in 1989 to 14.6 percent in 1997. This rise is consistent with the rise in the perceived risk of job loss over this period (figure 7.3). In both countries, this instrument confirms the view established earlier that insecurity was at a relatively high level in the mid-1990s.

Figure 7.6 also shows increasing insecurity between 1989 and 1997 in West Germany, the Netherlands, and Hungary. In Italy and in Israel the changes were small and insignificant. In Norway, workers were feeling more secure in 1997 than in 1989. In most cases these changes are

**Percent**

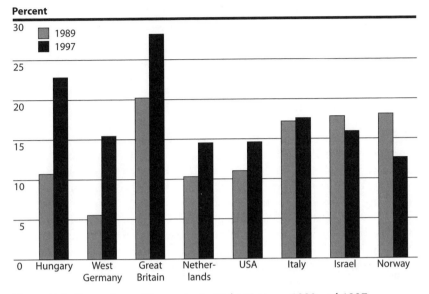

Figure 7.6. Perceptions of Insecurity in Eight Nations, 1989 and 1997
*Source*: International Social Survey Program.
*Note*: Chart shows proportion of workers who disagree or strongly disagree that their job is secure.

consistent with what one might expect. Workers in Hungary experienced a capitalist revolution during this interval, while those in West Germany went through the process of integration with East Germany and a rise in the aggregate unemployment rate from 5.6 percent to 9.9 percent. In Norway there was a small drop in the unemployment rate from 5 percent to 4.1 percent. The surprise is the Netherlands, where the increased insecurity came despite the fall in the unemployment rate from 6.9 percent to 5.2 percent. Thus, the Netherlands were similar in this respect to the United States and Britain, in having unusually high perceived insecurity in the mid-1990s.

For Britain, an intriguing picture of insecurity trends in an earlier period is derivable from a similar instrument, whereby survey respondents were asked to rate their job on a four-point scale, ranging from "very secure" to "very insecure." A trend can be extracted from the work histories recorded as part of the Social Change in Economic Life Initiative surveys in 1986. Allowing that there are potential problems of recall reliability in inferring trends from retrospective work histories, Burchell (2002) shows a picture of comparative stability in the 1960s and 1970s, with blue-collar workers traditionally bearing the brunt of economic insecurity. A very modest rise in this period makes way for a substantial hike in perceived insecurity after 1979. As in later years with the perceived risk of job loss, these changes in perceived insecurity also track the macroeconomic environment quite closely, for it was after 1979 that unemployment soared in Britain.

## Objective Proxies for Risk

The story so far is that two of the major elements of job insecurity as perceived by workers—the risk and cost of job loss—have moved in accordance with the macroeconomic and labor market environment in recent decades, but exhibit no clear long-term secular trend. Perceptions of insecurity in Britain rose from the 1970s to the 1980s. In the latter part of the 1990s, both elements declined in both the United States and Britain, as their economies grew and aggregate unemployment declined. Prior to that, the perceived risk of job loss in the mid-1990s was unusually high for professional workers and long-tenured workers in Britain and for white-collar workers in the United States.

Are these trends in the *ex ante* perceptions of insecurity consistent with movements in the *ex post* frequencies of job loss and wage loss?

### Risk of Job Loss

On both sides of the Atlantic the frequency with which employees entered into unemployment exhibits no secular upward trend over recent decades. In Britain, approximately 1.8 percent of male employees enter unemployment each month; the proportion naturally oscillates with the cycle and was falling from 1992 onward, but there has been virtually no secular trend since at least the late 1960s (Nickell et al., 2002).[19] From 1995 until 2002, there have been approximately eight redundancies per thousand employees every spring quarter.[20] In the United States, studies of job instability have proliferated and, unfortunately, present an inconsistent picture, in part associated with differences in data sets and definitions. Most recent studies, however, reveal at most small changes in the *ex post* frequency of job separations between the 1980s and 1990s (Gottschalk and Moffitt, 1999). Some studies show an increase in job separation rates from the 1970s to the 1980s—for example, Bernhardt et al. (1999), using data from the National Longitudinal Studies for young men. Some authors are able to distinguish voluntary from involuntary separations. Thus, Polsky (1999) finds a small increase in the rate of involuntary job separations between 1976–81 and 1986–91, especially for long-tenured workers. Valletta (1999) also finds that there was a significant increase between 1976 and 1991 in the frequency of job loss owing to permanent layoffs or being fired, especially for long-tenured workers. This increase, even after controlling for the macroeconomic environment, can be interpreted as evidence of a decline in the honoring of long-term employment contracts and an increase of insecurity for men. In contrast, there was no overall change in job security for women according to this indicator.

While the involuntary job separation rate is the most valid *ex post* indicator of job insecurity, other indicators of job stability have been investigated on the grounds that security is associated with stability. That these two concepts are not the same thing implies that findings on job stability are less informative in this respect. One approach is to measure the proportions of workers who are in very short tenure jobs. Since those with short tenure are typically more insecure, any rise in this proportion is said to indicate an overall rise in insecurity. Jaeger and Stevens (1999) find relatively little change in this indicator of stability between the 1980s and 1990s in the United States. Another approach focuses on broader indicators of the distribution of job tenures. One justification for such an approach is the oft-cited cliché that labor market changes were signaling the "end of jobs for life." Analysis has shown, however, that changes in job tenures through recent decades have been modest. While job tenure is declining for older workers and for less skilled men, a significant minority of men are still in jobs likely to last twenty years or more (Gregg and Wadsworth, 1995; Burgess and Rees, 1996, 1997). The average job tenure of men declined somewhat from the mid-1970s to the mid-1990s, but this was offset by a rise in the job tenure of women, especially those with dependent children (Gregg and Wadsworth, 1999). That rise could be interpreted as an effect of the introduction of regulations in Britain on maternity rights. However, a parallel pattern of change is also found in the United States. While the overall length of tenure of jobs remained broadly stable from 1973 onward, there was a switch away from long tenure among men's jobs, and toward longer-lasting jobs for women (Farber, 1995). This story of stability in job tenure is replicated for all industrialized countries throughout the 1990s (Auer and Cazes, 2000, 2003).

Job insecurity is also associated with type of job contract, leading researchers to identify insecurity by measures of the contract composition of the workforce. Temporary-contract jobs are inherently insecure, and table 7.3 confirms that temporary-contract workers do feel less secure than permanent-contract workers. Temporary-contract workers also experience substantially lower wages, poorer working conditions, and lower levels of job satisfaction (OECD, 2002). It is questionable, however, whether the proportion of a nation's workforce on temporary contracts is a good indicator of job insecurity in the whole nation. That proportion reflects a combination of legislation and regulation (in respect of both temporary and permanent contracts), employer strategies, and cyclical conditions.

Conceivably, more protection for "permanent" workers could stimulate a rise in the use of temporary workers; and countries with strong employment protection legislation (e.g., Spain) can have a high proportion of temporary workers, while others (e.g., the UK) have weak protection for all workers and comparatively few temporary workers. The impact of being temporary on insecurity is likely to vary across firms and space. Thus, only large secular changes in the proportion of temporary workers, plus the condition that this is not associated with more security for temporary or permanent workers, could be taken to validly indicate an increase in overall insecurity.

In fact, there were substantive increases between the 1980s and 1990s in the proportionate use of temporary workers in Australia, Finland, France, Italy, the Netherlands, and Spain; a decline in Greece; and only modest changes elsewhere in the industrialized world where measures are available on a consistent basis (Mangan, 2000; Booth et al., 2002; Auer and Cazes, 2000). By far the most spectacular case is that of Spain, where through the 1990s a third of workers were on temporary contracts, a historical reflection of the failure to reform restrictive employment protections in the post-Franco era, and the early introduction of permissive legislation for temporary contracts (Dolado et al., 2002). The change since the early 1980s constituted a genuine rise in the average level of insecurity, as well as a significant re-distribution of insecurity and a segmentation of the labor market. Also remarkable is the case of Australia, which saw a substantive increase through the 1990s in the use of casual employment, up to as much as 28 percent of the workforce by 1998. As with Spain, this increase in insecurity for substantial sections of the workforce was driven in Australia by deregulation of a strongly controlled labor market and made feasible through the pressure of mass unemployment (de Ruyter and Burgess, 2000; Burgess and Strachan, 2000). For most countries, however, temporary work contracts are still used sparingly.

*Accident Risk*

While job loss through redundancy is central to the notion of insecurity, also uncertain is whether a worker will lose income as well as good health through workplace accidents and diseases. Indeed, the casual disregard of employee safety has been the stuff of legend in certain industries. The chance of suffering accidents is thus another important aspect of the quality of work life.

In this respect, the quality of work life has generally been improving in the industrialized economies. The relative decline of heavy manufacturing industry, together with ever more effective legislation, have secured substantial reductions in the danger of suffering debilitating or fatal accidents at work in recent decades.

The trends for all types of industrial injury over the long term are not accurately known; however, in more recent history, consistent measures have been compiled for most industrialized nations. The indices of fatal accidents and of serious accidents (resulting in more than three days' absence from work) both fell significantly in the European Union and the United States, from the 1994–96 period to the 1997–2000 period.[21] Though there were changes in methodology, the fall was almost certainly a continuation of a longer-term trend. For example, in Britain the rate of serious injury fell from 761 per 100,000 in 1986–87 to 607 per 100,000 in 1995–96.[22] Fatal injuries are probably more accurately recorded. In Sweden, for example, the numbers dying each year from accidents at work declined from over four hundred in the mid-1950s to less than fifty at the millennium.[23] Although there are exceptions (Ireland's occupational injury rates deteriorated in the 1990s), improvements in this aspect of the risks workers face have generally continued into the modern era. Note, however, an important caveat to this conclusion: the above figures do not take into account health losses that are not associated with accidents.[24]

### Cost of Job Loss

Although it is well-established that workers suffer wage losses after unemployment (e.g., Jacobsen et al., 1993) there are few studies of the changing consequences of job loss using objective indicators. In the case of Britain, Nickell et al. (2002) find an increase in the cost of job loss, using two indicators. From 1982–86 until 1992–97, the permanent wage loss after a spell of unemployment rose from approximately 7.8 percent to 15.5 percent. Studies in the United States, by contrast, have failed to uncover any substantive trend in the consequences of job changing between the 1980s and 1990s (Farber, 1993; Gottschalk and Moffitt, 1999).

The cost of job loss is also affected by the expected duration of unemployment and the benefits a worker expects to receive over this period. An increase in unemployment duration occurred in many countries with the return of mass unemployment in the 1980s. Whatever the conditions and character of any subsequent job, the risk of a longer spell of unemployment, should one lose a job, raises job insecurity. It is not surprising that the perceptions of the difficulty of regaining employment tend to track the economic cycle. In addition, the cost of being unemployed changes if the replacement ratio (the ratio of out-of-work benefits to wages) changes. Consistent measures of this ratio are difficult to obtain, however, as the level of benefits depends on the period unemployed, and on the level of earnings. In Britain, the average replacement ratio fell somewhat during

the 1980s, thus compounding the rising wage losses experienced by unemployed men; but the general trend in most countries between the
1960s and the start of the 1990s was for either stable or increasing replacement ratios (OECD, 1994).

## Conclusion: Risk and the Quality of Work Life

In the uncertain realm of work life, the harshest consequences are reserved
for those unlucky enough to lose their job, whether through redundancy
or ill health. For those actually becoming unemployed, the negative impact on their well-being is normally stark and beyond serious doubt
(Clark and Oswald, 1994). This chapter has focused, not on the actual
experience of unemployment, but on the threat of unemployment for those
who are working. The distance of the state of working from the state of
being unemployed is part of the quality of the job. If there is a cyclical or
secular change in aggregate unemployment, this affects the quality of
work life for those still employed, because it alters their sense of security.
When the capitalist world entered a long period of instability following
the end of the postwar "golden age" of capitalism, and more especially
the era of persistent mass unemployment which arrived for many countries in the 1980s, the rising insecurity of all workers constituted a decline in the quality of work life.

Studies of the rise and decline of unemployment are, however, plenti-
ful. What has motivated this chapter is the proposition that, especially in
the past two decades, the structure of the labor market has become more
flexible and has thereby engendered an increase in insecurity that somehow transcends the movements in actual unemployment. This view has
been put most forcefully with respect to the American labor market, but
has also been applied with considerable vigor to labor markets in many
other industrialized nations. Insecurity has substantive detrimental effects on the quality of work life (Nolan et al., 2000); so if there has been
a secular rise in insecurity this could, just in itself, mean a substantial deterioration in the quality of work life in industrialized economies.

But earlier expositions and evaluations of this picture were erected on
a somewhat fragile evidence base. It has been possible to arrive at a
clearer verdict by combining new survey material and several recent
studies. The findings, using both *ex ante* and *ex post* measurement approaches, are summarized in table 7.4.

   1. For those countries about which most is known—the United States,
Britain, and Germany—the idea that the risk of job loss has risen relative to
unemployment is hard to substantiate. Depending on definitions, somewhere

between 5 percent and 15 percent of workers report high fears of job loss. Yet both objective and subjective measures agree that the chances of losing one's job have changed largely in synch with the unemployment cycle. In the United States and in Britain there is some evidence that, in the mid-1990s, insecurity was temporarily on the high side, but the return to low unemployment rates by the end of the 1990s was matched by low levels of insecurity. Fears of unemployment in the United States were understandably reignited after the collapse of the dotcom boom. In Germany's case, the temporary rise in unemployment fears in the early 1990s is attributable to the East German labor market's transition to capitalist processes.

2. For other countries, good measures of the fear of job loss are not available over time. Yet substantial rises in the deployment of temporary work contracts do suggest an increase in and redistribution of insecurity in Spain and Australia, and more modestly in Finland, France, Sweden, and Italy.

3. The risk of accident or injury at work, with attendant consequences for income and health, has generally been falling in the current era.

4. One element of the cost of job loss—the diminished wage in post-displacement jobs–may have risen for British males. No such change can be detected in the United States. Moreover, the subjective perceptions of the difficulty of regaining equivalent employment have not had a secular increase in either country, experiencing in particular a sharp decline in the late 1990s.

5. There has some been some redistribution of insecurity. It is by no means always the lower skilled workers who have experienced the worst increases in insecurity. In Britain, relatively skilled workers in the finance industry and professional workers generally became unusually insecure during the mid-1990s. The finance industry insecurity reflected a technology-induced shakeout in that industry. In the United States, white-collar workers had the greater increase in insecurity. These redistributive effects might suggest an explanation for the rising concern of the media in the idea of job insecurity in the mid-1990s, even though comparatively high levels of insecurity had been the experience of low-status occupations for a long time.

6. Global economic integration may be starting to have an effect on at least the distribution of insecurity. In Britain in 2001, insecurity was substantially higher for workers in companies with foreign ownership or facing competition from low-wage economies.

Taken together, these findings imply that it is not accurate to describe work in the modern industrialized world as especially insecure, beyond the fact that this has been an era of high unemployment which in some but not all countries has persisted throughout the recent decade. Despite impressive findings linking insecurity to loss of well-being in workers, one cannot scientifically sustain proclamations of a decline in the quality of work life on account of a *secular* upward shift in insecurity. To do so

**TABLE 7.4.**
Summary of Evidence on Trends in Job Insecurity

|  | *Validity* | *Study* | *Finding* |
|---|---|---|---|
| *Risk of Job Loss* | | | |
| Direct survey instruments for *ex ante* insecurity | ✓✓✓✓ | Schmidt (1999); Green et al. (2000); this chapter; Manski and Straub (2000). | Rises and falls with cycle; rose above trend in mid-1990s in both U.S. and U.K. |
| Unspecific survey instrument for *ex ante* job insecurity | ✓✓ | This chapter. | 1989–97 rises in Hungary, Germany, Britain, Netherlands, U.S.; fall in Norway. |
| Average frequency of exit to unemployment | ✓✓✓ | Nickell et al. (2002). | No secular change in U.K. since 1968. |
|  |  | Gottschalk and Moffitt (1999). | No increase in U.S. displacement rates, 1980s to 1990s. |
| Job separation rate: | | | |
|   Involuntary | ✓✓✓ | Polsky (1999). | Rise, U.S., 1976–81 to 1986–91. |
|   Overall | ✓✓ | Valletta (1999). | Rise, U.S., 1976–91, rate of permanent layoffs and dismissals. |
|   Overall | ✓✓ | Bernhardt et al. (1999). | Increased instability for young U.S. men, 1960s–70s to 1980s–90s. |
| Job tenure: | | | |
|   % with short tenure | ✓ | Jaeger and Stevens (1999). | No change in U.S. in 1980s and 1990s. |
|   Average tenure | ✓ | Burgess and Rees (1996); Gregg and Wadsworth (1999). | Britain, 1975–98: small fall for men, small rise for women. |
|   — | ✓ | Farber (1995). | U.S. job tenure stable since 1973. |
|   Retention rates | ✓ | Neumark et al. (1999). | No secular decline in U.S job stability. |
|   Range of stability indicators | ✓ | Auer and Cazes (2000, 2003). | Stability in job tenures in most industrialized countries. |
| Proportion of workers on temporary or casual employment contracts | ✓ | Mangan (2000); Booth et al. (2002); Auer and Cazes (2000). | Rises in Australia, Spain, Finland, France, Sweden, Netherlands, Italy; no big change in U.K., Germany, Denmark, Belgium; fall in Greece. |

TABLE 7.4. (*continued*)

| | Validity | Study | Finding |
|---|---|---|---|
| *Cost of Job Loss* | | | |
| Workers' perception of difficulty of regaining "as good employment" | ✓✓ | Schmidt (1999); Green et al. (2000); this chapter. | Fallen with unemployment in both U.S. and U.K. |
| Wage loss after unemployment | ✓✓✓ | Nickell et al. (2002). | Secular rise for British men from 1982–86 to 1992–97. |
| Wage loss after job change | ✓✓✓ | Farber (1993). | No change in U.S., 1982–83 to 1990–91. |
| | | Gottschalk and Moffitt (1999). | No change in U.S., 1980s and 1990s. |
| Probability of nonemployment after job exit | ✓✓✓ | Gottschalk and Moffitt (1999). | No change in U.S., 1980s and 1990s. |

✓ The number of ticks (up to 4) summarizes this author's judgment of how far the measure conforms to an element of the concept of job insecurity as defined in this chapter. This is neither a judgment about reliability nor a reflection on the studies which were aiming to measure something other than insecurity.

would be to hide from memory the experiences of millions of workers in earlier economic crises.

There have indeed been many changes affecting the quality of work life in the current era, including rising skill requirements, often more wages, and periods of substantive intensification of work. Working life continues to be insecure for significant minorities of the employed population, who bear the brunt of economic restructuring. However, to take job insecurity as the prime source of low job quality in the current period would be to attach an unwarranted badge of modernity to a problem that is endemic in capitalist economies.

# *Eight*

## Workers' Well-Being

### A Question of Well-Being

If recent decades of material affluence have been an age of progress in the achievement of higher living standards—as far as the industrialized world is concerned—one might expect there to have been also a step toward fulfillment and greater well-being in this central area of life. Does not economic growth bring along with it a better quality of working life?

It should be possible to answer this question with some confidence regarding the present era. The major ingredients of job quality—skill, effort, autonomy, pay, and security—are now all more open to measurement and scrutiny than in previous ages. Yet the problem in reaching a verdict is that, according to all the evidence examined in this book, these elements tell an ambiguous story. On average, jobs have been using higher levels of skills in the "knowledge economy," although in several countries there is also a growth of lower-skilled jobs in the service sectors. In most countries higher wages are being paid than were paid twenty years ago, and fewer accidents are scarring the workplace. Yet there have been widespread bouts of work intensification and, at least in Britain (though not in Finland), a decline in workers' task discretion. The endemic insecurity of jobs in capitalist economies remains. In the absence of a satisfactory means of weighing these contradictory trends, no single conclusion as to improvement or decline can be made.

A closely related question has, perhaps, a better chance of receiving a decisive answer: what has been happening to workers' "subjective well-being" associated with work? It is true that workers' emotional responses to work are affected not just by the quality of the job. Their personalities and psychological characteristics are greatly relevant. If one worker expresses a greater level of affective well-being than another, this could be owing to the former's sunnier and more optimistic outlook on life rather than anything inherent in the jobs they do. Yet the *change* over time in the work-related well-being of a given population gives a good clue as to the change in the quality of their jobs. The personalities of populations are unlikely to see much alteration, at least over the medium term. It is now possible to gauge the changes in subjective well-being of national working populations, through the lenses of series of representative social surveys. What does this picture reveal? What, if anything, can be deduced about the quality of jobs in modern developed nations?

## A Digression on the Notion of Subjective Well-Being

Before addressing these questions, it is instructive to dwell a little on what the idea of subjective well-being might mean in the world of economics. To a neoclassical economist, there can be only one logical notion of subjective well-being: it is called "utility." Economics is built upon the foundation of utility theory which it inherited from the utilitarian tradition in philosophy. The marginalist revolution in the late nineteenth century appended to this tradition the pivotal idea of marginal utility—the extra utility obtained from the consumption of one more unit of a commodity—and its association with optimizing behavior (sometimes referred to as "rational" behavior). To make this optimizing conception of human behavior a practical science with consistent predictive powers, the law of diminishing marginal utility was invoked, capturing the idea of consumers becoming increasingly satiated with products. Finally, in the early twentieth century it was discovered that it was not necessary to assume that utility was measurable against a known scale: all the necessary theorems about consumer behavior could be derived by assuming that individuals had a consistent ordinal ranking of preferences over what they consumed, which they revealed through their actions—what they bought or did. In the mainstream neoclassical economic tradition that has followed, and which still dominates all economics teaching across the industrialized world, individuals are at the center of the analysis, but their well-being is regarded as in principle unmeasurable. Such ironies are apt to go unnoticed in any "normal" mode of science.[1]

To any scholar working entirely within this tradition, the material to be scrutinized in this chapter will seem alien and irrelevant. Yet to many less conventional economists, the ideas behind twentieth-century utility theory became philosophically and empirically untenable. J. K. Galbraith's famous tract, *The Affluent Society*, is the best known of a line of dissident studies that has called into question the assumption that wants would diminish with increased wealth. To Marxist economists, the individualistic basis of utility theory is also a source of criticism. For them, well-being is determined by the extent to which human needs are satisfied, and those needs are molded in society from the material and creative sides of human nature.[2] More recently, Amartya Sen's reconceptualization of well-being has broadened its scope beyond subjective feelings and at the same time has questioned the assumption that well-being is not measurable. Indeed, the resurgence of concern with unequal income distributions implicitly presupposes the possibility of interpersonal comparisons of well-being. While Marxist economists have been easier to marginalize, being outside the paths of mainstream economic science, the established positions of other dissidents have helped to support a certain heterogeneity in schools of thought, despite the ever-narrower technicism that governs what currently prevails in the training of economists.

Psychology has now also intruded upon economics. Not only have experimental studies found wanting some of the key predictions about rational economic behavior, empirical studies of "happiness" and "life satisfaction" have begun seriously to undermine an important pillar of welfare economics, namely the prime importance of income in determining well-being. Though happiness is found to be positively correlated with income, especially among groups of poor countries, the relationship is weak among richer countries. Over time consistent measures of happiness, derived from survey instruments, have not increased in industrialized countries, and have even shown decreases in some countries, despite economic growth (Easterlin, 1995; Oswald, 1997; Blanchflower and Oswald, 2004; Frey and Stutzer, 2002a, 2002b). Part of the reason is that reports of well-being are normally influenced by perceptions of relative position in the economy or society. These findings are consistent with the relative income theory and the important dissident traditions in economics. It remains a serious blot on modern economics, which prides itself as a science, that the relative income theory is rarely taken seriously despite providing fruitful explanations for human behavior and despite never having been empirically refuted.

One aspect of life satisfaction is satisfaction with one's work. Job satisfaction has traditionally been a focus for industrial psychology and sociology, but it has become recognized that job satisfaction data, though subjective, convey information that helps to predict objective behavior, such as quitting one's job and absenteeism (Freeman, 1978; Hamermesh, 1977, 2001; Borjas, 1979; Clark et al., 1998). A coterie of economists have now gone against the grain of their professional training in maintaining that economists ought to embrace quantitative measures of well-being, and that job satisfaction data are an approximate measure of happiness at work.[3] In this light, comparative data on job satisfaction across countries and between groups are argued to be informative about the different levels of utility or well-being (Sousa-Poza and Sousa-Poza, 2000). This contention is remarkable, and if supported would throw wide open the study of economic welfare. Yet there are significant problems in accepting it. Job satisfaction depends not just on the well-being that the job conveys but also on the well-being that one normally expects to gain. It is likely that someone with limited expectations—perhaps because of lesser education, or for reasons of family and social background—will express higher satisfaction than is reported (for the same job) by another person with greater expectations. Moreover, the concept of job satisfaction does not adequately encapsulate the whole range of emotional responses to jobs. According to extensive research in occupational psychology, the main dimensions across which responses differ are the extent to which the job "arouses" individuals, and the extent to which it gives "pleasure" or "displeasure" (Warr, 1987); an adequate measure of affective well-being should include indicators that cover both these dimensions. For example, a job might be found to give a worker a pleasurable, anxiety-free environment, but to be lacking in stimulation.[4] In short, comparisons of job satisfaction levels between individuals or between groups or across nations suffer from a validity deficit: exactly what do they signify?

Comparisons of *trends* in job satisfaction are, however, a potentially valid guide to trends in well-being because, for given norms and expectations, job satisfaction bears a stable relation to worker well-being. People's norms and expectations do not usually change very much over the medium term. Over a decade or two, if there were substantial changes in job satisfaction, one can infer that these indicate changes in well-being. Though an imperfect measure of change, the national-level data on job satisfaction provide almost the only available indications of changing subjective well-being at work in the modern era. Historians of earlier periods have no quantitative indices of this nature to go by. What, then, has been happening in recent times?

## A Picture of the Changing Well-Being of Workers in the Industrialized World

The trends over modern times in subjective well-being of several national populations of workers are shown in figures 8.1 to 8.5 and in table 8.1, which capitalize on enquiries into job satisfaction within national-level surveys over three decades, and on the foresight of those survey designers (unfortunately not all) who saw the wisdom in maintaining identical instruments over time. The result is a stark and remarkable finding: despite the growing affluence of industrialized economies in the current era of prosperity, and despite also the relative decline of smokestack industries and back-breaking physical jobs attending to the mines and the smelters, the average job satisfaction of nations is generally either stationary or falling.

Britain falls into the latter category. Through the 1970s there was considerable stability in job satisfaction, even through the shocks to the labor market that reverberated from the oil price hikes in 1974 and 1979, and from the various incomes policies of the late 1970s (figure 8.1a).

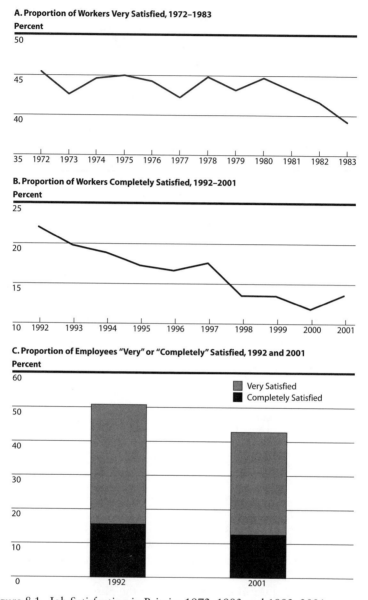

Figure 8.1. Job Satisfaction in Britain, 1972–1983 and 1992–2001
a. *Source*: General Household Survey.
*Note*: 5-point scale; base is workers aged 18–65.
b. *Source*: BHPS.
*Note*: 7-point scale; base is workers aged 18–65.
c. *Source*: EIB and the 2001 Skills Survey.
*Note*: 7-point scale; base is employees aged 20–60.

TABLE 8.1.
Job Satisfaction in Seven Industrialized Nations, 1989 and 1997

|  | 1989 | | 1997 | |
|---|---|---|---|---|
|  | Low[1] | High[2] | Low[1] | High[2] |
| Britain | 16.5 | 39.6 | 21.2 | 35.6 |
| Germany (West) | 15.3 | 43.8 | 18.6 | 39.0 |
| Hungary | 23.1 | 13.5 | 37.8 | 23.2 |
| Italy | 19.3 | 33.9 | 21.4 | 35.3 |
| Netherlands | 15.1 | 40.1 | 10.1 | 48.1 |
| Norway | 15.5 | 42.6 | 17.9 | 36.7 |
| United States | 12.9 | 50.1 | 16.6 | 48.4 |

*Source*: International Social Survey Program.
*Notes*:
[1] Percentage completely, very, or fairly dissatisfied or neither satisfied nor dissatisfied.
[2] Percentage completely or very satisfied.

Thereafter, signs indicate that job satisfaction was beginning to fall from about 1980. No data exist regarding what happened in the 1980s after 1983 (when the General Household Survey designers decided to stop asking about job satisfaction, perhaps because there was no longer a policy demand for this information in the early period of Margaret Thatcher's government). During the 1990s, however, three separate sources confirm that job satisfaction declined (see figures 8.1b and 8.1c, and table 8.1). Although some specific domains of job satisfaction (including satisfaction over pay and security) modestly increased, overall job satisfaction was unambiguously lower by the end of the decade. Gardner and Oswald (2002) found that public-sector workers, in particular, had suffered declines in this period. Unless there is cause to maintain that workers' norms of what counts as satisfactory in a job had for some reason substantially increased during the decade, one can only conclude that workers' well-being had genuinely fallen.

As noted above, in the future job satisfaction may not be the ubiquitous instrument of choice in social surveys. More accurate instruments have been developed to capture the different dimensions of well-being, and some are simple enough to use in large-scale surveys. For the most part these have not been in use long enough to generate a picture of change. One exception is a straightforward "work strain" instrument, consisting of three questions about the frequency with which workers "after (they) leave work keep worrying about job problems," "find it difficult to unwind at the end of a workday," and "feel used up at the end of a workday." Responses to these questions, each against a six-point scale, can be

**Percent**

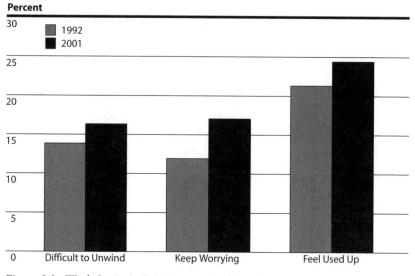

Figure 8.2. Work Strain in Britain, 1992 and 2001
  *Source*: EIB and the 2001 Skills Survey.
  *Note*: Proportion of workers who for much, most, or all the time: "find it difficult to unwind at the end of a workday," "keep worrying about job problems after leaving work,"
or "feel used up at the end of a workday."

combined to form a valid index of work strain which ranges in principle
from 1 to 18.[5] The mean level of work strain across the British nation
rose from 7.27 in 1992 to 7.52 in 2001. Figure 8.2 shows that the frequency of all three experiences was higher in 2001 than in 1992. This decline in well-being confirms again the impression gleaned from the job
satisfaction trend data.

Britain's story of declining subjective well-being at work is not unique.
In Germany there was a remarkable slump in job satisfaction from 1984
until 1997, after which there was a slight recovery (figure 8.3). The decline between 1989 and 1997 is confirmed from the separate source used
in table 8.1. Again making the assumption that the norms against which
job satisfaction is assessed change little over the medium term, one can
infer that German workers also have been experiencing declining well-
being. In the United States there was a decline in job satisfaction from
1973 onward, but here the decline was very modest, only detectable over
a long period throughout the 1970s and 1980s, and appears to have
ceased around the early 1990s (see figure 8.4 and table 8.1). This small
decline over such a long period is hardly worthy of note, and might easily
be seen as deriving from slowly changing work norms rather than from
genuinely changing well-being at work. Finally, there was a more sub-

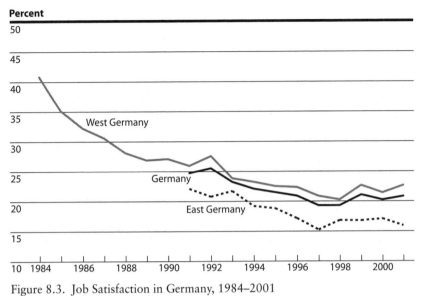

Figure 8.3. Job Satisfaction in Germany, 1984–2001
*Source*: GSOEP.
*Note*: Proportion responding at top two points of 10-point job satisfaction scale. Base is workers aged 18–65.

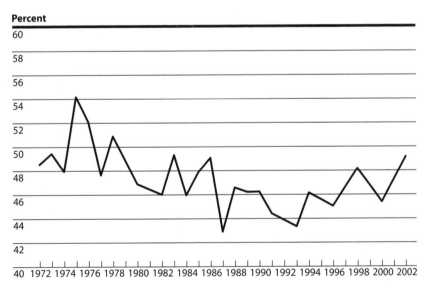

Figure 8.4. Job Satisfaction in the United States, 1973–2002 (Proportion of workers *very satisfied* ).
*Source*: General Social Survey.
*Note*: 4-point scale; base is workers aged 18–65.

stantial recorded fall in job satisfaction in Norway, between 1989 and 1997 (table 8.1); but it should be noted that there are no corroborative sources.

In most other European Union countries the story is less clear and not so decisively pessimistic (figure 8.5). While, in Denmark, the proportion of completely satisfied workers has tracked down from 42 percent in 1994 to 26 percent in 2000, the decline in average satisfaction levels is not quite significant at conventional levels of statistical significance. A similar story holds for each of France, Spain, Austria, Belgium, Denmark, Finland, Italy, Portugal, and Greece. However, this is too short a time period to identify as statistically significant on the radar screen anything but a major slump or increase in job satisfaction. Slower changes would only be revealed in a longer time span. A slightly longer period is afforded in the ISSP data (table 8.1). In Italy there was no change over 1989 to 1997, while in Hungary job satisfaction became polarized after the transition from the planned to free-market economy, generating both more highly satisfied and more highly dissatisfied workers. In the Netherlands, job satisfaction was significantly higher in 1997 than in 1989; however, since the ECHP panel data (in figure 8.5) recorded a downward shift from 1996 to 2000, any change over 1987 to 2000 is overall very small.

Should this mixed picture of stability and decline be taken seriously? Some social scientists—and, especially, this is the conventional wisdom of economics—will be skeptical to the point of dismissal. There are some potentially serious objections, and reasoned responses to each:

- The observed changes over time might be a statistical illusion generated by the vagaries of survey design. Though the question series meticulously use identical questions over time, not all set the questions in the same context. If preceding questions differ, the responses could be influenced in hard-to-predict ways that change over time. However, those sources that do not keep the same context are corroborated by those that do. Hence, this would seem an unlikely dismissal of the facts.
- In the panel data series, respondents could be influenced by their memory of the previous year's questioning. Yet, when this artificial source of change has been investigated (by, for example, inspecting only those interviewed for the first time), it does not account for the observed declines in job satisfaction (e.g., Jürges, 2003).
- The economic cycle could affect responses and generate a false sense of trend in any short series. This point is valid, and qualifies the conclusions one can draw from the seven-year series recorded in figure 8.3, and the various comparisons of two single points of time. Yet, the overall picture does not suggest that job satisfaction is especially volatile. Where longer series are available, they do not obviously react to macroeconomic shocks or move with

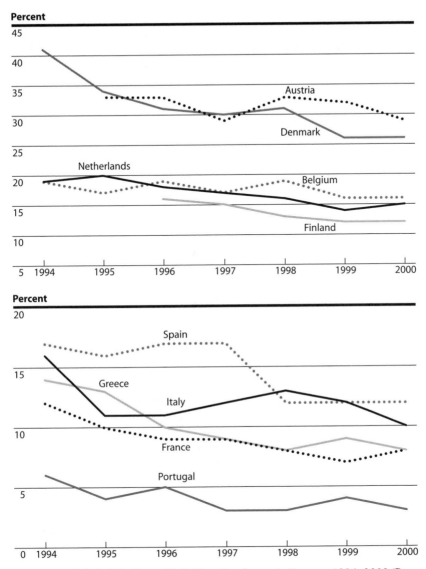

Figure 8.5. Job Satisfaction of Full-Time Employees in Europe, 1994–2000 (Proportion of workers *completely satisfied* with their jobs)

*Source*: European Community Household Panel (ECHP). http://www.datashop.org/en/bases/echp.html

*Note*: Satisfaction with work or main activity for employees working full-time is measured on a scale 1 ("completely dissatisfied") to 6 ("completely satisfied").

the cycle (e.g., figure 8.1),[6] and the longer series (GSOEP and BHPS) corroborate the two-point comparisons.

- Declines in job satisfaction might reflect the progressive replacement of old by young cohorts who are inherently more dissatisfied, perhaps because newer cohorts have greater expectations of work than older cohorts had previously nurtured. If so, the emphasis should be on the social sources of changing expectations rather than changing job quality. Jürges (2003) found evidence for a cohort effect in the case of West Germany. However, the effect was not linear (since satisfaction increased for older cohorts but only up to a point, beyond which it declined); moreover, it was not of sufficient magnitude to account for very much of the overall decline in job satisfaction.[7]

In short, in spite of these potential objections (which will continue to require serious consideration in future studies of trends in job satisfaction) the recent picture, made evident in figures 8.1 to 8.5 and in table 8.1, is sufficiently robust to require some explanation. If in some countries subjective well-being in the workplace is declining, is this because the overall quality of jobs is waning? If, elsewhere, well-being is largely unchanged, how can one explain the absence of progress in work life even amidst a continually growing general affluence?


## Well-Being and the Quality of Jobs

To begin to answer these questions, one can draw on the now considerable understanding of social scientists about what makes for higher or lower levels of job satisfaction (see, e.g., Spector, 1997). The determinants of job satisfaction can be classified into aspects of an individual's personality, aspects of her/his job and the match between the job and the individual. The job is the environment that conditions the individual's emotional responses to work. Some time ago, occupational psychology set itself the task of understanding the features of jobs that led to more positive emotional responses and those that were the trigger for dissatisfaction. Very many aspects of jobs have been found to affect job satisfaction. There seems to have been virtually no attempt, however, to use this understanding to develop an explanation of how changes in the features of jobs in the modern era have impacted the affective well-being of workers in the aggregate. Theories of aggregative change in the structure of the global economy, and of specific national economies and national institutions, are common and have frequently been referred to in this book. What is lacking so far, however, is a link between these global changes drawn on the wide canvas of political economists and the changes and continuities affecting the well-being of workers. To begin to build this link, attention is to be focused here on those aspects of jobs whose impact on satisfaction have received considerable attention by work specialists, and which have been examined in the preceding chapters as substantive elements in the quality of work life: skill, work effort, personal discretion and control, pay, and security.

In a remarkable recent study, Jürges (2003) conducted a search for factors underlying the decline in job satisfaction in West Germany. After a painstaking and thorough investigation, he drew a blank. First, he found that the slight rise in the sense of job insecurity in Germany (which in the 1990s ran parallel with rising unemployment rates) could only explain a small part of the decline in job satisfaction. In a similar vein, Blanchflower and Oswald (1999) had previously found that insecurity was not behind the more modest decline of job satisfaction in the United States between 1973 and 1996. Second, Jürges found that several measures of job characteristics were stable or changing in the wrong direction to account for decline in satisfaction. For example, the proportion of jobs with "undesirable working conditions" (such as cold, heat, damp, gases, or chemicals) fell from 24 percent to 20 percent not a spectacular improvement, but hardly the occasion for declining well-being.

Unfortunately it is here that one runs up against an issue for all secondary data analysts: if only the right questions had been asked, one could have understood better what was going on. The necessary questions about job quality are for the most part quite poorly covered in the questionnaire of the German Socioeconomic Panel, on which Jürges's study is based. It is likely that many aspects of job skill, work effort, and autonomy are not well enough measured to pick up changes in these factors occasioned by the structural changes in labor markets that so many writers have identified; a fortiori it is not possible to identify the extent to which these factors account for changes in the workers' well-being.[8] In the case of Britain, the researchers' lot is yet more frustrating: it is especially unfortunate that the British Household Panel Study with its good information about job satisfaction includes hardly any questions about the main sources of job satisfaction that had been identified in many studies since the 1960s. The same practical problem plagues the study of changes in well-being at the national level in the other countries.

The best opportunity for understanding these changes resides, instead, in the two British surveys—Employment in Britain and the 2001 Skills survey. Though these provide measures of change between just two data points, the surveys offer a unique combination of detailed work characteristics and well-being measures in nationally representative samples. Using these surveys and other supporting evidence, one can examine how the changes in job quality discussed in this book are associated with changes in the job satisfaction of British workers.

*Skill*

It would be an odd story if rising average skill levels (discussed in chapter 2) were behind a decline in subjective well-being. One of the claimed advantages of getting better educated is, after all, said to be the opportunity to take up more fulfilling work. Yet the connection between skill and well-being is a bit more complex than that. Empirical studies do not produce a strong correlation between education and job satisfaction, and sometimes the relationship is nonlinear or even goes into reverse. Though this has not yet been proven, the likely reason is that better educated workers have higher expectations of their jobs, and hence report job satisfaction in relation to these higher norms. Another reason why higher skills may not mean more satisfaction is that skills and effort tend to come in a package in modern industry. Gallie et al. (1998), for example, found that those workers who reported skill upgrading disproportionately also reported work intensification, substantially above those whose job skills were not being upgraded. In the pooled data from the 1992 Employment in Britain survey and the 2001 Skills Survey, the correlation between work strain and required qualification level was 0.28 and highly significant statistically. So skilled jobs might be more fulfilling, but they are also more demanding. It is thus not surprising to find that higher skill levels in jobs do not signal more job satisfaction. In the two surveys the correlation coefficient between required qualification level and job satisfaction is just 0.01 and statistically insignificant. The rising qualification requirements of jobs, and other indicators of skill change reported in chapter 2, are not, therefore, in themselves a reason to expect large changes in job satisfaction.

Another skills factor, however, is relevant: the extent to which workers are in jobs for which they are appropriately qualified. Over-education is a manifestation of a person-job misfit—which itself is a reason to expect dissatisfaction (Allen and van der Velden, 2001; Green and McIntosh, 2002). Similarly, those under-qualified for their jobs might also be expected to register dissatisfaction. The proportion of "matched" workers (where their own qualification matches their job's requirements) who were very or completely satisfied in the two surveys was 48.5, compared with 44.7 for those who were not matched. This difference is modest but statistically significant; it is relevant because of the increase in over-education during the 1990s (see chapter 2).

A useful dynamic way of seeing the effect that this might have on job satisfaction is to look at how particular cohorts change over time, as shown in table 8.2. Cohorts of groups of workers in a given occupation, within a narrow age-band, can be traced over the period 1992 to 2001. On average, the proportion of matched workers declined by 5.9 percentage

TABLE 8.2.
Correlation between Within-Cohort Changes in Job Satisfaction and Within-Cohort Changes in Job Characteristics over 1992–2001[1]

| | Mean Within-Cohort Changes in Each Variable | Partial Correlation Coefficient between Within-Cohort Changes in Job Satisfaction and Each Variable | Proportion of Decline in Job Satisfaction Accountable by Change in Each Variable (%)[7] |
|---|---|---|---|
| Required Qualification Level[2] | 0.017 | 0.051 | 0.2 |
| Matched Qualification[3] | −0.059 | 0.135 | 16.4 |
| Work Intensity[4] | 0.068 | −0.365* | 36.8 |
| Task Discretion[5] | −0.186 | 0.293* | 50.9 |
| Wages[6] | 0.104 | 0.002 | 2.4 |

*Source*: EIB and the 2001 Skills Survey.
*Notes*:
* Indicates that the correlation coefficient is significantly different from zero with probability 5%.

[1] Job satisfaction was classified into three levels: High ("very satisfied" or "completely satisfied"), Medium ("fairly satisfied" or "neither satisfied nor dissatisfied"), and Low ("fairly dissatisfied," "very dissatisfied," or "completely dissatisfied"). The mean within-cohort change in job satisfaction was –0.088. Eight date-of-birth cohorts at four-year intervals were defined, each divided into 9 major occupation groups, giving 72 cohorts and 144 observations over the two surveys. The oldest cohorts were 56–60 in 2001, while the youngest were 20–24 in 1992. Thus, for example, one cohort is the group of professional workers who were born between 1957 and 1960, who were thus between 32 and 36 in 1992, then between 41 and 45 in 2001. For the analyses in this table the cohorts have been weighted by the number of cases in each cohort, so as not to give undue weight to smaller cohorts.

[2] Average required qualification level in cohort; see notes to table 2.3.

[3] Proportion of workers in cohort holding qualifications that match those required for current recruitment to job.

[4] Proportion of workers in cohort for whom "required effort" (see table 3.5) was at its highest level.

[5] Mean Task Discretion Score, as defined in table 5.1.

[6] Log of hourly pay in 1992 pounds sterling.

[7] Computed from the multivariate analysis given in table A8.1. The estimates for each variable are derived by multiplying the coefficient in column (6) of table A8.1 by the mean within-cohort change, dividing by the mean within-cohort change in job satisfaction, and multiplying by 100.


points. Those cohorts for whom the decline in matching was more extensive registered modestly higher declines in job satisfaction, as shown by the correlation coefficient of 0.135 between the within-cohort changes in job satisfaction and qualification-matching, reported in the second column.[9] Thus, although the rising average skill level is not in itself an important factor in understanding changes in job satisfaction, the changing extent to which the education system, employers, and labor market institutions are bringing about a match between individuals and jobs is of some importance. In the case of Britain, a declining match is associated with some of the decrease in job satisfaction.

## Effort

Intensification of work effort is, in contrast to rising skill, a serious candidate to account for at least some of the decline in subjective well-being. Small-scale psychological studies have shown that, as expected, work overload has a negative impact on various measures of well-being. Economics assumes it to be so. The detrimental effect is confirmed with this nationally representative data from the 2001 Skills Survey and from the Employment in Britain survey. Extra hard work is associated with greater levels of work strain. For example, among those workers whose job requires hard work ("strong agreement"), work strain (on the 1 to 18 scale) is recorded as 8.59, as compared with 6.77 for other workers, the difference being highly significant. Since work strain is precisely a measure designed to capture those dimensions of workers' response to jobs that are most affected by hard work, the association is entirely to be expected. More telling is the finding that hard work is also negatively associated with job satisfaction: those cohorts whose effort was intensified more over 1992 to 2001 tended to be those with the greater drops in job satisfaction (as shown by the negative correlation coefficient, −0.365, reported in table 8.2, between the within-cohort changes in work intensity and satisfaction).

## Discretion

The importance for job satisfaction of personal influence and discretion over the tasks to be performed has long been widely recognized from the findings of small-scale studies, as discussed in chapter 5. Expanding individual autonomy has, accordingly, been central to the mission of job redesign since the start of this movement more than three decades ago. In subsequent developments it also came to be believed that maintaining personal control was especially important for offsetting the dissatisfaction that occurred in situations of excessively hard work.[10] In the current setting, job satisfaction is strongly positively associated with the Task Discretion Score (see chapter 5): the correlation coefficient is 0.23. The decline in task discretion, noted in chapter 5, is therefore a potential candidate to account for the fall in job satisfaction.

Since the correlation coefficient across the cohorts between the change in job satisfaction and the change in discretion is 0.293 (table 8.2), this means that cohorts whose discretion declined more than average registered greater than average falls in job satisfaction. The average decline in the Task Discretion Score was also considerable: it was $-0.186$, which is just under a quarter of the gap between the cohort with the least and the cohort with the most discretion.[11]

## Pay

It is typically found that pay has a comparatively modest impact on job satisfaction. The reasons have been rehearsed before: the key is the "comparison pay" that individuals expect to receive given their skills and given what others are receiving. Being in receipt of pay above the comparison pay leads to higher job satisfaction, and vice versa. But since in a cross-section those workers with high pay tend also to have a high comparison pay, the direct effect of pay on satisfaction is attenuated. With the two surveys here, pay has a positive but small association with job satisfaction, with a correlation coefficient of just 0.03. When examined over time, there is a negligible link between a cohort's rise in pay and its change in job satisfaction.

## A Multivariate Summary Account

The foregoing analysis tells the story that rising work effort and falling task discretion were major factors associated with the decline in job satisfaction between 1992 and 2001. However, these and other change factors overlap, and the above correlation coefficients do not signify whether part or all of the story has been uncovered. To do so, a multivariate analysis is required, which takes into account the simultaneous impact of multiple changes.[12] While the full findings are shown in the appendix to this chapter, the implications of this analysis are presented in table 8.2. The final column shows how important each of the job quality variables are in accounting for the overall decline in job satisfaction within the cohorts between 1992 and 2001.

Roughly half of the decline in job satisfaction is directly attributable to the decline in task discretion. In other words if, hypothetically, the level of task discretion had not fallen during these years, while all other variables changed in the way they did, average job satisfaction would still have declined but by only half as much. Another third of the fall in job satisfaction resulted from the work intensification that took place during the decade. An additional small proportion of the fall is accounted for by the decreasing extent to which workers' qualifications and job requirements are matched.

No other personal factors that were changing over this period could account for any part of the decline in job satisfaction: neither the changing gender balance of the workforce, nor the hours they worked, nor the age of the cohorts had any effect. Nor did structural changes like the falling proportion of workers who work in large establishments, or the proportion covered by trade union bargaining arrangements, affect job satisfaction. Other aspects of the work itself also had virtually no effect on well-being, including the extent to which computers are used in the job and the prevalence of team working. The absence of any contributions to the explanation from these other variables puts in perspective the remarkably large impact of the declining discretion and work intensification.[13]

A final word can be added about the effect of job insecurity in Britain. As is found elsewhere, job insecurity is unsettling and a significant and substantial generator of job dissatisfaction. In the 2001 Skills Survey, of those who thought that job loss was quite likely or very likely, only 23.1 percent were very or completely satisfied with their jobs, as compared with 43.9 percent for the remainder of workers who felt more secure. This association almost certainly reflects causation and is supported in multivariate, longitudinal studies (e.g., Jürges, 2003). The role of job insecurity in accounting for change in job satisfaction cannot be directly investigated in Britain owing to lack of an identically constructed variable to measure insecurity in both 1992 and 2001. Nevertheless, as was seen in the previous chapter, job insecurity *fell* in the period from 1992 to 2001 as the unemployment rate gradually dropped. So consideration of the issue of job insecurity, far from helping to explain the recorded decline in well-being, makes this fall the more surprising: job satisfaction declined in spite of the improving job market.


### Conclusion: The Quality of Work Life Is Strained

The main findings of this analysis are, perhaps, startling, but at the same time unsurprising in light of previous knowledge. It might seem rather obvious that allowing workers the possibility to plan and control what they are doing, in the daily business of their work life, is central to their well-being. This centrality was a tenet of Marxist and other conceptions of work for more than a century. Various facets of autonomy that were thought to be crucial have been investigated empirically in industrial psychology for several decades. The problem is that previous knowledge about the importance for welfare of designing more fulfilling jobs has been ignored or insufficiently appreciated by employers and policy makers.

Lack of appreciation derives ultimately from the genuine conflict of interest in the workplace: the employer's interest is to extract the best performance from workers, not to generate their maximum well-being. It has been argued that workers who are more satisfied, with greater levels of subjective well-being, will deliver better performance. Absenteeism, for example, can be reduced by addressing the sources of job dissatisfaction.

Management gurus take the point much further in proposing that empowering and freeing up the initiative of the workforce is an essential ingredient of corporate success (Peters, 1988; Kanter, 1989); conversely, failure stems from a management mind-set that prefers closer control of the workforce. Nevertheless, specific instances where firms have lost out through an obsession with control do not prove that *in general* the workplace is a "win-win" game, where what is good for workers is always right for the firm. One has to hold to a very rosy ideology about capitalism to accept the story that all one needs is enlightened managers. In general, individual jobs are designed by employers for maximum productivity relative to their wage cost, given their knowledge of production techniques in the industry. Since the knowledge of what is best is far from perfect and strongly dependent on variable management cultures, so too jobs are designed and changed in differing ways. The analysis in this chapter is therefore only an "account" of declining satisfaction, which lays the blame at the door of falling discretion and work intensification but does not produce a deep explanation for the strategic direction taken during the 1990s by the British management classes.

What *is* emphasized by this analysis is that, whatever the impact on performance, the taste for reducing workers' control over their daily tasks has had a very considerable effect on their well-being. The lesson is that, for the benefit of working people, there needs to be less intervention and control from above, and more discretion and self-determination from below even within the confines of a job.

Attributing half of the decline in job satisfaction to declining discretion is, at least in one respect, an optimistic finding. There is nothing necessary or inherent in modern technology that requires managers to choose more regimented forms of work control (whether bureaucratic or technical). As has been seen, no decline of personal control has been witnessed, for example, in Finland. Policies that can lead to an alteration of management culture need not be at the expense of sacrificed productivity. The same cannot so easily be said of work effort. Though excessive work effort leading to burn-out may be costly in the long run for workers and firms, in general it is beneficial for firms to extract more effort where possible from workers. In chapter 4 it was argued, further, that technological changes in the modern era had led to an increased demand for workers able and prepared to put in high levels of effort. Resistance to this tendency must come either from the individual or the collective will, of which more will be said in the next chapter, rather than through a spurious argument that it would be in both parties' interests to reduce work effort.

Though the findings reported here for Britain are robust to many different ways of looking at the data, and are suggestive of what can happen in other countries, ultimately they require corroboration. The British decline in job satisfaction has been confirmed from three data sources, but only in one case is it possible to address possible explanations. This is because most of the social surveys that are telling this interesting story about well-being over time unfortunately have had too little questionnaire space to examine people's jobs in sufficient detail. Having just one data series is insufficient to make generalizations about even proximate explanations for changing well-being more widely in the modern era of capitalism. The slump in job satisfaction in Germany remains a puzzle. The decline in job satisfaction in the United States during the 1970s and 1980s is also unexplained but it is also a very modest decline, which might just be a reflection of slowly changing expectations. There were no major changes in average pay over this period, though increasing inequality may have caused more "surprises" in pay leading to some polarization of the distribution of job satisfaction (Hamermesh, 2001). Nevertheless, if the results from Britain are anything to go by, increasing average pay levels in already-rich countries is not likely to generate major increases in job satisfaction over the long term. It will be more important to seek to re-design work in the interests of workers rather than bureaucrats and employers, and to seek ways to control the pace of work.

### Appendix: Multivariate Analyses

In table A8.1, the determinants of within-cohort job satisfaction are analyzed where cohorts are defined as in the notes to table 8.2. The coefficient estimates are obtained from fixed-effects panel estimations which, in this context of two periods, are equivalent to OLS (ordinary least squares) regressions in first differences. Column (1), the benchmark specification, confirms the decline in job satisfaction through the negative coefficient on the year for 2001. Subsequent columns introduce possible variables to "account for" the decline, either separately (columns 2 to 5) or together (column 6). Column (2) shows only small and insignificant direct effects from the skill variables. Column (3) shows a considerable negative impact from hard work on job satisfaction, and a significant decline in the magnitude of the year dummy coefficient. Column (4) shows that a rise in task discretion would lead to a rise in job satisfaction.

The fact that task discretion fell underpins the substantial decline in the magnitude of the 2001 year dummy coefficient. Column (5) shows that, as expected, pay had no impact on the decline in satisfaction. Finally, column (6) confirms the significant effects of task discretion, work intensity, and qualifications match when combined in a multivariate analysis, and shows that the entire decline in job satisfaction has been accounted for by the combined changes in the independent variables, since the 2001 year dummy is now small and insignificantly different from zero.

**TABLE A8.1.**
Within-Cohort Analysis of Job Satisfaction, Britain, 1992 and 2001

|                        | (1)          | (2)          | (3)          | (4)          | (5)          | (6)          |
|------------------------|--------------|--------------|--------------|--------------|--------------|--------------|
| Year – 2001            | −0.087       | −0.076       | −0.061       | −0.029       | −0.088       | 0.009        |
|                        | (0.015)***   | (0.018)***   | (0.016)***   | (0.026)      | (0.016)***   | (0.029)      |
| Required               |              | 0.011        |              |              |              | −0.010       |
| Qualification          |              | (0.045)      |              |              |              | (0.042)      |
| Qualification          |              | 0.182        |              |              |              | 0.278        |
| Match                  |              | (0.170)      |              |              |              | (0.155)*     |
| Work Intensity         |              |              | −0.463       |              |              | −0.474       |
|                        |              |              | (0.139)***   |              |              | (0.137)***   |
| Task Discretion        |              |              |              | 0.273        |              | 0.241        |
|                        |              |              |              | (0.105)**    |              | (0.101)**    |
| Wages                  |              |              |              |              | 0.088        | −0.020       |
|                        |              |              |              |              | (0.097)      | (0.092)      |
| Constant               | 1.425        | 1.308        | 1.577        | 0.755        | 1.406        | 0.903        |
|                        | (0.011)***   | (0.113)***   | (0.047)***   | (0.257)***   | (0.174)***   | (0.281)***   |
| Observations           | 144          | 144          | 144          | 144          | 144          | 144          |
| R-squared              | 0.70         | 0.71         | 0.74         | 0.73         | 0.70         | 0.78         |

*Notes*: See notes to table 8.2.
* significant at 10%; ** significant at 5%; *** significant at 1%

The pattern of these findings is robust to a number of alterations. Work intensity was measured instead using an index combining the high speed, high tension, and required effort indicators described in chapter 3. The pattern of findings was the same. The Required Qualification Index was replaced by the Composite Skill Index described in chapter 2, again with the same findings. Other variables were included, which had no impact on satisfaction and none on the decline in satisfaction as indicated by the year dummy coefficient. These include: sex, hours of work, trade union coverage, establishment size, computer usage, team working, and age of cohort. In the case of sex, one might not expect to capture significant effects using this within-cohorts estimation method, since the gender proportions of cohorts will change relatively little. The gender effect is more appropriately estimated in a cross-section. Finally, cohort size is an issue in pseudo-panel estimates of this nature (Deaton, 1985). In this analysis the average size of cohort is 49. The above estimates allow for weights according to cohort size, but the general pattern of findings holds whether or not weights are used.

# Nine

## Summary and Implications for Policy on the Quality of Work Life

### The Rewards and Demands of Work in the Affluent Economy

Tracing the evolution of job quality in modern capitalism is no simple matter; nor should one expect to find any unidirectional changes indicating unambiguous betterment or deterioration in the experiences of workers. As was argued in chapter 1, an interdisciplinary understanding of the concept of job quality is called for, which points to several features that are, according to the theories of both economics and other social sciences, important aspects of job quality. This book has focused on five central aspects of job quality: skill, work effort, personal discretion, pay, and security. If these features are changing in opposing ways, there is no neat solution as to how to weigh their respective contributions to workers' welfare. And while this book has often dealt with national averages, as a way of summing up the experiences of all workers in a national economy, there are enough cases of divergence among different sectors to warn against oversimplifying the verdict in respect of any of the features of job quality. The evidence on job quality is also geographically sketchy, reflecting as it does the uneven availability of suitable social survey data across the industrialized world. The most complete picture has been constructed for Britain, but even here there are many gaps in knowledge.

Taken overall, however, there are several scientifically based findings from the survey and other evidence that, together, permit an overview of trends in the key aspects of job quality and support a discussion of policy implications. That is the purpose of this closing chapter.

Pay and the fairness of pay are key features of job quality. Have these indicators been improving in recent decades? Those in search of a good story can be reluctant to record improvements in economic or social life. The fact is that, in terms of wages, most groups of workers in the advanced industrialized economies are receiving substantially higher wages than they were two or three decades ago. In most nations, the average wage rate has risen, giving workers a share of national economic growth. In one case, Spain, wages rose by a factor of two and a half since 1970; much of the increase in the 1970s was a recovery from the immiseration forced upon the Spanish working class by four decades of repressive dictatorship. In other industrialized nations, wage increases have been more modest yet still sufficient to signal a substantial rise in job quality. The major exception is the United States, where there was no substantial increase in the average wage from 1973 until the latter half of the 1990s. The American workforce comprises a third of all those in the richest industrial nations, so the failure of its wage rate to rise is a substantive judgment on advanced capitalism in this era. True, American wage rates were a lot higher than elsewhere in the 1970s—for them, there was no other example to be followed. Yet, despite continuing economic growth, American workers on average appear not to have received a noticeable share of it. Among the industrialized nations, only the workers of Canada and New Zealand have endured a similar fate.

Underlying the trend in the average wage, however, is an even more remarkable feature of wages in the United States: a very substantial widening of wage dispersion. Between 1973 and 1989, the wages of the poorest half of the workforce fell, while those in the top third were rising. By 1989, the wages of the ninety-fifth percentile were more than five times that of the tenth percentile, and still rising. It was only in the late 1990s' technology-led boom that wages in the bottom half turned the corner and started to grow.

The United States may be exceptional with regard to average wage trends, but with regard to increasing wage inequality it is far from alone: the majority of richer economies have seen rises in wage inequality over long periods. Of the larger nations, neither Italy nor Britain were far behind the United States in drifting further away from equality in the labor market. High on the economists' list of suspects have been the entry of third-world, low-wage economies in the "South" into the manufacturing markets of the "North," and an accelerated burst of skill-biased technological change. Either or both of these are thought to have generated increased demand for skilled workers relative to unskilled workers, outstripping the rate at which, through education, the supply of skilled workers has been augmented. Market forces took their anointed course and the result is a deterioration in the relative wages of the lower-skilled jobs. Nevertheless, the evidence is far from overwhelming. A powerful alternative explanation is that institutional changes, such as reduced trade union power and falling minimum wages, were the source of the greater dispersion. Reduction in the federal minimum wage under President Reagan in the 1980s accounts for a substantial part of rising inequality in the United States. In general, institutional differences can explain why there is variation in the extent that inequality has changed in different countries.

In short, an assessment in terms of wages of the quality of jobs in modern-day advanced capitalism presents a mixed picture. In most nations the record is one of betterment, tinged with the divisiveness of inequality. Unfortunately, the most populous industrialized nation, the United States, is the major exception.

Increasingly skilled work is one potential source of rising wages and productivity. It is also a way for workers to gain more fulfillment through their jobs. A happy coincidence is therefore at the heart of the concept of the "knowledge economy." According to this perspective, the main way for firms in the advanced economies to compete with each other, and with those based in low-wage economies like China, is through superior knowledge. For this, high-level skills are required. The only way forward, it is claimed, is for all workers to acquire new competencies and abilities. Thus, just as with the economists' more prosaic postulate of skill-biased technological change, the assumption of proponents of the "knowledge economy" is that a preponderance of employers will have been offering the prospect of steadily more skilled work in the recent era. Unfortunately, it is less clear as to how far the knowledge economy is expected to penetrate the whole workforce. One cannot help wondering, for example, what the evangelists of the knowledge economy think of the quality of work life experienced by garbage clearance workers they see scurrying down their street, the sales and packaging workers in the supermarkets, or the health-care workers nursing their older relatives: are these, too, part of the knowledge society? The truth, which should be obvious to anyone who is not so keen to see change around every corner, is that there is a very substantial continuity in the mix of skills used in the jobs required in modern industries. If anyone had imagined that unskilled jobs would somehow disappear, or become deeply fulfilling in this information age, they would soon have become disappointed.

The average skills required in jobs have nevertheless been slowly increasing over recent decades—a positive story, in principle, for the quality of work life. Jobs have become more complex; and several generic skills such as problem-solving, communications, verbal and literacy skills, and above all computing skills, have increased in importance in recent years. The complexity of jobs is shown by indices of the time taken to learn to do them (any job you can pick up in one week is probably very simple), of the cumulative training time required, and of the academic or vocational qualifications required to get and do jobs. In Germany, for example, the proportion of jobs with a higher education entry requirement rose from 11 percent to 16 percent between 1985 and 2001. The increase in required qualifications is only partially circumscribed by the presence of credentialism—employers raising their qualifications requirements in response to a rising tide of supply because they want to recruit from the same relative place in the ability spectrum.[1]

While the quality of jobs is improved by the opportunity to perform more complex and fulfilling work, also important is the match between the worker and the job. On one side, the worker who has not acquired enough skills to cope with a job becomes stressed and unproductive. On the other side are those with qualifications and skills that they cannot utilize. Western writers have, for a long time, been apt to question the wisdom of the oversupply of Ph.D.s in developing nations like India. Yet in recent decades, a number of Western countries have been experiencing an increase in the proportions of people with educational qualifications taking jobs that have no equivalent requirements. In Britain, for example, the proportion of workers who find themselves overqualified for their jobs rose from 31 percent in 1992 to 37 percent by 2001. Some of these job-holders are students and others with no intention to make the jobs a permanent part of their lives. Others are less fortunate, perhaps condemned to a career of boredom at the workplace.

One major reason why one thinks of skilled jobs as being of high quality is that, on balance, the more complex jobs are ones where workers themselves have a lot of say about how the jobs are done, unlike less skilled jobs which, even if not routine, are usually more closely controlled by rules or by immediate bosses. Indeed, workers need skills if they are to do their jobs effectively using individual discretion and flexibility. Yet the converse does not hold: higher skill requirements do not mean that workers have to be granted extra discretion. The attitudes and culture of management have a strong effect on how jobs are designed—whether workers, either individually or in teams, are given leeway to determine their tasks within the objectives of the organization, or whether their tasks are more tightly prescribed and monitored. It is not known which of these contrasting management cultures is most conducive to the profits of the organization. However, the evidence is unequivocal that higher levels of personal discretion and influence over job tasks have a strong beneficial impact on workers' well-being.

So, what has been happening to the extent of workers' discretion and control? The picture is mixed, and distinctly patchy (if confined to periods of about a decade or more, only two countries present evidence). To start with the good news, in Finland there is some evidence of improvement in the 1980s. In fact, in all of Scandinavia levels of discretion have been high compared to elsewhere, reflecting the quality of work-life policies enacted in these countries; but there are no conclusive data on the trends, other than for Finland.

In contrast, the 1980s and 1990s saw a steady decline in the levels of discretion experienced by British workers. Though participation in some higher-level decision-making increased slightly (through, for example, managers holding consultation meetings with groups of workers), on average British workers experienced a fall in their perceived influence over their daily work tasks. They reported less choice over the way they did their jobs, and less personal influence over what tasks they did, how they did them, how hard they worked, and to what quality standards. This decline in influence has had substantial, unambiguously detrimental effects on the satisfactions that British workers experienced in their jobs.

If the skills and discretion story is an equivocal one for the quality of work life, the evidence of a widespread intensification of work effort and its detrimental impact on well-being is unambiguous. An early indication that the knowledge economy was a mixed blessing came when it was found in social survey research that workers who reported that their work was requiring increased skills were especially likely also to report an intensification of their work effort. In contrast to the psychologists' invocation to "work smart, not hard," the reality facing many is that the demands of work have increased in both dimensions.

Intensification of work effort could be seen as a symptom of employers gaining the upper hand at work. Remarkably, however, effort intensification is also rife in that majority of nations where wages and other work conditions have been improving. In Britain, for example, although the hourly wage rose by a quarter between 1992 and 2001, effort had, according to six separate indicators, also increased substantially. One robust explanation links this intensification to technical and organizational changes in the workplace, which made it possible to improve the flow of work to workers. New technologies can improve the productivity of all workers, but especially those who work hard and take advantage of the improved workflow possibilities. In chapter 4 this process, termed "effort-biased technological change," has been described in some detail. Innovations like the mobile phone and the laptop computer—devices that enable work to be carried out at what, previously, had been idle times—are only the most tangible signs. Call centers, which have the facility to deliver work instantaneously to workers, with near-perfect monitoring of work effort, are another visible example of workflow optimizing. Ongoing work reorganizations using management tools like Total Quality Management in conjunction with the new technological possibilities, often involving flexible working and multi-skilling, are the widespread proximate sources of work intensification. In services where competitive pressures are high, a more direct source of intensification is the increase of customer-driven work flows—a strategy that is more likely to work in public organizations and elsewhere where workers have a strong professional commitment to service delivery.

Although some workers may enjoy working hard, the increased effort within work hours has, on average, been unambiguously detrimental for workers. The high effort also contributes to the perceptions of another growing problem, referred to quirkily in Britain as the "work/life balance" and more directly in North American commentary as the "time squeeze." The experience of not having sufficient time to do all one's tasks, inside and outside work, is partly triggered by the "closing up" of the working day—the filling out of previously slack moments. But it is also set off by an increasing concentration of work time among households. Largely, this is a reflection of increasing participation of women in the workplace. A common experience in Britain and the United States is for the total hours commitment of multiple-person households to be rising substantially. In the United States, for example, married couples increased their joint working time from fifty-three to sixty-three hours per week between 1970 and 1998. Coming on top of the increased tension and speed of work during work hours, it is perhaps unsurprising that the time squeeze came by the turn of the century to be seen as a pervasive social and personal dilemma. When viewed in this social context, therefore, the quality of work life seems to have diminished.

Yet, from another perspective the story is different. In most countries, hours of work for the average employee have fallen in recent decades—a continuation of long-term trends and undoubtedly a reflection of the rising affluence of the age. France is one of the more dramatic instances, with annual working time falling by 311 hours between 1979 and 2003. The main exception, again, is the United States. Controversy has reigned over the measurement of hours trends in the United States: according to some commentators the average hours of employees have even increased. What is certain is that since the 1970s working hours have failed to come down from their already relatively high levels. The absence of a sufficiently strong labor movement to fight for hours reductions is the chief source of American excess. In Britain, average working hours were also static from 1980 through to the mid-1990s, but have since re-started their long-term historic decline. Overall, however, the deteriorating work-life balance issue is a question of household hours supply rather than the average hours of jobs or individual employees.

Among the arguments that modern-day capitalism is engendering a lower quality of work life, the issue of allegedly declining security has attracted more attention than any other. It has not been ignored by the media: the *New York Times* and *Boston Globe*, for instance, together contrived to report some item about job security or insecurity virtually once a day at the time of peak interest in 1996. It is also, however, the aspect of job quality about which myth and nostalgia have led furthest away from reality. Scholars of this age have the foresight of social survey designers to thank for rescuing the modern era from an inappropriate christening as capitalism's special age of insecurity.

Insecurity, in fact, is firmly linked with the actual experience of unemployment, which has been endemic in capitalist societies, and is not peculiar to the present. The worst fear for a worker is the risk of losing the job and becoming unemployed. That fear demoralizes workers, impairs their mental health, and hurts other members of their households. For many countries, the golden age period of capitalism that followed World War II was a time when comparatively few experienced the fear of unemployment on a regular basis. The 1970s and 1980s signaled a return to more normal times, with many countries having persistent periods of mass unemployment extending to more than 10 percent of the workforce and correspondingly high insecurity even among the many who managed to avoid job loss. Nevertheless, with the unemployment rate at the millennium below 6 percent in the United States, Japan, and several European countries (including Britain, the Netherlands, and most of the Nordic countries), it would be hard to characterize the present era as one with especially wide and high insecurity. At 9 percent, unemployment in Germany and France in 2002 was of great concern, though not nearly as bad as in most developing countries.

In the industrialized nations, fears of job loss have been falling and rising with the objective danger of unemployment facing workers. The mid-1990s, when media interest was at its height, were, it is true, times of considerable uncertainty. In Britain and the United States, perceptions of insecurity were unusually high, given the actual unemployment rates at the time. These enhanced fears were linked to several well-publicized waves of downsizing and job displacement, especially for white-collar workers;[2] in Britain, they were associated with the technological culling of the financial sectors, where a few years before large segments of workers, who had never before felt a significant threat of redundancy, had suddenly experienced job losses. But this particular distribution of insecurity has a tale in itself to tell: it was the middle classes who were experiencing more uncertainty in that period. Workers in the manufacturing industries were, by contrast, enjoying a period of stability and security—unlike a decade before, when U.K. manufacturing jobs were being lost in large numbers. The mid-1990s stories of insecurity were stimulated the more easily by journalists' closer identification with the affected sectors.[3] The ability of high-quality, nationally representative, surveys to debunk the biased impressions of sectional interests is a manifestation of the democracy of statistics when at their best. As might have been expected, fears of job loss were reduced in Britain and the United States through the end of the 1990s as the unemployment rate fell. They correspondingly rose in Germany as the rate of unemployment there crept up to a peak of over 9 percent in 1997.

The myth of recent exceptional insecurity has also surfaced as an assertion about newly unstable jobs in modern economies. There is some logic in linking stability to security: many of those who only manage to stay a short while in jobs may be in temporary-contract jobs or otherwise quite in fear of early redundancy and layoffs. The connection is loose, since longer-stay workers are also threatened and are likely to have more to lose. Yet the view that global and structural changes in the economy have undermined job stability by reducing average tenure is difficult to sustain. In some countries there have been modest declines in the average job tenure of male workers. Yet female workers have experienced some increases in job tenure, as they have become ever more integrated into the labor market and as pockets of progressive legislation have afforded some job protection surrounding pregnancy. The overall picture is one of comparatively little change in job instability over the years. The myth of declining stability is, however, hard to dispel—no matter how many times analysts report the above story of little change, the clarion call of "an end to jobs for life" seems to re-appear, not least from the lips of those who would threaten the living and working standards of workers, urging them not to resist what is asserted to be inevitable change, to take up the mantel of training, or to sign up to a challenging but halcyon vision of having multiple careers in one lifetime.[4]

With some major aspects of the quality of work life improving, others deteriorating, no overall verdict about changing quality can be made without making judgments about the relative value of those aspects. A single-index account of how advanced industrial capitalism is treating workers has its attractions, and job satisfaction is one such index. Job satisfaction should not be treated as a measure of the level of worker well-being. But changes in job satisfaction over time within representative populations are a plausible guide to changes in workers' well-being.

Remarkably, despite the increase in wages of the modern era, and the putative emergence of the knowledge economy with its wider provision of skilled and potentially more fulfilling work, there are no advanced industrialized nations for which there is evidence that workers have been becoming increasingly happy with their work life. In most cases, job satisfaction has not changed very much over a period of some years, though the record of what happened is very sketchy. American workers' job satisfaction was largely stable for as much as three decades; if anything, it drifted very slowly downward. This stagnation is hardly surprising given the failure of average wages to rise, increasing inequality and reports of work intensification. In two countries job satisfaction fell significantly: in Germany from the 1980s to the mid-1990s, and in Britain through most of the 1990s. In Britain's case the decline in satisfaction is directly accounted for by the intensification of work effort and the decline in workers' discretion.

## Policy Implications

What, if anything, is to be done to redress adverse trends in the quality of work life in modern affluent societies? Conscious responses to these trends have been widespread and multilayered, but how effective can they be? Can enlightened individuals, unions, or governments better harness the still-growing abundance of the industrialized world to produce a more fulfilling and rewarding experience when people go off to their daily work?

Individual resistance against work intensification comes, for example, in the form of absenteeism, or more drastically through job mobility where that is possible, but these responses are limited by the disciplines of the labor market and by personal commitment to the employing organization. Instead, individuals have the option of developing personal strategies for dealing with more intensive work. Over time they learn how to use new technologies more efficiently and, with forethought, can limit their impact on work effort. Consciousness-raising movements have come into existence, such as "Take Back Your Time" day in the United States, which draws inspiration in part from what Americans see in Europe: much shorter working hours (de Graaf, 2003). Tactics of job-sharing, partial retirement, and sabbatical leave have been used. A determined few can opt to "downshift" into less stressful jobs with lower pay, which in turn is sustainable if workers accept a simpler way of living with less money and material goods.[5] In addition to personalized coping strategies, individuals are now offered the advice of a burgeoning self-help industry, which provides training in time management, stress control, and other desirable personal practices.

Some such courses are also offered by larger employing organizations, anxious to treat their employees well and avoid legislative suits. However, employer policies to remedy stress rarely go beyond the relief of symptoms and the development of coping mechanisms. Internal social support has been shown to help the management of stress, though it does not always materialize (Wichert, 2002). A criticism is that such organization-led policies can easily shift apparent responsibility for problems from the employer to the employee. Nevertheless, it has also been argued that the costs that arise from poor decision-making due to organizational stress, and the increasing damage suits from employees claiming to be harmed by stress, provide sources of counterpressure that may oblige firms to change their practices (Mankelow, 2002). For most employees, however, the opportunities to mitigate the pressures of hard work or to move away from undesirable jobs are limited.

A second potential level of resistance to detrimental trends in the quality of work life is through trade unions and other collective representative units such as works committees. Unfortunately, unions have not been all that effective at resisting work intensification. The evidence reviewed in chapter 4 implied that the presence of unions reduced the extent of work intensification somewhat, and that union derecognition was the occasion for very substantial increases in work effort. However, much of the intensification of work would have happened even if there had been no decline in the bargaining powers of unions over recent decades. Moreover, there is no evidence that they have been instrumental in resisting the decline in task discretion that took place in Britain. These findings should not be surprising since hours, work effort, and work organization have not always been at the forefront of unions' collective bargaining agenda. The unions' prime emphasis has been on pay. In recent years, however, even their influence on wages has been diminishing (Blanchflower and Bryson, 2003).

Trade unions remain, however, the main collective instrument for workers to resist reductions in the quality of working life. They provide an efficient voice for identifying cases of extreme stress within large organizations, and for facilitating redress either through ensuring the enforcement of rights or at the bargaining table. Some unions already are prioritizing issues of job quality. Since the problems of excessive hard work and long hours are often an organizational imperative rather than merely an individual pathology, the best hope for many workers is that their trade unions take a lead on quality of work life bargaining at their workplaces. If work intensification is as important for job quality as has been maintained in this book, any such lead is likely both to find support from remaining trade union members and to raise unions' attractiveness to potential new members.

The third level at which adverse trends in job quality should be addressed is that of the state. The traditional efficiency rationale for state intervention is to redress cases of "market failure." The concept of market failure recognizes that for various reasons (most prominently, externalities and information asymmetries) private agents acting in their own interests do not bring about a socially optimal allocation of resources. Some aspects of the quality of work life fall into this category, most notably health and safety. It is inefficient for individuals to acquire full information about and evaluate the health and accident risks attendant upon working in various organizations. Such information is a public good, which governments typically evaluate on their citizens' behalf and accordingly regulate workplaces by systems of proscription and constraint, backed by fines and the threat of serious criminal prosecutions.[6] Skill acquisition is another area where the state intervenes. Training investments have external benefits when skills are potentially transferable to a few firms other than that which is funding them; individuals are often constrained by borrowing restrictions from supporting their own training (Stevens, 1999).

Governments therefore make loans available for skill acquisition, oversee the socialization of training practices within sectors, and provide occasional elements of public subsidy. Governments also have the general obligation to manage the macro-economy in a stable manner: to mitigate the effects of external shocks and to avoid hyperinflationary financing and other destabilizing practices. Indeed, the minimization of unemployment may be the single most important economic function of government, which must see not only to the quantity of jobs but also to the quality of the work life that they offer. The impact of job insecurity on worker well-being is substantial and far-reaching.

Governments also intervene in the quality of working life on equity grounds, for example by imposing minimum-wage requirements on whole sectors or economies. In this case, the intervention may or may not be beneficial for the efficiency of a labor market, depending on its competitive structure and on how the minimum wage dovetails with out-of-work benefit systems.

But the role of governments cannot be reduced just to that of redressing market failures and relieving inequalities. Governments are not neutral players, as is witnessed by shifts in political sentiment about the level of minimum wages and other pro-worker legislation. Moreover, there can also be widespread "government failure" in many areas of the public economy, where for diverse reasons governments are systematically inefficient in their quest to address market failures (Booth and Snower, 1996).

The failures include the state's oversight of the quality of work life. An instance of government failure is the systematic understating of the true costs of controlling labor processes in the state sector. Take, for example, the education sector. With growing affluence, and under the rhetoric of the knowledge economy, one of the biggest sources of increased demands on the public purse is for the expansion of public education systems. Yet, especially in those economies that have become much more unequal in the modern era, there is also a reluctance to find extra resources for the state. The consequence is a fiscal squeeze and simultaneously an impetus to ensure the accountability and to raise the quality of public education services. Increasingly intrusive central controls on what state school teachers and lecturers actually do, enable state bureaucrats to more closely manage the delivery of public services. Yet the costs of accountability and closer control are underestimated, and normally hidden from the public account, to be manifested only in the long term in unrest, absenteeism, and high turnover. The hidden costs lie in the reductions in discretion and the freedom to do satisfying work, and in the intensification of work effort that is necessary to meet the increasing demand for education services. Similar remarks apply to other public services and to areas of intervention in the private sector where the costs of compliance with rules are rarely evaluated. The costs remain hidden in part because they serve the interests of the bureaucracies that impose them.

Where, then, should governments intervene to improve the quality of jobs? On the question of skill, the most significant implication of the evidence is not that the concept of the "knowledge economy" is wrong, but that it is too simplistic. The survey findings strongly support the view that the utilization of skills in modern workplaces has been increasing, and it remains the function of governments to ensure that the skills of the workforce are adequately supplied through each nation's education system. There is no reason for governments to renounce this mission.

Yet the knowledge economy rhetoric neglects the considerable growth of traditionally low-skilled though nonroutine jobs in the service sectors. Linked to this same tendency, the rhetoric also overlooks the potential problem of increasingly severe education/job mismatches. The prevalence of overeducation in the economy has hitherto been a problem of quite moderate severity, but it is increasing. Unfortunately, not enough is known about the dynamic costs of over-education—in particular, it is not known how long workers in different countries remain in jobs where their education is being under-utilized. Nevertheless, over-educated and under-educated workers are found to be substantially less satisfied at work than those who are well matched to their job requirements. Excess supplies of education may be effective in the long run in giving firms the incentive to demand and use more highly educated labor. Yet governments concerned so much with ensuring an expanded supply of educated workers may also need to consider how best to stimulate firms to raise their skills demands, while ensuring that their education systems continue to generate useful skills for modern workplaces and society. In other words, the responsibilities of governments should not be limited just to the supply side of the skills market; they should concern the matched expansion of both the supply of and the demand for skills.[7] Policies to change employers' demands for skills are hard to construct and to articulate in the context of a liberal economy where the deployment of labor is seen as the business of the employer, not the state. Nevertheless, governments can affect incentives to use low-skilled labor, for example through taxation and minimum-wage policies; they also have a public function of diffusing best practice, which can sometimes involve the pursuance of high-skill strategies.

The reduction in the exercise of task discretion seems to have been devastating for the level of job satisfaction experienced by the British workforce, but the sources of this decline are as yet poorly understood. Official remedies, therefore, cannot be confidently recommended. Nevertheless, it seems likely that the extent of discretion afforded to ordinary workers is a reflection of managerial culture; if so, it could like all styles be open to public influence. Moreover, the state itself, as employer and regulator, can heed the evidence about the detrimental impacts of low-discretion jobs on workers' well-being. It should be explicit about the costs of policies which reduce trust in workers and which impose limitations on workers' discretion. Evidence that politics makes a difference, even to the private sphere of work organization, comes from Scandinavia where, from the 1970s onward, several government policies became oriented toward raising the quality of work life. Express frameworks were legislated into existence for social partners to negotiate changes in work organization which could raise elements of the quality of work life, including discretion, variety, and participation in workplace decisions. Firms came under a legal obligation to use professional health and safety services. Opportunities for teamwork and for self-development expanded substantially in Finland. The fruits of the plethora of quality of work-life policies were shown also in a cross-national survey in 1996, which revealed that Scandinavian workplaces generally exhibited high levels of workplace quality relative to the rest of Europe (Gallie, 2003).

Whether and how governments should intervene to affect wage rates is an old conundrum. In the large majority of cases it is normally assumed that wage-setting is not the job of government in liberal economies. In corporatist economies, governments participate in tripartite agreements (with unions and employers' organizations) to control wage growth, with varying degrees of intensity and success, and provide legislative frameworks for the support of nationwide and sectorwide agreements. Through its influence on the labor market, as well as through the skill formation processes, the institutions of government have had far-reaching effects on the levels and trends of inequality. Though real wages have grown in many nations in response to economic growth, the issue that requires attention is the stagnation of wages for very large numbers of poorer American workers, and to a lesser extent of European workers. The growth of low-paid jobs has put a high burden on those doing this work. The public instrument of choice for redressing the degradation of work through low pay has been the minimum wage. Since even Britain now has a national minimum-wage law, along with most other industrialized nations, the issue is the level at which it is set. Governments may have been responsible for the declines suffered by low-paid workers, as for example during the 1980s in the United States under the Reagan presidency (Card and Di-Nardo, 2002). In Britain, the Labor Government has been too timid in raising minimum thresholds, and so has missed opportunities for providing better legal support for millions of its citizens (Dickens and Manning, 2003). Although caution was understandable in the early stages of its introduction, given the fear of unemployment going back to earlier high levels, the cost of keeping the minimum wage too low has been a relatively disappointing impact on poverty and on the gender-pay gap.

Finally, given the widespread experience of work intensification, and the dominant role of new technologies, the space for enlightened governments to intervene to reduce excessive work pressures is constrained. Within the bounds of the capitalist ethos, how hard somebody works is seen as a matter between the employer and employee. Governments have traditionally intervened, usually in response to deep and strong political forces, to place constraints on working hours. In the nineteenth century, the most significant moral drives concerned the super-exploitation of children in workplaces. In the modern era, the European Union has introduced its Directive on Working Time, on the grounds of the health and safety of workers. This legislation obliges governments to limit working time to no more than forty-eight hours per week, on the face of it a serious restriction on work. However, its implementation is in practice quite loose. The restriction concerns the hours averaged over many weeks, and there are varied exclusion clauses. In the case of Britain, workers have been permitted to opt out of this weekly hours restriction, and the main effect of the legislation has been to increase the availability of paid holiday rights for lower paid workers (no mean achievement) (Green, 2003). The weekly hours restriction may not be in workers' own interests: commonly, many who work longer hours express greater levels of job satisfaction than those who work less than forty-eight hours, so the legislation is a questionable restriction of choice, where that choice is genuine. Moreover, if the quality of work life has been in decline in some countries, this has not been because of increases in the length of working hours. In France, the experience of legislating shorter hours (in that case, in a contested attempt to share employment more evenly among the active population) has met with the problem that this has exacerbated the intensification of work effort during the constrained shorter hours.

Though hours restrictions are thus at best a loose way of tackling the detrimental effects on worker well-being that come from work intensification, governments can still make a difference. It remains up to governments to support trade unions in their objectives to provide the appropriate representations for their members; and, especially where there are no unions, to oblige companies on grounds of health and safety to ensure that work effort is held within bounds in all sectors of companies, whether through the enforcement of rights or through processes of regulation. The protection of citizens from undue stress is a social necessity, not a private choice at the whim of companies that may or may not choose to take care of the interests of their employees. Notwithstanding environmental and political instability, the prospect remains for continued economic growth across the industrialized world in the coming decades. It will be important for governments to become increasingly active in helping to ensure that this affluence is expressed in a better quality of work life.

# Data Set Appendix

THE FOLLOWING LISTS and describes the survey data sets used in this book. Other data sources have been referenced where appropriate. The original data creators (other than myself in the case of sources 7 and 8), depositors, holding archives, and funders of these data sets bear no responsibility for the analyses and interpretations made in this book.

## 1. British Household Panel Study (BHPS)

The BHPS is a nationally representative panel data set of individuals and households residing in Britain. All adults in sampled households are interviewed once a year. The original sample, selected following a stratified random sampling procedure, was first interviewed in 1991. It comprises some 5,500 households and 10,300 individuals. New households formed by members splitting from their "old" household are added to the sample. Members leave through death and through sample attrition. The panel is also periodically refreshed with new samples. Full details are available at www.iser.essex.ac.uk/bhps.

Funding Source: The UK Economic and Social Research Council.

## 2. Employment in Britain (EIB)

The Employment in Britain research program comprised two surveys, one of employed people, the other of unemployed people, living in Britain in 1992 and aged twenty to sixty. Only the survey of employed people is used in this book. It comprised an achieved sample of 3,869 individuals. Stratified random sampling was used to select households from sectors drawn from the Postal Address File. One person was interviewed per household, chosen randomly from those who were found and eligible at each address. Interviews were face to face, and involved three parts: the respondent's work history, the main interview concerning current and recent experiences of work, and a short self-completion interview, completed in the presence of but without intervention by the interviewer. Weights were applied to correct for the differential probability of selection depending on the number of eligible persons at each address. Since the achieved sample slightly overrepresented women, compared with Labor Force Survey data, a second small correction was also applied, reducing the weight for women and raising the weight for men so as to match national data. See Gallie et al. (1998) for full details.

Funding Source: An industrial consortium, the UK Employment Department, the UK Employment Service, and the Leverhulme Trust.

### 3. First European Survey on the Work Environment, 1991–1992; Second and Third European Surveys on Working Conditions

These are surveys of nationally representative samples of employed people in member states of the European Union. The surveys focused on how workers experienced their working conditions, excluding pay, using a common questionnaire across countries. Not all questions were common to all three surveys. Multistage random sampling methods were used to select respondents in employment to be interviewed in each member country. One person was interviewed per household, chosen randomly from those that were found and eligible at each address. The respondents, who were at least fifteen, were interviewed face to face. In the first survey, the full sample comprised 12,819 respondents drawn from twelve countries. The second (1996) and third (2000) surveys, comprising 15,986 and 21,703 respondents respectively, were drawn from fifteen countries. Response rates varied substantially (for example, in the third survey from 41 percent in the Netherlands to 76 percent in Germany). The Labor Force Survey in each country was used, along with sampling weights, to generate analytical weights that correct for the differential probability of selection. For full details, see European Foundation for the Improvement of Living and Working Conditions (1992, 1997, and 2001).

Funding Source: European Commission.

### 4. The General Social Survey (GSS)

The GSS is a nationally representative survey of the U.S. population, conducted annually almost every year since 1972. Being the product of an admirable, early, act of far-thinking investment by an interdisciplinary team of social scientists, the GSS meticulously replicates both questions and question sequences in successive surveys, in order to allow researchers to track change and thereby inform public policy. It covers each year a broad set of core issues and other "add-on" modules devoted to specific topics. A work orientations module was included in 1989 and in 1997, while some basic employment data are included every year. Stratified random sampling methods are used nowadays, though sampling strategies in some early years used partial quota methods, which differed from random methods in complex ways. Since 1985, this survey has been part of the International Social Survey Program. The GSS sequence epitomizes the enhanced material suitable for understanding social change, available to analysts and future historians of recent decades, compared with what is possible for historians of earlier eras.

Full details are available at www.icpsr.umich.edu.

Funding Source: The main but not exclusive source has been the National Science Foundation.

### 5. The German Socio-Economic Panel (GSOEP)

The GSOEP is a nationally representative panel data set of individuals and households residing in Old and New Federal German States. Respondents are interviewed once a year. The original sample, selected following a stratified random sampling procedure, was first interviewed in 1984. New members are added each year through children attaining age sixteen, new households formed by members splitting from their "old" household. Members leave through death and through sample attrition. The panel is also periodically refreshed with new samples, including a new East German sample after reunification. Successive waves are thus designed to be representative of the relevant population in Germany. In 2001, there were approximately 12,000 households and 22,000 persons in the panel. Questionnaires include labor market histories since leaving education. Labor market information is collected every year, and job characteristics data every few years. Full details are available at www .diw.de/english/sop/.

Funding Source: The German Science Foundation.

### 6. International Social Survey Program (ISSP)

This program is not one particular survey, but a network that brings together national surveys in many different countries using comparable methodologies and a set of core questions. For example, in the United States the data come from the General Social Survey (see above). The objective is to support international comparative research in the social sciences. Each year the core questions are supplemented by one or more additional modules. In both 1989 and 1997, the added module was on the theme of "work orientations." Identical questions permit comparisons for eight countries that were surveyed in both years.

Details are available at www.issp.org.

Funding Sources: Various national sources.

## 7. The 1997 Skills Survey

The Skills Survey undertaken in 1997 surveyed individuals in employment aged twenty to sixty in Britain. The focus of the survey was the skills that individuals use in their jobs. Some questions were designed to replicate identically those in SCELI and in Employment in Britain. The achieved sample was 2,467 cases. Stratified random sampling was used to select households from sectors drawn from the UK Postal Address File. One person was interviewed per household, chosen randomly from those that were found and eligible at each address. Interviews were face to face, and averaged forty minutes. Weights were calculated to correct for the differential probability of selection depending on the number of eligible persons at each address. Since the achieved sample slightly overrepresented women, compared with Labor Force Survey data, another small correction was also applied, reducing the weight for women and raising the weight for men so as to match national data. See Ashton et al. (1999a) for full details.

Funding Source: The UK Economic and Social Research Council.

## 8. The 2001 Skills Survey

The 2001 Skills Survey surveyed individuals in employment aged twenty to sixty in Britain. The focus of the survey was the skills that individuals use in their jobs. Many of the questions were designed to replicate identically those in SCELI, Employment in Britain and in the 1997 Skills Survey. The achieved sample was 4,470 cases. Interviews were face to face, and averaged fifty-three minutes. Stratified random sampling was used to select households from sectors drawn from the U.K. Postal Address File. One person was interviewed per household, chosen randomly from those that were found and eligible at each address. Weights were calculated to correct for the differential probability of selection depending on the number of eligible persons at each address. Since the achieved sample slightly overrepresented women, compared with Labor Force Survey data, another small correction was also applied, reducing the weight for women and raising the weight for men so as to match national data. See Felstead et al. (2002) for full details.

Funding Source: The U.K. Government's Department for Education and Skills.

## 9. The Social Change and Economic Life Initiative (SCELI)

The Social Change and Economic Life Initiative comprised several surveys concerned with work. For this book, only the subsample of 4,047 comprising those aged twenty to sixty and in employment was used. The sample was drawn randomly from six large areas of Britain, which were selected to give a range of social and industrial conditions with varying degrees of prosperity. Although the survey was not explicitly designed to generate a random representative cross-section of Britain in 1986, subsequent checks using the Labor Force Survey have confirmed that the achieved sample was representative of Britain as a whole in terms of sex, age, employment status, social class, and ethnicity (Green et al., 2000). The main method of data collection was through face-to-face interview. For more details, see Penn et al. (1994). Weights were applied to correct for the differential probability of selection depending on the number of eligible persons at each address. Since the achieved sample slightly overrepresented women, compared with Labor Force Survey data, a second small correction was also applied, reducing the weight for women and raising the weight for men so as to match national data.

Funding Source: The U.K. Economic and Social Research Council.

## 10. Working in Britain, 2000

Working in Britain, 2000 surveyed individuals in employment aged twenty to sixty. The face-to-face interviews, which took place between June 2000 and January 2001, focused on employment relations and employment contracts, and were designed as part of a larger research program entitled "The future of work." Some of the questions were designed to replicate identically those in Employment in Britain. The achieved sample was 2,466 cases. Stratified random sampling was used to select households, and one person was interviewed per household, chosen randomly from those who were found and eligible at each address. Weights were calculated to correct for the differential probability of selection depending on the number of eligible persons at each address, and to correct for differential response rates across certain socioeconomic groups. Full details can be obtained from the U.K. Data Archive: White, M. et al., "Changing Employment Relationships, Employment Contracts and the Future of Work, 2000" [computer file]. Colchester, Essex: U.K. Data Archive [distributor], 4 April 2003. SN: 4641. http://www.data-archive.ac.uk/.

Funding Source: The U.K. Economic and Social Research Council.

## 11. The Workplace Bargaining Survey, 1994

The Workplace Bargaining Survey surveyed 1,060 establishments with at least ten workers in Australia. The survey focused on employee relations practices. A manager in each establishment was interviewed face to face, while separately data on the employment structure of the establishment were collected in a written form, entitled the "demographics question-naire." A random sample of employees was drawn from the population in each establishment, and each employee was sent a self-completion questionnaire which was to be returned by post; 11,296 completed employee questionnaires were obtained. Weights were calculated that allow analysts to correct for differing probabilities of being selected into the sample from the national population of establishments.

Further details are available from the Social Science Data Archive at Australian National University at http:/ssda.anu.edu.au.

Funding Source: The Australian Government's Department of Industrial Relations.

## 12. The Workplace Employee Relations Survey, 1998 (WERS98)

WERS98 is a representative survey of establishments in Britain with at least ten workers. Its focus is employment practices and industrial relations, and how these have changed over time. There are three cross-sectional elements to the survey: a face-to-face interview with a manager, a face-to-face interview with a worker representative (where available), and a self-completion questionnaire distributed to a random selection of employees. Only the first two of these are utilized in this book. (There is also a panel survey comprising surviving respondents to WIRS90.) There were successful management interviews in 2,191 establishments (giving a response rate of 80 percent); among these, 918 successful worker representative interviews were conducted, also with a response rate of 80 percent of the establishments where an eligible worker representative was present. Weights are provided that allow analysts to correct for sample selection probabilities, including the deliberate oversampling of establishments in certain categories. Topics in the questionnaire include: management of the personnel function; recruitment and training; consultation and communication; employee representation; payment systems and pay determination; grievance, disciplinary, and disputes procedures; equal opportunities; flexibility; workplace performance; and employee attitudes to work.

Full details are available at www.niesr.ac.uk/niesr/wers98/.

Funding Sources: U.K. Government's Department of Trade and Industry; the Advisory, Conciliation and Arbitration Service; the Economic and Social Research Council; and the Policy Studies Institute (all U.K.).

## 13. The Workplace Industrial Relations Survey, 1990 (WIRS90)

WIRS90 is a representative survey of 2,061 establishments in Britain with at least twenty-five workers. It is part of a series of surveys devoted to charting the pattern and change of industrial relations practices. Other surveys took place in 1980, 1984, and 1998. WIRS90 differs from its successor, WERS98 (described above) in not covering establishments in the size range 10–24, and in not including a survey of employees. For details, see Millward et al. (1992).

Funding Source: U.K. Government's Department of Trade and Industry; the Advisory, Conciliation and Arbitration Service; the Economic and Social Research Council; and the Policy Studies Institute (all U.K.).

# Notes

Preface
The Quest for "More and Better Jobs"

1. See European Commission (2001a, 2003).
2. *Observer*, August 30, 1998.


Chapter One
Assessing Job Quality in the Affluent Economy

1. Galbraith (1958).
2. See, e.g., Cronin (1984: chap. 9). A qualification to this judgment is that there was little or no reduction in this era in the extent of discrimination against women in the workplace.
3. Of course, many social scientists questioned whether such conditions could be maintained: they felt temporarily vindicated when economic conditions took a turn for the worse in the 1970s.
4. Also new is the growth of a more quantitatively competent social science research community.
5. In future times, much more will be learned about the changes taking place in both the developed and developing worlds' workplaces, as long as high-quality representative surveys continue to be supported by research funders and as the quantitative competencies of the research communities are expanded.
6. A distinction should also be made between reports of the individual's job situation, such as task discretion, and reports of personal well-being or statements of personal attitudes.
7. Several analysts support the paradigm of the "high-performance work organization," but research to establish a connection between high-involvement human resource practices and profitable performance remains incomplete; the research does not establish this as the universal best method for profit-seeking employers (Wood, 1999).
8. Autor et al. (2003b) offer a further reason for indeterminacy in the skills of "jobs"; while maintaining that the introduction of computerized technologies has unavoidable task skill requirements, they suggest that management decisions may affect the way that tasks are packaged into jobs.
9. The limitations of determinism are sometimes nicely demonstrated by taking theories at their word, as does Richard Freeman in his provocative title "Are your wages set in Beijing?" (Freeman, 1995).
10. See Borjas (2002: chap. 6) for an exposition.
11. The unanimity embedded in this constraint limited greatly what economics could say about the redistribution of income. Subsequent welfare economics

became embroiled in the issue as to whether, if losers could in principle be compensated by winners, this also constituted a gain in society's welfare.

12. For a typical example, relevant to Canada, see Lowe (2000). Galenson (1991) takes work quality to be shown through the use of quality circles, labor-management participation teams, and humanization of work. The emphasis of Biagi (2002) for Italy and elsewhere in Europe, and for Suwa (2002) on Japan has been on forms of participation.

13. This application of Sen's valuation system to the domain of work may be the first. Yet, one of the advantages of the capabilities perspective is its applicability to types of social evaluation other than egalitarianism whence the concept arose (Sen, 1993).

14. Tensions such as these were evident in reported discussions of the conference "For a Better Quality of Work" held in September 2001 under the Belgian presidency.

15. See Marginson (1998) for a discussion of the relative merits of survey work for industrial relations research.

## Chapter Two
## The Quality of Work Life in the "Knowledge Economy"

1. Department of Trade and Industry and Department for Education and Skill (2001: para 1.20). See also Stiglitz (1999). Earlier in the United States, Reich (1991) had argued that there was a growing demand for "symbolic manipulators" or "analysts." The optimism of the British state is echoed in the rhetoric of many other governments.

2. In Britain, this contrasts with the earlier postwar era, when privilege could be preserved more readily through traditional class networks, with less emphasis on academic achievement.

3. An example of an early study to make this argument is Bound and Johnson (1992). Though a consensus remains that technological change is skill-biased, more recent studies now question whether the rise of inequality in the 1980s in the United States can be explained by an acceleration in high skills demand (Autor et al., 1998; Card and DiNardo, 2002).

4. See Borghans et al. (2001) for further discussion of issues surrounding skill measurement from the point of view of economics.

5. The increase probably understates the changes in requirements, because the survey assumes no change in requirements for those respondents who stay in the same job. Consistent projection beyond 1997 is not possible due to classification changes.

6. A validating study broadly confirmed this proposition (Green, 2000c); however, there are some respondents who are able to pick up jobs quickly because they are able or well-educated, so this indicator is not perfect on its own.

7. See notes to table 2.3.

8. However, rises in the three indicators can only partly be accounted for by shifts in the occupational composition of the workforce (Green et al., 2003b).

9. The needs of older people are a factor driving the demand for low-skilled services; demographic change suggests this source of demand will increase in the coming decades.

10. Aggregate balance does not preclude many individual workers experiencing skills mismatches.

## Chapter Three
## Late Twentieth-Century Trends in Work Effort

This chapter is a substantially revised and updated version of my paper, Green (2001); copywright held by Blackwell Publishing/London School of Economics.

1. See, e.g., IRS Employment Trends, November 1995, no. 596.

2. Typically, the "New Man" was thought to be unable to materialize in a long-hours culture (e.g., *Guardian* headlines "Work ethic stunts New Man," June 6, 1995, and "Myth of 'new man' hides blight on families," June 9, 1996). Pressure groups such as the Fawcett Society advocated family-friendly policies to reduce male working hours.

3. Interview with Robert Levine on BBC2, "How to Beat the Clock," January 1, 1999. See also Levine (1997). The program also noted the seeming paradox that the production of countless time-saving devices coincided with less, not more, time to spare. Commentator Jonathan Rowe confidently asserted that "economists do not understand time."

4. E.g., London Hazards Centre (1994).

5. *Times*, January 16, 1990:11.

6. *Financial Times*, December 8, 1993:10.

7. For example, the *Financial Times* ran articles covering workplace stress just four times in 1990, and just five in 1991, but in the following five years, the topic was featured thirteen, ten, thirteen, twenty-one, and seventeen times, respectively.

8. It should also be recalled that the rise of the stress industry does not itself prove or even closely track the intensification of work. The perception of stress, and its portrayal as an individual neurosis, is partly a reflection of the individualization of work relations.

9. Hours were much higher in the early nineteenth century, in the thick of the early industrial revolution; however, this was almost certainly the culmination of a historical increase in working hours compared with those of pre-industrial times.

10. From U.K. Labour Force Survey, authors' analysis. The figures include paid and unpaid overtime.

11. A related potential source of the public perception of a time squeeze is that, in both Britain and the United States, there has been a trend to increasing inequality of work hours (Green, 2001; Cappelli et al., 1997: 193–195).

12. These authors use this within-household complementarity of work hours to help resolve conflicting stories about the trend in the burden of work hours for U.S. workers, sparked by Juliet Schor's controversial study of the "overworked American" (Schor, 1991). A supplement to this interpretation is the finding for

both Britain and the United States of a certain polarization in working hours, with more working very long hours and more working part time.

13. Hyman et al. (2003) examine ways in which pressures in modern industries combine with changes in the family in forming the tangible and intangible intrusions of work into life outside the workplace.

14. Unfortunately, "work effort" is sometimes used to mean hours of work; its definition needs clarification in every discussion.

15. The substitutability of skill and effort also underpins the ambiguities in the concept of skill—as competencies or behavioral attributes. See chapter 2.

16. Wherever rise in productivity is attributable to increased work effort is described as an improvement in efficiency, this is to disregard the worker's well-being—in economist's terms, to assume that workers have a zero marginal disutility of effort.

17. Justification for using self-report data has been provided by Guest (1990).

18. See Green and McIntosh (1998).

19. A further method evinced a decade ago was to use the Percentage Utilization of Labor (Bennett and Smith-Gavine, 1987), an index derived from work study data. It is ironic that evidence derived from "scientific management" methods, so long derided in social scientific discourse as ideological and as a means to intensify work, should have been adduced as evidence of increased work intensity under early Thatcherism. However, the validity and reliability of this index have been subject to a convincing conceptual and practical critique (Guest, 1990; Nichols, 1991).

20. Episodes of work intensification are widely held to have characterized eras such as the beginnings of industrial capitalism, the spread of Taylorism in the United States, and Henry Ford's discovery of the assembly line.

21. Some 27 percent of employees did not answer the questions, mainly because they were not in employment five years previously.

22. For survey details, see Millward et al. (1992).

23. "Working harder, working longer: managers' attitudes to work revisited," IRS Employment Review, 600, January 1996.

24. These questions had been used in the 1970s in the U.S. Quality of Employment Surveys (Bielby and Bielby, 1988).

25. Readers struck by the magnitude of these changes may like to note that the frequency responses to most variables change by very much less between the two surveys, indicating continuity in most aspects of working life.

26. For survey details, see Cully et al. (1999).

27. For Employment in Britain, however, an additional factor ("the targets you are set") was included in the list. Thus, even though this factor is excluded from the Effort Pressure Sources Index, comparison of Employment in Britain with the other surveys is not strictly valid. The year 1992 is included in table 3.7 because the changes are sufficiently large to dwarf any likely errors induced by the slightly different response card.

28. Other than this sectoral difference, there is no evidence of significant polarization in the experience of work intensification: all occupational groups experienced work intensification and all experienced increased work pressures.

29. The rise in average effort for the EU 12 countries from 3.40 to 3.46 is statistically significant.

30. The rises in the importance of technical constraints on effort have been interpreted as a persistence of Fordist and Taylorist forms of organization (Cézard et al., 1992; Valeyre, 2002).

31. It is also possible to run a check on data reliability using inter-rater comparisons of effort intensification (see Green, 2001, 2004).

## Chapter Four
## Accounting for Work Intensification

1. In a conventional economic framework, rising wages could raise or lower the supply of work effort, depending on whether the "substitution effect," resulting from the increased opportunity cost of nonwork time, outweighed the "income effect," whereby workers choose more nonwork time as their income rose. In addition, rising wealth deriving from their ownership of physical or financial assets would also lead people to spend this affluence on more leisure time, that is, by giving up some of their work hours. The balance between these opposing forces favored declining hours for most of the twentieth century.

2. This result follows formally from a standard effort model such as Barzel (1973), except effort here is work intensity rather than the length of the working day.

3. Consumers assess their utility by seeing their current consumption in relation to past experience and to other people's consumption behavior in their reference group (Duesenberry, 1949).

4. Using a similar argument, Clark (1994) attributes an earlier episode of work intensification, during the industrial revolution in Britain, to increasing capital costs per worker; but he overlays the argument with the hypothesis that coercion through a system of factory discipline was necessary to "persuade" workers to give up their autonomy.

5. Management writer Stephen Roach deplores the irony that such labor-saving technology was unfortunately not making work life any better (Roach, 1996), something that Ricardo and Marx had noted in the nineteenth century.

6. For more on this reading of the literature, see Green (2004a).

7. Bain and Taylor (2000) also join others in contesting the validity of the "panopticon" as a metaphor for the modern or future workplace.

8. For further examples, see Adams et al. (2000) and Sinclair et al. (1996).

9. There is evidence that working longer hours (often associated with highly intensive work effort) leads to increased wages in the long term (Bell and Freeman, 2001; Francesconi, 2001).

10. Rents are the surpluses above the level at which other organizations or persons would be prepared to enter the market.

## Chapter Five
## The Workers' Discretion

1. In the view of neo-Marxian sociology, autonomy has been seen as a dimension of skill itself, not just something that is closely correlated with skill. As outlined by Attewell (1990), this conception arose from dual concerns about the erosion of both autonomy and skill in the craft worker, but it is more satisfactory to regard autonomy and skill as separate concepts.

2. The same cry has also obscured the generation of extremes of inequality.

3. Moreover, in a noncompetitive market where efficiency wages are paid, wages would be higher where monitoring is less frequent, which is likely to be the case where workers' discretion is greater.

4. Of course, economics does see choice as the means toward generating more efficient markets, and hence cheaper goods; in this sense, its value is "derived" from the value of the extra commodities made possible in a more competitive economy.

5. The analysis of the British trends draws on more detailed analyses given in Felstead et al. (2002) and in Gallie et al. (2004).

6. Analysis in OECD (2003: 46) shows change also from 1990 to 1996; however, the survey questions were changed in 1996, rendering this earlier comparison invalid.

7. The correlation coefficients in table 5.3 are all significantly different from zero at the 5 percent level. The pattern is unaltered if small cohorts are excluded, or if the correlations are weighted by cohort size. The pattern of a negative correlation between the change in discretion and the change in use of advanced technology is robust to the introduction of many other control variables in multivariate analyses.

8. Their concern with work-life quality underpins the commissioning of the survey series, from 1977 onward, from which figure 5.1 is drawn.


## Chapter Six
## The Wages of Nations

1. Galbraith's *Affluent Society* is just one book in a distinguished line, from Thorstein Veblen's *Theory of the Leisure Class* onward, of criticisms from within social science of the assumption of beneficial growth. Two recent contributions are Schor (1999) and Frey and Stutzer (2002a).

2. Formally, $\dot{w} \equiv \dot{o}_w + \dot{y} - \dot{p}$, where $\dot{w}$ is the rate of change of wages, and $\dot{o}_w$, $\dot{y}$, and $\dot{p}$ are the rates of change of the wage-bill share, GDP per capita, and the participation rate, respectively.

3. Note that the figures for the growth rates of wages cannot be taken as very precisely measured. There are no sampling distribution statistics with which to perform significance tests. This author's judgment, no more than an experienced guess, is that differences between countries' real wages growth of less than about 5 percent over three decades should be disregarded, as they could arise because of sampling errors and methodological changes within countries.

4. U.S. wages showed gains in the late 1990s (Mishel et al., 2003: chap. 2), but again ceased growing in the post-dotcom recession from 2001.

5. The estimated wage-growth rates differ from those underlying figure 6.1 since they refer to compensation per employee rather than hourly wages, to a different segment of the workforce, and to different time periods.

6. OECD (2003), table 1.A1.1.

7. OECD (2003), table 1.A1.3.

8. The deviations may also arise in part from methodological differences in the construction of the series. One difference worth noting is that the GDP series are from national accounts sources and use GDP price deflators, while real wages series have been deflated by consumer price indices.

9. In most other OECD countries the participation rate rose by a lesser amount, or fell a little (OECD, 2003, table 1.A1.3).

10. It should be remembered that the manufacturing sector employs a declining minority of the workforce in industrialized economies.

11. Kuznets (1955) identified demographic factors and the "dynamism of a growing and free economic society" (p.11) as underpinning the equalizing trend.

12. In the United States, this ratio was 4.33 in 2000 (Mishel et al., 2003: table 2.6).

13. Mishel et al. (2003): table 2.6.

14. For a given level of educational achievement, the decline is still more striking. For those with high school–level education, hourly pay fell from $13.36 in 1973 to $11.95 in 1995, recovering only to $12.81 by 2001 (Mishel et al., 2003: table 2.17).

15. For overviews, see Katz and Autor (1999) or Card and DiNardo (2002).

16. Of course, discrimination extends also to other spheres outside the labor market.


**Chapter Seven**
**The Workers' Risk**

1. Standing (1999) proposes a list of eight elements of job insecurity.

2. From OECD *Labour Force Statistics* 1981–2001 (Paris: OECD).

3. Even if the uncertainty has an upside, a wider distribution of potential future rewards, for a given expected value, is a reduction of welfare for the majority of workers who would normally be assumed to be risk averse.

4. For reviews see Burchell (1994); Wichert (2002); or Nolan et al. (2000).

5. Even in the mid-1990s the evidence for chronic uncertainty was thought by some critics to be somewhat fragile (Godard, 1998).

6. The concept of "present value" refers to the sum total of present and discounted future income.

7. This characterization makes the concept consistent with standard assumptions in risk analysis. Nickell et al. (2002) adopt a simpler interpretation of job insecurity which focuses only on the mean loss.

8. Formally, the "expected loss" is written as

$$(\Pi_{JL}) \times E(CJL) + (1 - \Pi_{JL}) \times \Pi_{WL} \times E(CWL)$$

where $\Pi_{JL}$ is the perceived probability of job loss; CJL is the cost of job loss in terms of foregone wages net of benefits while unemployed, and possibly lower wages in the next job; $\Pi_{WL}$ is the probability of wage loss in the same job; and CWL is the cost to the worker of such a wage reduction. The first expression is the expected reduction of value from job loss, while the second expression is the expected reduction of value resulting from wages being less than the norm.

9. Attitudes toward subjective measures of expected future events may be becoming more favorable; see, e.g., Manski and Straub (2000).

10. Unfortunately the scale was changed slightly in 1998 to: definitely, probably, probably not, definitely not. In fact this made no obvious break in the series. After 1998, the question and scale were both substantially altered, and comparisons are invalid.

11. Multidimensional instruments for measuring job insecurity have also been tested, but are not available in representative surveys over time.

12. The statistical relationship between perceived risk of job loss and local unemployment rates is positive as expected, but too loose to establish whether the perceived risk has fallen by less than could be predicted by that relationship.

13. The confidence intervals around the means in the General Social Survey remain relatively large, a consequence of its quite small sample size; this limitation restricts the researcher's ability to make definitive judgments about the trends.

14. Nevertheless, the generally heightened research focus on insecurity in the mid-1990s also reflects the temporary increase in average fears of unemployment.

15. This indicator is taken from a follow-up survey of the employers of some of the 2001 Skills Survey respondents, the Employer Perspectives Survey (Green et al., 2003a).

16. Homeworking (not shown in the table) had no significant correlation with insecurity. Taken together, these findings mean that it makes no sense to link the undifferentiated concept of "nonstandard" work to insecurity.

17. The above bivariate associations all remain significant in multivariate analyses of the determinants of job insecurity using ordinal probit estimation methods.

18. International comparisons of the level of security are not possible with this data, because responses are affected by translation and by national norms; only changes over time can be meaningfully compared.

19. Booth et al. (1999) present a contrasting picture of rising rates of displacement through layoffs from the 1950s through to the 1980s, based on respondents' memory of their work histories. But they note that the measure of layoffs is negatively correlated with aggregate unemployment, and this casts some doubt on the reliability of the measure of layoffs obtained through distant recall.

20. From Sly (2000), and *Labour Market Trends*, November 2002, table C.42.

21. From Swedish Work Environment Authority at www.av.se/statistik/eng/showdoceng.asp, which quotes original sources: Eurostat—ESAW (European Statistics on Accidents at Work); U.S.: Bureau of Labor Statistics—U.S. Department of Labor.

22. From Health and Safety Executive; see www.hse.gov.uk/statistics/xl/histrate.xls.

23. From Swedish Work Environment Authority; see "Fatalities in Occupational Accidents, Sweden 1955–2001." Available at www.av.se/statistik/eng/showdoceng.asp.

24. Stress caused by work intensification is likely to have deteriorated, given the evidence of chapter 3. Measurement difficulties preclude accurate confirmation of the trend in stress, but the U.K. Health and Safety Executive publishes "roughly comparable" self-reported data on illnesses caused or made worse by stress and related conditions at work. The rate doubled between 1990 and 2001. The problem is nontrivial. Approximately 563,000 people were found to be suffering from work-related stress, depression, or anxiety in 2001, with an average of twenty-nine working days lost for each of these people. See www.hse.gov.uk/statistics/causdis/stress.htm.

## Chapter Eight
## Workers' Well-Being

1. See Kuhn (1962).

2. See Fine and Leopold (1993): chap. 4, for a critique of utility theory from this perspective.

3. Examples are: Clark and Oswald (1996); Frey and Stutzer (2002a, 2002b).

4. Instruments for the measurement of more complex dimensions are now available, but have not been applied widely across countries or over a period of time.

5. This instrument was designed by Professor Peter Warr of Sheffield University, to whom thanks are due for advice on its expected properties. Cronbach's alpha is a suitable statistic for assessing how well a group of items captures a unidimensional latent construct, in this case work strain. For the samples in Employment in Britain and the 2001 Skills Survey, Cronbach's alpha was 0.78; this compares with a typical acceptability threshold of 0.70.

6. Another objection might be that overall job satisfaction data obscure different trends in satisfaction over specific domains of the job. In Britain, pay satisfaction showed a modest rise in the 1990s, which is unsurprising given rising wages. Yet, specific domains each only present a partial picture, while an overall measure is relevant to the overall evaluation of job quality.

7. Distinguishing cohort effects from age and period effects in panels requires contestable assumptions about identifying restrictions and are hard to demonstrate beyond all doubt.

8. For example, effort is only covered by a single question: "Ist ihre Arbeit mit hoher nervlicher Anspannung verbunden?"; for English-speaking users this question has been translated variously in different years as "Is your work mentally strenuous?" and "Does your work involve a high level of stress?"

9. This correlation coefficient just fails to reach statistical significance at conventional levels. However, the relevant coefficient *is* significant in the multivariate analysis discussed below (table A8.1).

10. Whether discretion moderates the impact of stressors on work strain—that is, interacts with the stressors—or simply offsets the impact equally at high

or low levels, is an issue that has been widely debated and investigated, without a consensual resolution.

11. This within-cohort decline is somewhat less than the decline reported and discussed in chapter 6 because as each cohort becomes older and more experienced at work, they would normally expect to acquire more control and influence: indeed, it is found that age is positively correlated with discretion (Gallie et al., 2004).

12. Green (2004b) reports a pooled cross-section analysis of the decline in job satisfaction, in which task discretion is the most important variable explaining the downward trend of job satisfaction. See also Green and Tsitsianis (2005).

13. The absences are indicated by the fact that, when entered into the multivariate analyses, the relevant variables had small and statistically insignificant coefficients.

## Chapter Nine
## Summary and Implications for Policy on the Quality of Work Life

The arguments and claims in this section are supported by the evidence reported earlier in this book; they are not separately referenced here.

1. Another reservation, almost impossible to measure, is that qualifications standards might be partially degraded over time.

2. American downsizing in the early 1990s, the "middle-class nightmare," was largely the occasion for churning workers, not for overall employment reductions (Baumol et al., 2003).

3. Moreover, a wider experience of some insecurity may be countered by a reduction in the depth of insecurity. Who is to say whether 20 percent of the workforce thinking that there is a one in four chance of job loss is worse, or better, than just 10 percent facing an even chance of job loss?

4. The idea that the computer age represents an era of unprecedented change (to which one must adapt) is itself part of a repressive ideology; it is also an insult to earlier generations of workers who passed through much more radical changes in their World War II experiences.

5. Bunting (2004: chap. 10) reports some successful cases of downshifting.

6. Health and safety regulation also stems from the hard-contested social imperative to treat workers as human beings, not as commodities with the costs and benefits which are implied in a market perspective. A social, rather than a market, value is thus placed upon the protection of workers.

7. Dual concern for both sides of the skills market is especially effective and necessary in rapidly developing countries which are simultaneously transforming their economies and their skill formation systems in parallel (Ashton et al., 1999b).

# References

Ackroyd, S., and S. Bolton (1999). "It is not Taylorism: Mechanisms of work intensification in the provision of gynaecological services in a NHS Hospital." *Work, Employment and Society* 13(2): 369–387.

Adams, A., E. Lugsden, J. Chase, S. Arber, and S. Bond (2000). "Skill-mix changes and work intensification in nursing." *Work, Employment and Society* 14(3): 541–555.

Adams, J. S. (1965). "Inequality in social exchange." *Advances in Experimental Social Psychology* 2: 267–299.

Akerlof, G. A. (1982). "Labor contracts as partial gift exchange." *Quarterly Journal of Economics* 97 (November): 543–569.

Allan, C., P. Brosnan, and P. Walsh (1999). "Human resource strategies, workplace reform and industrial restructuring in Australia and New Zealand." *International Journal of Human Resource Management* 10(5): 828–841.

Allen, J., and R. van der Velden (2001). "Educational mismatches versus skill mismatches: Effects on wages, job satisfaction, and on-the-job search." *Oxford Economic Papers* 53(3): 434–452.

Andrews, M., and R. Simmons (1995). "Are effort bargaining models consistent with the facts? An assessment of the early 1980s." *Economica* 62(August): 313–334.

Appelbaum, E., T. Bailey, P. Berg, and A. L. Kalleberg (2000). *Manufacturing Advantage: Why High-Performance Work Systems Pay Off.* Ithaca and London: Cornell University Press.

Appelbaum, E., A. Bernhardt, and R. J. Murnane (2003). "Low-Wage America: An Overview." In *Low-Wage America*, edited by E. Appelbaum, A. Bernhardt, and R. J. Murnane. New York: Russell Sage, 1–32.

Ashton, D., B. Davies, A. Felstead, and F. Green (1999a). *Work Skills in Britain.* Oxford, ESRC Centre for Skills, Knowledge and Economic Performance, Oxford and Warwick Universities.

Ashton, D., F. Green, D. James, and J. Sung (1999b). *Education and Training for Development in East Asia: The Political Economy of Skill Formation in East Asian Newly Industrialised Economies.* London and New York: Routledge.

Askenazy, P. (2002). *Réduire le temps de travail, flexibilité et intensification.* Conference Proceedings: "Organisation, Intensité du Travail, Qualité du Travail." Centre d'études de l'emploi, Cepremap, Paris, November 2002.

Atkinson, A. B. (2002). *Income Inequality in OECD Countries: Data and Explanations*, mimeo. Oxford: Nuffield College,

Attewell, P. (1990). "What Is Skill?" *Work and Occupations* 17(14): 422–448.

Auer, P., and S. Cazes (2000). "The resilience of the long-term employment relationship: Evidence from the industrialized countries." *International Labour Review* 139(4): 379–408.

Auer, P., and S. Cazes, eds. (2003). *Employment stability in an age of flexibility.* Geneva: International Labour Office.

Autor, D. H., L. F. Katz, and A. B. Krueger (1998). "Computing inequality: Have computers changed the labour market?" *Quarterly Journal of Economics* 113(4): 1169–1214.

Autor, D. H., F. Levy, and R. J. Murnane (2003a). "The skill content of recent technological change: An empirical exploration." *Quarterly Journal of Economics* 118(4): 1279–1334.

Autor, D. H., F. Levy, and R. Murnane (2003b). "Computer-based technological change and skill." In *Low-Wage America*, edited by E. Appelbaum, A. Bernhardt, and R. J. Murnane. New York: Russell Sage.

Bacon, N. (1999). "Union derecognition and the new human relations: A steel industry case study." *Work, Employment and Society* 13(1): 1–17.

Bain, P., and P. Taylor (2000). "Entrapped by the 'electronic panopticon'? Worker resistance in the call centre." *New Technology, Work and Employment* 15(1): 2–18.

Ballantine, J. W., Jr., and R. F. Ferguson (2003). "Plastic manufacturers: How competitive strategies and technology decision transformed jobs and increased pay disparity among rank-and-file workers." In *Low-Wage America*, edited by E. Appelbaum, A. Bernhardt, and R. J. Murnane. New York: Russell Sage.

Barro, R. J., and J. W. Lee (1996). "International measures of schooling years and schooling quality." *American Economic Review, Papers and Proceedings* 86(2): 218–223.

Barro, R. J., and J. W. Lee (2001). "International data on educational attainment: updates and implications." *Oxford Economic Papers* 53(3): 541–563.

Bartel, A. P., C. Ichniowski, and K. Shaw (2003). " 'New technology' and its impact on the jobs of high school educated workers: A look deep inside three manufacturing industries." In *Low-Wage America*, edited by E. Appelbaum, A. Bernhardt, and R. J. Murnane. New York: Russell Sage.

Barzel, Y. (1973). "The determination of daily hours and wages." *Quarterly Journal of Economics* 88: 220–238.

Batstone, E., and S. Gourlay (1986). *Unions, Unemployment and Innovation.* Oxford: Blackwell.

Baumol, W. J., A. S. Blinder, E. N. Wolff, and J. N. May (2003). *Downsizing in America: Causes, Consequences and Cures.* New York: Russell Sage.

Bell, L., and R. Freeman (2001). "The incentive for working hard: Explaining hours worked differences in the U.S. and Germany." *Labour Economics* 8(2): 181–202.

Bennett, A., and S. Smith-Gavine (1987). "The percentage utilisation of labour index (PUL)." In *Working Below Capacity*, edited by D. Bosworth and D. Heathfield. London: Macmillan.

Bernhardt, A., L. Dresser, and E. Hatton (2003). "The coffee pot wars: Unions and firm restructuring in the hotel industry." In *Low-Wage America*, edited by E. Appelbaum, A. Bernhardt, and R. J. Murnane. New York: Russell Sage.

Bernhardt, A., M. Morris, M. S. Handcock, and M. A. Scott (1999). "Trends in job instability and wages for young adult men." *Journal of Labor Economics* 17(4)(Part 2): S65–S90.

Biagi, M. (2002). "Quality of work, industrial relations and employee involvement in Europe: thinking the unthinkable. In *Quality of Work and Employee Involvement in Europe*. The Hague: Kluwer Law International.

Bielby, D. D., and Bielby, W. T. (1988). "She works hard for the money: Household responsibilities and the allocation of work effort." *American Journal of Sociology* 93(5): 1031–59.

Blanchflower, D., and A. Bryson (2003). *What Effect Do Unions Have on Wages Now and Would What Do Unions Do? Be Surprised?* Working Paper 9973, National Bureau of Economic Research.

Blanchflower, D. G., and A. J. Oswald (1999). *Well-Being, Insecurity and the Decline of American Job Satisfaction*, mimeo. University of Warwick, available at www.andrewoswald.com.

Blanchflower, D., and A. Oswald (2004). "Well-being over time in Britain and the USA." *Journal of Public Economics* 88: 1359–1386.

Blanchflower, D. G., A. J. Oswald, and A. Stutzer (2001). "Latent entrepreneurship across nations." *European Economic Review* 45(4–6): 680–691.

Blau, F. D., and L. M. Kahn (1996). "International differences in male wage inequality: Institutions versus market forces." *Journal of Political Economy* 104(4): 791–837.

Blau, F., and L. M. Kahn (1997). "Swimming upstream: Trends in the gender wage differential in the 1980s." *Journal of Labor Economics* 15(1): 1–42.

Blauner, R. (1964). *Alienation and Freedom. The Factory Worker and His Industry*. Chicago: University of Chicago Press.

Boggis, J. J. (2001). "The eradication of leisure." *New Technology, Work and Employment* 16(2): 118–129.

Booth, A., and D. Snower (1996). "Introduction: does the free market produce enough skills?" In *Acquiring Skills*, edited by A. Booth and D. Snower. Cambridge: Cambridge University Press.

Booth, A. L., J. J. Dolado, and J. Frank (2002). "Introduction: Symposium on temporary work." *Economic Journal* 112(480): F181–F188.

Booth, A. L., M. Francesconi, and C. Garcia-Serrano (1999). "Job tenure and job mobility in Britain." *Industrial and Labor Relations Review* 53(1): 43–70.

Borghans, L., and A. de Grip, eds. (2000). *The Over-Educated Worker? The Economics of Skill Utilisation*. Cheltenham: Edward Elgar.

Borghans, L., F. Green, and K. Mayhew (2001). "Skills measurement and economic analysis: an introduction." *Oxford Economic Papers* 53(3): 375–384.

Borjas, G. (1979). "Job satisfaction, wages and unions." *Journal of Human Resources* 14(1): 21–40.

Borjas, G. (2002). *Labor Economics*. 2nd ed. New York: McGraw-Hill.

Bound, E., and G. Johnson (1992). "Changes in the structure of wages in the 1980s: An evaluation of alternative explanations." *American Economic Review* 92: 371–392.

Braverman, H. (1974). *Labor and Monopoly Capital*. New York: Monthly Review Press.

Bresnahan, T. F. (1999). "Computerisation and wage dispersion: An analytical reinterpretation." *Economic Journal* 109(June): F390–F415.

Bresnahan, T. F., E. Brynjolfsson, and L. M. Hitt (2002). "Information technology, workplace organization and the demand for skilled labor: Firm-level evidence." *Quarterly Journal of Economics* 117(1): 339–376.

British Government (1992). *People, jobs, and opportunity.* Command Papers. Cm; 1810. London: HMSO.

Brown, P., and A. Hesketh (2004). *The Mismanagement of Talent.* Oxford: Oxford University Press.

Bruton, H., and D. Fairris (1999). "Work and development." *International Labour Review* 138(1): 5–30.

Bué, J., and C. Rougerie (1999). *L'organisation du travail: entre contrainte et initiative.* Premières Synthèses, DARES, 32.1, August.

Bulmer, M., K. Bales, and K. K. Sklar (1991). "The social survey in historical perspective." In *The Social Survey in Historical Perspective, 1880–1940*, edited by M. Bulmer, K. Bales, and K. K. Sklar. Cambridge: Cambridge University Press, 1–48.

Bunting, M. (2004). *Happy Slaves. How the Overwork Culture Is Ruling Our Lives.* London: Harper Collins.

Burchell, B. (1994). "The effects of labour market position, job insecurity and unemployment on psychological health." In *Social Change and the Experience of Unemployment*, edited by D. Gallie, C. Marsh, and C. Vogler. Oxford: Oxford University Press.

Burchell, B. (2002). "The prevalence and redistribution of job insecurity and work intensification." In *Job Insecurity and Work Intensification*, edited by B. Burchell, D. Lapido, and F. Wilkinson. London: Routledge, 61–76.

Burchell, B. J., D. Day, M. Hudson, D. Ladipo, R. Mankelow, J. Nolan, H. Reed, I. Wichert, and F. Wilkinson (1999). *Job Insecurity and Work Intensification; Flexibility and the Changing Boundaries of Work.* Joseph Rowntree Foundation report.

Burgess, J., and G. Strachan (1999). "The expansion in non-standard employment in Australia and the extension of employers' control." In *Global Trends in Flexible Employment*, edited by A. Felstead and N. Jewson. London: Macmillan, 121–140.

Burgess, S., and H. Rees (1996). "Job Tenure in Britain 1975–92." *Economic Journal* 106(March): 334–344.

Burgess, S., and H. Rees (1997). "Transient jobs and lifetime jobs: dualism in the British labour market." *Oxford Bulletin of Economics and Statistics* 59(3): 309–328.

Bynner, J. (1994). *Skills and Occupations. Analysis of Cohort Members' Self-Reported Skills in the Fifth Sweep of the National Child Development Study.* Social Statistics Research Unit, City University, London.

Campbell, D., A. Carruth, A. Dickerson, and F. Green (2001). "Job insecurity and wage outcomes in Britain." Discussion Paper 01/09, Department of Economics, University of Kent.

Cappelli, P. (1993). "Are skill requirements rising? Evidence from production and clerical jobs." *Industrial and Labor Relations Review* 46(3): 515–530.

Cappelli, P., L. Bassi, H. Katz, D. Knoke, P. Osterman, and M. Useem (1997). *Change at Work.* Oxford and New York: Oxford University Press.

Card, D., and J. E. DiNardo (2002). "Skill-biased technological change and rising wage inequality: Some problems and puzzles." *Journal of Labor Economics* 20(4): 733–783.

Caroli, E., and J. Van Reenen (2001). "Skill-biased organizational change? Evidence from a panel of British and French establishments." *Quarterly Journal of Economics* 116(4): 1449–1492.

Cartron, D., and M. Gollac (2002). *Fast work et maltravail.* Conference Proceedings: "Organisation, intensité du travail, qualité du travail." Centre d'études de l'emploi, Cepremap, Paris, November.

Castells, M. (1996). *The Information Age. Economy, Society and Culture. The Rise of the Network Society, Volume 1.* Oxford: Blackwell.

Cézard, M., F. Dussert, and M. Gollac (1992). "Taylor va au marché. Organisation du travail et informatique." *Travail et emploi* 54(4): 4–19.

Clark, A. E. (1998). *What Makes a Good Job? Evidence from OECD Countries.* Orléans, Centre de Recherche Sur l'Emploi at la Production, Document de Recherche 1998–26.

Clark, A. E., and A. J. Oswald (1994). "Unhappiness and unemployment." *Economic Journal* 104(May): 648–659.

Clark, A. E., and A. J. Oswald (1996). "Satisfaction and comparison income." *Journal of Public Economics* 61(3): 359–381.

Clark, A. E., Y. Georgellis, and P. Sanfey (1998). "Job satisfaction, wages and quits: Evidence from German panel data." *Research in Labor Economics* 17: 95–121.

Clark, G. (1994). "Factory Discipline." *Journal of Economic History* 54(1): 128–163.

Clarkberg, M. (1999). "The Time-Squeeze in American Families: From Causes to Solutions." Paper presented to Economic Policy Institute Symposium, Washington D.C., June 15, 1999.

Cooper, R. (1973). "How jobs motivate." *Personnel Review* 2(2): 4–12.

Cronin, J. E. (1984). *Labour and Society in Britain 1918–1979.* London: Batsford Academic and Educational.

Cully, M., S. Woodland, A. O'Reilly, and G. Dix (1999). *Britain At Work.* London: Routledge.

Davis, L. E. (1966). "The design of jobs." *Industrial Relations* 6: 21–45.

Deaton, A. (1985). "Panel data from a time-series of cross-sections." *Journal of Econometrics* 30: 109–126.

de Graaf, J., ed. (2003). *Take Back Your Time.* San Fancisco: Berrett-Koehler.

Delbridge, R., P. Turnbull, and B. Wilkinson (1992). "Pushing back the frontiers: Management control and work intensification under JIT/TQM factory regimes." *New Technology, Work and Employment* 7(2): 97–106.

Department of Trade and Industry and Department for Education and Skill (2001). *Opportunity for all in a world of change.* UK Government [Cm 5052]; http://www.dti.gov.uk/opportunityforall/pages/contents.html.

de Ruyter, A., and J. Burgess (2000). "Job security in Australia: broadening the analysis." *Australian Journal of Social Issues* 35(3): 215–234.

de Vries, M.F.R.K., and K. Balazs (1997). "The downside of downsizing." *Human Relations* 50(1): 11–50.

DfEE (2000). *Skills for All: Research Report from the National Skills Task Force.* Sudbury: UK Department for Education and Employment.

Dickens, R., and A. Manning (2003). "Minimum wage, minimum impact." In *The Labour Market Under New Labour*, edited by R. Dickens, P. Gregg, and J. Wadsworth. Basingstoke: Palgrave Macmillan.

Dobbin, F., and T. Boychuk (1999). "National employment systems and job autonomy: Why job autonomy is high in the Nordic countries and low in the United States, Canada and Australia." *Organization Studies* 20(2): 257–292.

Dolado, J. J., C. Garcia-Serrano, and J. F. Jimeno (2002). "Drawing lessons from the boom of temporary jobs in Spain." *Economic Journal* 112(480): F270–F296.

Duesenberry, J. S. (1949). *Income, Saving, and the Theory of Consumer Behavior.* Cambridge, Mass.: Harvard University Press.

Easterlin, R. (1995). "Will raising the incomes of all increase the happiness of all?" *Journal of Economic Behaviour and Organization* 27: 35–48.

Edwards, P., M. Collinson, and C. Rees (1998). "The determinants of employee responses to total quality management: Six case studies." *Organization Studies* 19(3): 449–475.

Edwards, P., and C. Whitston (1991). "Workers are working harder—effort and shop-floor relations in the 1980s." *British Journal of Industrial Relations* 29(4): 593–601.

Edwards, R. C. (1979). *Contested Terrain.* New York: Basic Books.

Edwards, R. C., D. M. Gordon, and M. Reich (1982). *Segmented Work, Divided Workers: The Historical Transformation of Labor in the United States.* Cambridge: Cambridge University Press.

Ehrenreich, B. (2002). *Nickel and Dimed.* London: Granta Books.

Elger, T. (1990). "Technical innovation and work reorganization in British manufacturing in the 1980s: continuity, intensification or transformation?" *Work, Employment and Society* 4(Special Issue, May): 67–102.

Elliott, L., and Atkinson, D. (1998). *The Age of Insecurity.* London and New York: Verso.

European Commission (2001a). *Employment and Social Policies: A Framework for Investing in Quality.* Communication from the Commission to the Council, the European Parliament, the Economic and Social Committee and the Committee of the Regions, COM(2001) 313 final.

European Commission (2001b). *Employment in Europe 2001.* European Commission, Directorate-General for Employment and Social Affairs.

European Commission (2002). *Employment in Europe 2002.* European Commission, Directorate-General for Employment and Social Affairs.

European Commission (2003). *Improving Quality in Work: A Review of Recent Progress.* Communication from the Commission to the Council, the European Parliament, the Economic and Social Committee and the Committee of the Regions, COM(2003) 728 final.

European Foundation for the Improvement of Living and Working Conditions (1992). *First European Survey on the Work Environment.* Luxembourg: Office for Official Publications of the European Communities.

European Foundation for the Improvement of Living and Working Conditions (1997). *Second European Survey on Working Conditions*. Luxembourg: Office for Official Publications of the European Communities.

European Foundation for the Improvement of Living and Working Conditions (2001). *Third European Survey on Working Conditions 2000*. Luxembourg: Office for Official Publications of the European Communities.

Fairris, D., and M. Brenner (2001). "Workplace transformation and the rise in cumulative trauma disorders: Is there a connection?" *Journal of Labor Research* 22(1): 15–28.

Farber, H. S. (1993). "The incidence and costs of job loss: 1982–91." *Brookings Papers on Economic Activity: Microeconomics* 1: 73–119.

Farber, H. S. (1995). *Are Lifetime Jobs Disappearing? Job Duration in the United States: 1973–1993*. Working Paper No. 5014, National Bureau of Economic Research.

Felstead, A., D. Gallie, and F. Green (2002). *Work Skills in Britain 1986–2001*. Nottingham: DfES Publications.

Felstead, A., N. Jewson, and S. Walters (2005). *Changing Places of Work*. Basingstoke: Palgrave Macmillan.

Fernie, S., and D. Metcalf (1998). *(Not) Hanging on the Telephone: Payments Systems in the New Sweatshops*. Centre for Economic Performance, London School of Economics.

Fine, B., and E. Leopold (1993). *The World of Consumption*. London: Routledge.

Foster, D., and P. Hoggett (1999). "Change in the benefits agency: Empowering the exhausted worker?" *Work, Employment and Society* 13(1): 19–39.

Fostin, N., and T. Lemieux (1997). "Institutional change and rising wage inequality: Is there a linkage?" *Journal of Economic Perspectives* 11(2): 75–96.

Francesconi, M. (2001). "Determinants and consequences of promotions in Britain." *Oxford Bulletin of Economics and Statistics* 63(3): 279–310.

Freeman, R. (1978). "Job satisfaction as an economic variable." *American Economic Review. Papers and Proceedings* 68(2): 135–141.

Freeman, R. (1995). "Are your wages set in Beijing?" *Journal of Economic Perspectives* 9(3): 15–32.

Freeman, R., and J. L. Medoff (1984). *What Do Unions Do?* New York: Basic Books.

Freeman, R., and R. Schettkatt (2001). "Skill compression, wage differentials and employment:Germany vs. the US." *Oxford Economic Papers* 53(3): 582–603.

Frey, B. S., and A. Stutzer (2002a). *Happiness and Economics: How the Economy and Institutions Affect Human Well-Being*. Princeton: Princeton University Press.

Frey, B. S., and A. Stutzer (2002b). "What can economists learn from happiness research?" *Journal of Economic Literature* 40(2): 402–425.

Friedman, A. L. (1977). *Industry and Labour*. London: Macmillan.

Friedmann, Georges (1946). *Machine et humanisme*. Paris: Gallimard.

Friedman, M., and R. Friedman (1980). *Free to Choose: A Personal Statement*. Harmondsworth: Penguin.

Galbraith, J. K. (1958). *The Affluent Society*. London: Hamish Hamilton.

Gale, H. F., T. R. Wojan, and J. C. Olmsted (2002). "Skills, flexible manufacturing technology, and work organization." *Industrial Relations* 41(1): 48–79.

Galenson, W. (1991). *New Trends in Employment Practices: An International Survey*. New York: Greenwood Press.

Gallie, D. (1996). "Skill, gender and the quality of employment." In *Changing Forms of Employment: Organisations, Skills and Gender*, edited by R. Crompton, D. Gallie, and K. Purcell. London: Routledge.

Gallie, D. (2002). *Work Intensification in Europe 1996–2001?* Conference on Work Intensification, Centre D'Etudes De L'Emploi, Paris, November 22–23.

Gallie, D. (2003). "The quality of working life: Is Scandinavia different?" *European Sociological Review* 19(1): 61–79.

Gallie, D., M. White, Y. Cheng, and M. Tomlinson (1998). *Restructuring the Employment Relationship*. Oxford: Clarendon Press.

Gallie, D., A. Felstead, and F. Green (2004). "Changing patterns of task discretion in Britain." *Work, Employment and Society* 18(2): 243–266.

Gardell, B. (1977). "Autonomy and participation at work." *Human Relations* 30(6): 515–533.

Gardner, J., and A. J. Oswald (2002). *What Has Been Happening to the Quality of Workers' Lives in Britain?* Mimeo. University of Warwick, Department of Economics.

Gera, S., W. L. Gu, and Z. X. Lin (2001). "Technology and the demand for skills in Canada: An industry-level analysis." *Canadian Journal of Economics* 34(1): 132–148.

Giret, J. F., and J. M. Masjuan (1999). "The diffusion of qualifications in the Spanish labour market." *Journal of Education and Work* 12(2): 179–199.

Glyn, A. (2001). *Inequalities of Employment and Wages in OECD Countries*, mimeo. University of Oxford, Department of Economics.

Godard, J. (1998). "Review of *Change at Work* by P. Cappelli, L. Basi, H. Katz, D.Knoke, P. Osterman, and M.Useem," *British Journal of Industrial Relations* 36(3): 501–503.

Godard, John (2001). "The transformation of work and high performance? The implications of alternative work practices for the experience and outcomes of work." *Industrial and Labor Relations Review* 54(4): 776–805.

Goldthorpe, J. H. (1969). *The Affluent Worker in the Class Structure*. Cambridge: Cambridge University Press.

Goldthorpe, J. H., D. Lockwood, F. Bechhofer, and J. Platt (1968). *The Affluent Worker: Industrial Attitudes and Behaviour*. Cambridge: Cambridge University Press.

Goos, M., and A. Manning (2003). *Good jobs and bad jobs. Changes in UK employment, 1975–2000*. Discussion Paper, London School of Economics, Centre for Economic Performance.

Gottschalk, P., and R. Moffitt (1999). "Changes in job instability and insecurity using monthly survey data." *Journal of Labor Economics* 17(4)(Part 2): S91–S126.

Green, F. (1979). "The neo-fisherian theories of saving: A theoretical and empirical evaluation." Ph.D. thesis, Economics, Birkbeck College, London University.

Green, F. (2000a). *Why has work effort become more intense? Conjectures and evidence about effort-biased technical change and other stories.* Discussion Paper 2000/3, Department of Economics, University of Kent.

Green, F. (2000b). "The impact of company human resource policies on social skills: Implications for training sponsorship, quit rates and efficiency wages." *Scottish Journal of Political Economy* 47(3): 251–272.

Green, F. (2000c). An *investigation into the interpretation of questions about broad skill levels in the Skills Survey.* Report presented to the UK Government, Department for Education and Employment, June.

Green, F. (2001). "It's been a hard day's night: The concentration and intensification of work in late 20th century Britain." *British Journal of Industrial Relations* 39(1): 53–80.

Green, F. (2003). "The demands of work." In *The Labour Market Under New Labour. The State of Working Britain 2003*, edited by R. Dickens, P. Gregg, and J. Wadsworth. Basingstoke: Palgrave Macmillan, 137–149.

Green, F. (2004a). "Why has work effort become more intense?" *Industrial Relations* 43(October): 709–741.

Green, F. (2004b). "Work intensification, discretion and the decline in well-being at work." *Eastern Economic Journal* 30(4): 615–625.

Green, F., D. Ashton, B. Burchell, B. Davies, and A. Felstead (2000). Are British workers getting more skilled? In *The Over-Educated Worker? The Economics of Skill Utilisation*, edited by L. Borghans and A. de Grip. Cheltenham: Edward Elgar.

Green, F., D. Ashton, and A. Felstead (2001). "Estimating the determinants of supply of computing, problem-solving, communication, social and teamworking skills." *Oxford Economic Papers* 53(3): 406–433.

Green, F., B. Burchell, and A. Felstead (2000). "Job insecurity and the difficulty of regaining employment: an empirical study of unemployment expectations." *Oxford Bulletin of Economics and Statistics* 62 (December): 855– 884.

Green, F., A. Felstead, and D. Gallie (2003). "Computers and the changing skill-intensity of jobs." *Applied Economics* 35(14): 1561–1576.

Green, F., K. Mayhew, and E. Molloy (2003). *Employer Perspectives Survey 2002.* Sheffield: Department for Education and Skills.

Green, F., and S. McIntosh (1998). "Union power, cost of job loss, and workers' effort." *Industrial & Labor Relations Review* 51(3): 363–383.

Green, F., and S. McIntosh (2001). "The intensification of work in Europe." *Labour Economics* 8(2): 291–308.

Green, F., and S. McIntosh (2002). *Is there a Genuine Underutilisation of Skills Amongst the Over-qualified?* Discussion Paper, Centre for Skills, Knowledge and Organisational Performance, Oxford and Warwick Universities.

Green, F., S. McIntosh, and A. Vignoles (2002). "The utilization of education and skills. Evidence from Britain." *The Manchester School* 70(6): 792–811.

Green, F., and N. Tsitsianis (2005). "An investigation of national trends in job satisfaction in Britain and Germany." *British Journal of Industrial Relations* 43(3), forthcoming.

Greenan, N. (2003). "Organisational change, technology, employment and skills: an empirical study of French manufacturing." *Cambridge Journal of Economics* 27(2): 287–316.

Gregg, P., K. Hansen, and J. Wadsworth (1999). "The rise of the workless household." In *The State of Working Britain*, edited by P. Gregg and J. Wadsworth. Manchester: Manchester University Press, 75–89.

Gregg, P., S. Machin, and S. Szymanski (1993). "The disappearing relationship between directors' pay and corporate performance." *British Journal of Industrial Relations* 31(1): 1–9.

Gregg, P., and J. Wadsworth (1995). "A short history of labour turnover, job tenure, and job security, 1975–93." *Oxford Review of Economic Policy* 11(1): 73–90.

Gregg, P., and J. Wadsworth (1999). "Job Tenure, 1975–98." In *The State of Working Britain*, edited by P. Gregg and J. Wadsworth. Manchester: Manchester University Press.

Gregory, M., B. Zissimos, and C. Greenhalgh (2001). "Jobs for the skilled: How technology, trade, and domestic demand changed the structure of UK employment, 1979–90." *Oxford Economic Papers* 53(1): 20–46.

Grimshaw, D., F.-L. Cooke, I. Grugulis, and S. Vincent (2002). "New technology and changing organisational forms: implications for managerial control and skills." *New Technology, Work and Employment* 17(3): 186–203.

Grimshaw, D., and J. Rubery (2001). *The Gender Pay Gap: A Research Review.* Manchester: Equal Opportunities Commission.

Guest, D. (1990). "Have British workers been working harder in Thatcher's Britain? A reconsideration of the concept of effort." *British Journal of Industrial Relations* 28(3): 293–312.

Hall, P., and D. Soskice (2001). "An introduction to varieties of capitalism." In *Varieties of Capitalism*, by P. Hall and D. Soskice. Oxford: Oxford University Press.

Hamermesh, D. (1977). "Economic aspects of job satisfaction." In *Essays in Labor Market Analysis*, edited by O. Ashenfelter and W. Oates. New York: Wiley.

Hamermesh, D. S. (2001). "The changing distribution of job satisfaction." *Journal of Human Resources* 36(1): 1–30.

Handel, M. (2000). *Trends in Direct Measures of Job Skill Requirements.* Working Paper No. 301, Annandale-On-Hudson, Jerome Levy Economics Institute.

Handel, M. J. (2005). "Trends in perceived job quality, 1989 to 1998." *Work and Occupations* 32(1): 66–94.

Hartog, J. (2000). "Over-education and earnings: Where are we, where should we go?" *Economics of Education Review* 19: 131–147.

Haskel, J., and Y. Heden (1999). "Computers and the demand for skilled labour: industry- and establishment-level panel evidence for the UK." *Economic Journal* 109 (March): C68–C79.

Hasluck C., T. Hogarth, G. Pierre, D. Vincent, and M. Winterbottom (2000). *Work-Life Balance 2000: Results from the Baseline Study: Summary.* London: Department for Education and Employment.

Hausman, D. M., and M. S. McPherson (1996). *Economic Analysis and Moral Philosophy.* Cambridge: Cambridge University Press.

Head, S. (2003). *The New Ruthless Economy*. New York: Oxford University Press.

Heery, E., and J. Salmon (2000). "The insecurity thesis." In *The Insecure Workforce*, by E. Heery and J. Salmon. London: Routledge.

Herzberg, F., B. Mausner, and B. Snyderman (1957). *The Motivation to Work*. New York: Wiley.

Hjalager, A. M. (1999). "Technology domains and manpower choice in the restaurant sector." *New Technology, Work and Employment* 14(1): 62–74.

Hollanders, H., and B. ter Weel (2002). "Technology, knowledge spillovers and changes in employment structure: evidence from six OECD countries." *Labour Economics* 9(5): 579–599.

Holzer, H. J. (1998). "Employer skill demands and labor market outcomes of blacks and women." *Industrial and Labor Relations Review* 52(1): 82–98.

Howell, D., and E. Wolff (1991). "Trends in the growth and distribution of skill in the U.S. workplace, 1960–1985." *Industrial and Labor Relations Review* 44(3): 481–501.

Huselid, M. (1995). "The impact of human resource management practices on turnover, productivity and corporate financial performance." *Academy of Management Journal* 38(5): 635–672.

Huselid, M., and B. Becker (1996). "Methodological issues in cross-sectional and panel estimates of the human resource-firm performance link." *Industrial Relations* 35(3): 400–422.

Hyman, J., C. Baldry, D. Scholarios, and D. Bunzel (2003). "Work-Life Imbalance in Call Centres and Software." *British Journal of Industrial Relations* 41(2): 215–240.

Ichniowski, C., T. A. Kochan, D. Levine, C. Olson, and G. Strauss (1996). "What Works At Work: Overview and Assessment." *Industrial Relations* 35(3): 299–333.

International Labor Office (2001). *Reducing the Decent Work Deficit: A Global Challenge*. Geneva: Internation Labour Office.

Jacobs, J. A., and K. Gerson (2001). "Overworked individuals or overworked families?" *Work and Occupations* 28(1): 40–63.

Jacobsen, L., R. Lalonde, and D. Sullivan (1993). "Earnings losses of displaced workers." *American Economic Review* 83 (September): 685–709.

Jaeger, D. A., and A. H. Stevens (1999). "Is job stability in the United States falling? Reconciling trends in the current population survey and panel study of income dynamics." *Journal of Labor Economics* 17(4)(Part 2): S1–S28.

Jencks, C., L. Perman, and L. Rainwater (1988). "What is a good job? A new measure of labor-market success." *American Journal of Sociology* 93 (May): 1322–1357.

Johnson, G. D., C. Formichella, J. S. Thomas, D. Bhaumik, F. Degruy, and C. A. Riordan (1998). "Stress and distress among Gulf of Mexico shrimp fishermen." *Human Organization* 57(4): 404–413.

Jürges, H. (2003). "Age, cohort, and the slump in job satisfaction among West German workers." *Labour* 17(4): 489–518.

Kalleberg, A. (forthcoming). *Good Jobs, Bad Jobs: Changing Work and Workers in America*. New York: Russell Sage.

Kanter, R. M. (1989). *When Giants Learn to Dance*. London: Unwin Hyman Limited.

Karasek, R. A. (1979). "Job demands, job decision latitude, and mental strain: Implications for job redesign." *Administrative Science Quarterly* 24: 285–308.

Karesek, R., and T. Theorell (1990). *Healthy Work. Stress, Productivity and the Reconstruction of Work Life*. New York: Basic Books.

Katz, L. F., and D. H. Autor (1999). "Changes in the wage structure and earnings inequality." In *Handbook of Labor Economics*, edited by O. Ashenfelter and D. Card. Amsterdam: North-Holland 3, 1463–1555.

Keep, E., and K. Mayhew (1999). "The assessment: Knowledge, skills, and competitiveness." *Oxford Review of Economic Policy* 15(1): 1–15.

Kelly, J. E. (1982). "Economic and structural analysis of job redesign." In *Autonomy and Control at the Workplace*, edited by J. E. Kelly and C. W. Clegg. London: Croom Helm.

Knights, D., and D. McCabe (1998). " 'The times they are a changin?' transformative organizational innvoations in financial services in the UK." *International Journal of Human Resource Management* 9(1): 168–184.

Kochan, T., H. Katz, and R. McKenzie (1986). *The Transformation of American Industrial Relations*. New York: Basic Books.

Krueger, A. B. (1993). "How computers have changed the wage structure—evidence from microdata, 1984–1989." *Quarterly Journal of Economics* 108(1): 33–60.

Kuhn, T. (1962). *The Structure of Scientific Revolutions*. London: University of Chicago Press.

Kuznets, S. (1955). "Economic Growth and Income Inequality." *American Economic Review* 45(1): 1–29.

Ladipo, D., and F. Wilkinson (2002). "More pressure, less protection." In *Job Insecurity and Work Intensification*, edited by B. Burchell, D. Lapido, and F. Wilkinson. London: Routledge.

Lankshear, G., P. Cook, D. Mason, S. Coates, and G. Button (2001). "Call centre employees' responses to electronic monitoring: Some research findings." *Work, Employment and Society* 15(3): 595–605.

Lavoie, M., R. Roy, and P. Therrien (2003). "A growing trend toward knowledge work in Canada." *Research Policy* 32(5): 827–844.

Lazear, Edward P. (2000). "Performance pay and productivity." *American Economic Review* 90(5): 1346–1361.

Lee, D. S. (1999). "Wage inequality in the U.S. during the 1980s: Rising dispersion or falling minimum wage?" *Quarterly Journal of Economics* 114(3): 941–1023.

Lehto, A.-M., and H. Sutela (1999). *Efficient, More Efficient, Exhausted*. Helsinki: Statistics Finland.

Levine, R. (1997). *A Geography of Time*. New York: Basic Books.

Levy, F., and R. J. Murnane (2004). *The New Division Of Labor*. New York and Oxford: Russell Sage Foundation and Princeton University Press.

Levy-Garboua, L., and C. Montmarquette (2004). "Reported job satisfaction: What does it mean?" *Journal of Socio-Economics* 33(2): 135–151.

Lloyd, C. (1997). "Microelectronics in the clothing industry: Firm strategy and the skills debate." *New Technology, Work and Employment* 12(1): 36–47.

London Hazards Centre (1994). *Hard Labour*. London: London Hazards Centre Trust.

Lowe, G. S. (2000). *The Quality of Work: A People-Centred Agenda*. Ontario: Oxford University Press.

Machin, S., and J. Van Reenen (1998). "Technology and changes in skill structure: Evidence from seven OECD countries." *Quarterly Journal of Economics* 113(4): 1215–1244.

Madison, A. (1982). *Phases of Capitalist Development*. Oxford: Oxford University Press.

Mangan, J. (2000). *Workers Without Traditional Employment*. Cheltenham: Edward Elgar.

Mankelow, R. (2002). "The organisational costs of job insecurity and work intensification." In *Job Insecurity and Work Intensification*, edited by B. Burchell, D. Lapido, and F. Wilkinson. London: Routledge, 137–153.

Manski, C. F., and J. D. Straub (2000). "Worker perceptions of job insecurity in the mid-1990s." *Journal of Human Resources* 35(3): 447–479.

Marginson, P. (1998). "The Survey tradition in British industrial relations research: An assessment of the contribution of large-scale workplace and enterprise surveys." *British Journal of Industrial Relations* 36(3): 361–388.

Mason, G., B. van Ark, and K. Wagner (1994). "Productivity, product quality and workforce skills: Food processing in four European countries." *National Institute Economic Review*(February): 62–82.

Millward, N., A. Bryson, and J. Forth (2000). *All Change At Work?* London: Routledge.

Millward, N., M. Stevens, D. Smart, and W. R. Hawes (1992). *Workplace Industrial Relations in Transition*. Aldershot: Dartmouth Publishing.

Miozzo, M., and M. Ramirez (2003). "Services innovation and the transformation of work: The case of UK telecommunications." *New Technology, Work and Employment* 18(1): 62–79.

Mishel, L., J. Bernstein, and H. Boushey (2003). *The State of Working America 2002/2003*. New York: Cornell University Press.

Morehead, A., M. Steele, M. Alexander, K. Stephen, and L. Duffin (1997). *Changes at Work: The 1995 Australian Workplace Industrial Relations Survey*. Sydney: Longman.

Mowday, R.T., L.W. Porter, and R. M. Steers (1982). *Organizational Linkages: The Psychology of Commitment, Absenteeism and Turnover*. San Diego: Academic Press.

Nelson, M. K., and J. Smith (1999). *Working Hard and Making Do*. London: University of California Press.

Neumark, D., D. Polsky, and D. Hansen (1999). "Has job stability declined yet? New evidence for the 1990s." *Journal of Labor Economics* 17(4)(Part 2): S29–S65.

Nichols, T. (1991). "Labour intensification, work injuries and the measurement of percentage utilization of labour (PUL)." *British Journal of Industrial Relations* 29(4): 569–601.

Nichols, T. (1997). *The Sociology of Industrial Injury*. London: Mansell.

Nickell, S., P. Jones, and G. Quintini (2002). "A picture of job insecurity facing British men." *Economic Journal* 112(476): 1–27.

Nolan, P. (1989). "The productivity miracle?" In *The Restructuring of the UK Economy*, edited by F. Green. Hemel Hempstead: Harvester Wheatsheaf.

Nolan, J. P., I. C. Wichert, and B. J. Burchell (2000). "Job insecurity, psychological well-being and family life." In *The Insecure Workforce*, edited by E. Heery and J. Salmon. London: Routledge.

Oaxaca, R. (1973). "Male-female wage differentials in urban labor market." *International Economic Review* 14: 693–709.

OECD (1994). *The OECD Jobs Study: Evidence and Explanations. Part 2, Adjustment Potential of the Labour Market.* Paris: OECD.

OECD (2001). *OECD Employment Outlook 2001.* Paris: OECD.

OECD (2002). *OECD Employment Outlook 2002.* Paris: OECD.

OECD (2003). *OECD Economic Outlook 73.* Paris: OECD.

OECD (2004). *OECD Employment Outlook 2004.* Paris: OECD.

OECD, Human Resources Development Canada, and Statistics Canada (1997). *Literacy Skills for the Knowledge Society—Further Results from the International Adult Literacy Survey.* Paris: OECD.

Orwell, G. (1940). *Down and Out in Paris and London.* Harmondsworth: Penguin and Secker and Warburg.

Osterman, P. (1999). *Securing Prosperity.* Princeton and Oxford: Princeton University Press.

Osterman, P. (2000). "Work reorganization in an era of restructuring: Trends in diffusion and effect on employee welfare." *Industrial and Labor Relations Review* 53(2): 179–196.

Oswald, A. (1997). "Happiness and economic performance." *Economic Journal* 107: 1815–1831.

Pailhé, A. (2002). *L'Intensité du travail s'allège t'elle avec l'age.* Conference Proceedings: Organisation, Intensité du Travail, Qualité du Travail. Centre d'études de l'emploi, Cepremap, Paris, November.

Penn, R., M. Rose, and J. Rubery, eds. (1994). *Skill and Occupational Change.* Oxford: Oxford University Press.

Peters, T. (1988). *Thriving on Chaos: Handbook for a Management Revolution.* London: Macmillan.

Polsky, D. (1999). "Changing consequences of job separation in the United States." *Industrial and Labor Relations Review* 52(4): 565–580.

Reeder, E. (1989). "The fast food industry." In *Technology and the Labour Process,* edited by E. Willis. Sydney: Allen and Unwin.

Reich, R. B. (1991). *The Work of Nations: Preparing Ourselves for 21st Century Capitalism.* New York: Knopf.

Rifkin, J. (1995). *The End of Work.* New York: Tarcher/Putnam Books.

Roach, Stephen S. (1996). "The hollow ring of the productivity revival." *Harvard Business Review* 74(6): 81–86.

Robinson, H. (2003). "Gender and labour market performance in the recovery." In *The Labour Market Under New Labour. The State of Working Britain 2003*, edited by R. Dickens, P. Gregg, and J. Wadsworth. Basingstoke: Palgrave Macmillan, 232–247.

Robinson, J. P. (1991). "Trends in free time: A cross-sectional comparative analysis for seven industrial countries 1961–1985." In *The Changing Use of Time: Report from an International Workshop*. Shankill: European Foundation for the Improvement of Living and Working Conditions.

Rubery, J., and D. Grimshaw (2001). "ICTs and employment: The problem of job quality." *International Labour Review* 140(2): 165–192.

Schmidt, J. (2001). "Did job quality deteriorate in the 1980s and 1990s?" In *Sourcebook of Labor Markets: Evolving Structures and Processes*, edited by I. Berg and A. L. Kalleberg. New York: Kluwer Academic, 387–407.

Schmidt, S. R. (1999). "Long-run trends in workers' beliefs about their own job security: Evidence from the General Social Survey." *Journal of Labor Economics* 17(4)(Part 2): S127–S141.

Schor, J. B. (1991). *The Overworked American*. New York: Basic Books.

Schor, J. B. (1999). *The Overspent American: Why We Want What We Don't Need*. New York: Perennial.

Sen, A. (1987). *On Ethics and Economics*. Oxford: Blackwell.

Sen, A. (1993). "Capability and well-being". In *The Quality of Life*, edited by M. Nussbaum and A. Sen. Oxford: Clarendon Press.

Sewell, G., and B. Wilkinson (1992). "Someone to watch over me: Surveillance, discipline and the just-in-time labour process." *Sociology* 26: 271–289.

Shapiro, C., and J. E. Stiglitz (1984). "Equilibrium unemployment as a worker discipline device." *American Economic Review* 74(3): 433–444.

Sinclair, J., M. Ironside, and R. Seifert (1996). "Classroom struggle: Market-oriented education reforms and their impact on the teacher labour process." *Work, Employment and Society* 10(4): 641–661.

Sly, F. (2000). "Redundancies: Enhancing the coherence of Labour Force Survey estimates." *Labour Market Trends* (May): 225–229.

Sousa-Poza, A., and Sousa-Poza, A. A. (2000). "Well-being at work: A cross-national analysis of the levels and determinants of job satisfaction." *Journal of Socioeconomics* 29(6): 517–538.

Spector, P. E. (1997). *Job Satisfaction: Application, Assessment, Causes, and Consequences*. London: Sage.

Standing, G. (1999). *Global Labour Flexibility: Seeking Distributive justice*. Basingstoke: Macmillan.

Steedman, Hilary, and A. Murray. (2001). "Skill profiles of France, Germany, the Netherlands, Portugal, Sweden and the UK." *European Journal for Vocational Training* 1 (22).

Stevens, M. (1999). "Human capital theory and UK vocational training policy." *Oxford Review of Economic Policy* 15(1): 16–32.

Stiglitz, J. E. (1999). *Knowledge in the Modern Economy*. Conference Proceedings, *The Economics of the Knowledge Driven Economy*, London: Department for Trade and Industry and the Centre for Economic Policy Research.

Suwa, Y. (2002). "Employee involvement in Japan: Can the Japanese-style information/consultation system survive? In *Quality of Work and Employee Involvement in Europe*, edited by M. Biagi. The Hague: Kluwer Law International, 101–115.

Taplin, I. M. (1995). "Flexible production, rigid jobs—lessons from the clothing industry." *Work and Occupations* 22(4): 412–438.

Taylor, M. P. (1996). "Earnings, independence or unemployment: Why become self-employed?" *Oxford Bulletin of Economics and Statistics* 58(2):253–266.

Thelen, K. (2001). "Varieties of labor politics in the developed democracies." In *Varieties of Capitalism*, edited by P. Hall and D. Soskice. Oxford: Oxford University Press.

Timmons, S. (2003). "A failed panopticon: Surveillance of nursing practice via new technology." *New Technology, Work and Employment* 18(2): 143–153.

Tomaney, J. (1990). "The reality of workplace flexibility." *Capital and Class* 40(Spring): 29–60.

Toynbee, P. (2003). *Hard Work. Life in Low-Pay Britain*. London: Bloomsbury.

Valeyre, A. (2001). "Le travail industriel sous la pressions du temps." *Travail et emploi* 86: 127–149.

Valeyre, A. (2002). *Les Formes d'intensification du travail industriel et leurs déterminants*. Conference Proceedings: "Organisation, Intensité du Travail, Qualité du Travail," Centre d'études de l'emploi, Cepremap, Paris, November.

Valletta, R. G. (1999). "Declining job security." *Journal of Labor Economics* 17(4)(Part 2): S170–S197.

van den Berg, P. T., and R. Schalk (1997). "Type A behavior, well-being, work overload and role-related stress in information work." *Journal of Social Behavior and Personality* 12(1): 175–187.

Veblen, T. (1899) *The Theory of the Leisure Class*. New York: Macmillan.

Walton, R. E. (1985). "From control to commitment in the workplace." *Harvard Business Review* 85: 77–84.

Warr, P. (1987). *Work, Unemployment, and Mental Health*. Oxford: Oxford University Press.

Wazir, Burhan. 1999. "Life at the end of the line." *The Observer*, Nov. 21, 1999.

Weeks, J. (1999). "Wages, employment and workers' rights in Latin America, 1970–98." *International Labour Review* 138(2): 151–168.

Wichert, I. (2002). "Job insecurity and work intensification: The effects on health and well-being." In *Job Insecurity and Work Intensification*, edited by B. Burchell, D. Lapido, and F. Wilkinson. London: Routledge, 92–111.

Wolff, E. N. (2003). "Skills and changing comparative advantage." *Review of Economics and Statistics* 85(1): 77–93.

Wood, A. (1995). "How trade hurt unskilled workers." *Journal of Economic Perspectives* 9: 57–80.

Wood, S., ed. (1982). *The Degradation of Labour?* London: Hutchinson.

Wood, S., ed. (1989). *The Transformation of Work?: Skill, Flexibility and the Labour Process*. London: Unwin Hyman.

Wood, S. (1999). "Human resource management and performance." *International Journal of Management Reviews* 1(4): 367–413.

Wright, C., and J. Lund (1998). "Under the clock: Trade union responses to computerised control in U.S. and Australian grocery warehousing." *New Technology, Work and Employment* 13(1): 3–15.

# Index of Names

# General Index

absenteeism, 78, 86, 152, 166, 178, 180
accidents, xvii, xix, 18, 125, 144, 145, 148, 150, 179
affluent economy, xv, 6, 8, 84, 99
affluent society, 2, 151, 198
alienation, 2, 12, 26, 94, 98, 100
appraisal, 57, 58, 77, 90, 91
assembly line, xvii, 57, 59, 196
autonomy, xix, 2, 12, 15, 17, 19, 28, 42, 71, 79, 83, 94, 97, 98, 101, 110, 150, 161, 164, 166, 197, 198. *See also* task dicretion; decision latitude

British government, 4, 24
British Household Panel Study (BHPS), 133, 154, 160, 161, 185

call center, 70, 77, 174
capability, 13–15, 28, 70, 78
capitalism, varieties of, 101
collective bargaining, 87, 88, 179
commitment, of workers, 7, 41, 74, 79, 81, 83, 84, 87, 100, 174, 178
communication skills, 6, 35, 39, 172
compensating differentials, 9, 15, 16, 63, 68, 95, 96, 110
competition, international, xvi, 6, 7, 9, 79, 127–129, 138, 149
Composite Skill Index, 33, 34, 38, 104, 169
computers: and skill, 37–43, 193; and work effort, 70, 72, 73, 76, 91–93, 108, 174
consumerism, 68, 69
coping strategies, 129, 178
cost, of job loss, 79, 130, 138–140, 142, 145–47, 200
credentialism, 31, 32, 172

"decent work," xv, 19, 20
decision latitude, 96–99, 101–3, 106. *See also* autonomy; task discretion
degradation of labor, 12
Department for Education and Skill, 189
Department of Trade and Industry, 184, 191

de-skilling, 12, 28, 35, 39, 99, 107
Dictionary of Occupational Titles, 29
Difficulty of Re-employment Index, 137, 138
discretion. *See* task discretion; autonomy; decision latitude
Discretionary Effort, 53, 54, 56, 60, 64
discrimination. *See* gender equality
distrust. *See* trust

Economic Policy Institute, 119
efficiency wages, 16, 77, 198
Effort Pressure Index, 57, 93
effort. *See* work effort
employee involvement, 38, 84, 99–101
employment commitment, 68
employment in Britain, 51, 53, 72, 73, 93, 161, 162, 164, 185, 188, 189,196, 201
employment systems, 101
empowerment, 4, 17, 27, 83, 167
Enquêtes Conditions de Travail, 58
European Commission, 20, 21, 22, 111, 186, 193
European Community Household Panel (ECHP), 158, 159
European Directive on Working Time, 81, 86, 183
European Foundation for the Improvement of Living and Working Conditions, 22, 58, 105, 186
European Foundation for Living and Working Conditions, 22, 105
European Social Model, 20
European Surveys on Working Conditions, 59, 60, 106, 186

fear of job loss, 132, 148. *See also* risk of job loss
Fordism, 99
functional flexibility, 71–73

gender discrimination, 122, 123
gender equality, 19, 21, 22
General Social Survey, 135, 138, 139, 157, 186, 187, 200